FABULOUS FRY PAN FAVORITES

By Patricia Phillips

© 1984 by
National Presto Industries, Inc.
Eau Claire, WI 54703

First Printing ... June 1984

Printed in U.S.A

**Cover photo:
Roast Pork Loin
with Sweet-Sour Fruit,
page 40**

My grateful acknowledgement
to Sue Spitler for her many
contributions in the development
of this book.

Introduction

An electric fry pan brings you much greater convenience than you might ever guess. Its ample contours can hold anything from a saucy casserole to an airy soufflé. Its touch-of-the-dial heat control produces ideal conditions for techniques as diverse as deep-frying, steaming and baking. Its nonstick surface not only reduces the need for cooking fats but also truly makes cleanup a breeze. And certainly not the least of its assets is portability.

In planning and developing the contents of this book, much thought was given to those circumstances and occasions when the electric fry pan's multiple talents would most come in handy. The list kept growing and growing! It started with some that appeared obvious: hot hors d'oeuvres for parties and buffets, one-pan meals for casual get-togethers, and breakfasts to cook and serve tableside. Then it seemed appropriate to focus on all those times when the pan can be used instead of the oven—as on hot summer days or when you want to bake several dishes at once for a big holiday dinner; the results included big meat roasts, whole poultry, and all kinds of breads and cakes.

Because the pan's even, dependable heat ensures saucemaking success, both delicate and robust sauces were natural additions—as were otherwise-tricky chutneys, candies, and preserves. The pan's speed called forth an almost instant supply of sandwiches and snacks. Its ability to combine several functions made quick work of pasta and sauces, rice combinations, stews, chili, and pizza. The same ease prompted big batches of chicken and potato salads, as well as some novel hot green vegetable salads.

Not to be overlooked was basic concern for good nutrition. And here the fry pan's unmatched ability to produce fresh, tender cooked vegetables with a wide variety of techniques became a great source of inspiration. Broccoli, zucchini, and green beans never tasted so good!—whether steamed, sautéed, or simmered in a sauce; potatoes, onion rings, and vegetable fritters could be deep fried to golden perfection. It seemed as if vegetables alone would ensure everyday fry pan use. But that wouldn't do justice either to the pan or to the requirements of a balanced diet. So complete menus were conceived—a week's worth of breakfasts, lunches, dinners, and meals for just one or two diners, as well as a treasury of special meals for guests.

And still there was more that the fry pan could offer. It is splendid for stir-frying, steaming and fat-free cooking. So a showcase of Oriental dishes, especially light foods, and even a Christmas pudding was added. The fry pan is also a dessert-lover's best friend—as the mouthwatering abundance of pies, puddings, cakes, and other sweets in this book will confirm.

That's how over 300 recipes came to be included here. All have been tested in an 11-inch electric fry pan—and tasted with great delight! No adjustments are needed to prepare the recipes in a 12-inch fry pan. In a 15-inch fry pan, you may find that stews need a bit more liquid and that chutneys, preserves, and candies will cook faster. A few of the recipes in this book, including pizza, onion bread, souffléd omelets, and a pan-size potato pancake, are specifically suited to the surface area of an 11-inch or 12-inch pan. To adapt these to a 15-inch pan, shape the solid mixtures, such as the pizza, into a 10-inch square in the larger pan; cook the liquid mixtures, such as the omelets, in a 9×13-inch baking pan (greased or otherwise prepared as directed in the recipe) set in the larger fry pan.

If you would like to adjust yields to suit your family's needs, you can very often simply cut ingredient quantities in half or double them, keeping these electric fry pan capacities in mind: An 11-inch square pan will hold up to 15 cups, or from one to eight servings. A 12-inch square pan holds 18 cups, or from one to 12 servings. A 15-inch rectangular pan, with a wider base but lower sides, holds 16 cups, or 4 to 12 servings. When you are increasing or decreasing recipe yields, do watch the timing. Small quantities will cook faster and larger amounts will take longer.

It is a pleasure to be able to share the joys of electric fry pan cooking through the recipes in this book. But you will no doubt want to adapt other favorite foods to fry pan cookery too. The vast range of dishes included here should enable you to find a comparable recipe, note the temperature setting and timing, and apply the technique to your own recipe. You'll soon realize that electric fry pan cookery does not differ greatly from conventional stove techniques—it's just easier, more reliable, less messy, and often faster!

Fact About the Electric Fry Pan

The electric fry pan can handle almost any kind of cooking. So keep it out on a convenient surface in your

Roast Chicken with Garden Vegetables. Recipe on page 47.

kitchen, ready to use. You needn't worry about wear and tear for the pan is designed for durability.

The pans are made of aluminum or stainless steel, both of which conduct heat well and respond quickly to changes in heat level. Aluminum is somewhat more heat sensitive, and thus a better conductor than stainless steel; cast aluminum is preferable to stamped aluminum because it is virtually warp-proof.

The easiest-to-use pans feature one of the new generation of nonstick surfaces. These are much sturdier than earlier versions, but it is still wise to use wooden or plastic utensils with them. If used carefully, a metal whisk won't do any damage, but it's important that you not cut foods with a knife in the pan. Virtually all electric fry pans are totally immersible (without the electric cord and heat regulator, of course!), and most are dishwasher safe; check your manufacturer's manual for care and cleaning instructions. If the pan's plastic legs and handles should break or wear out, be assured that replacement parts are readily available from the service centers listed in the manual; so these small, inexpensive parts need not limit the long life of the pan.

The shape of the pan is one key to its versatility. The body combines the functions of a skillet and a deep fryer; with the domed lid in place, it becomes a baker, steamer, or Dutch oven. You can prevent excess steam from condensing on the underside of the lid and falling back into the food by leaving the lid slightly ajar; the recipes in this book will direct you to do so whenever necessary.

The other key to the pan's performance is the heat control unit. Settings range from Warm to 400°F, with 25° intervals from 200° to 400°. Choose the setting you want and the pilot light will go on, indicating that the pan is heating to that temperature. The light goes off when the temperature has been reached. The pan heats, goes off, and then reheats again to maintain the correct temperature; the light goes on and off accordingly. If you set the control at 350°, for example, the pan will heat continuously until that temperature is reached; then it will cycle on and off to maintain the temperature. This thermostat-controlled heating process is quite similar to that of a conventional oven. Speed and efficiency will vary according to the amount of electric current delivered to your home, the number of appliances that share the same circuit, and the amount of electricity in use in the area at any given time. In fact, you may notice that your pan heats faster at one time of day, perhaps in mid-morning, than it does at a time when many households are making maximum use of appliances, as at the dinner hour. This is normal, and the variance in cooking time will not be more than a few minutes.

Cooking with an Electric Fry Pan

Read through these explanations of electric fry pan techniques and you'll understand the "why's" behind the recipe instructions in this book. Refer to this list also when you are preparing your own recipes in the fry pan. In general, the efficiency of the electric fry pan means that much cooking is done at lower temperatures and for shorter amounts of time than you may be accustomed to, but basic procedures are quite similar to those of conventional cooking.

Melting Butter. Always use the Warm setting to melt butter for sautéing, sauces, and other uses, because the butter will burn at higher settings.

Simmering. By definition, simmering is cooking at a heat level slightly below the boiling point; when foods are simmering properly, small bubbles appear but do not break the surface of the liquid being cooked. In all electric fry pans, foods will heat to simmering at some point between the Warm setting and 200°. But the precise point will differ from pan to pan, according to electricity level, altitude, and other factors. So you have to find the simmer point of your pan when you're cooking. Heat the pan at 400° until the food boils; then reduce the heat to the simmer level by turning the heat control down until the pilot light goes out. If you don't want the food to boil, start at Warm and increase the heat until you reach the simmer point. You will find precise directions, whenever appropriate, in the recipes.

Pan-Frying and Sautéing. Follow the same logic with the electric fry pan that you would with conventional pans. As a general rule, vegetables are sautéed at 225° and meats are browned at 325°. Often the pan is preheated, so that when oil or shortening and food is added, the pan is hot enough to evenly brown and seal in juices for best flavor. Remember that if butter is the cooking fat used, it should be preheated at Warm, even if the food will be cooked at a higher setting. You'll find that bacon is less apt to spatter and shrink if you don't preheat the pan.

Deep Frying. You only need about one inch of vegetable oil or other fat to deep fry in an electric fry pan. Never fill the pan more than half-full with oil or it may bubble up and spatter badly. The temperature of the oil is critical to best results; if it is too high, the food may burn before it is thoroughly cooked, if too low the food may not get crisp or may taste oily. To make sure that the oil remains at the correct temperature, place a deep frying thermometer in the pan and leave it there throughout the cooking. By checking the thermometer, you may discover that you have to turn up the heat setting to maintain the temperature specified in the recipe. The major reason for this is that every time you add food, the temperature of the oil is reduced. So if you are frying a lot of food, you might have to adjust the heat control to 380° or even 400° to make sure that the oil remains at 375°. Another reason is the large surface area of the pan, which allows heat to escape; this can have an especially dramatic effect on the oil temperature if the kitchen or cooking area is cool. The oil used for deep frying can be reused if you let it cool and then strain it through a strainer lined with cheesecloth, a coffee filter, or paper toweling; discard strong-smelling or discolored oil.

It goes without saying that basic safety precautions should be used whenever deep frying.

It is a good idea to make sure that the power cord attached to the heat control does not hang over the counter where it could be entangled or pulled on, this is especially true if you use an extension cord. And if you do use an extension cord, its marked electrical rating should be at least as great as the electrical rating of the fry pan you are using.

When children are helping or present, close supervision is a must; always exercise caution when moving a fry pan full of hot cooking oil.

Steaming. To cook in steam, food must be placed on a rack **over** – not **in** – simmering liquid in a covered pan. Its domed lid and controlled heat make the electric fry pan an extremely efficient steamer. But you will need to supplement it with some kind of rack. For vegetables, an inexpensive steamer basket (available at hardware stores and housewares departments) is the best accessory, because its small perforations and curved sides ensure that small pieces won't fall into the liquid. For other foods, any rack at least one-half-inch high will work fine. A wire cake rack, a wok-style steaming rack, or a pressure cooker rack can be used; if necessary, raise the rack above the liquid by placing crumpled aluminum foil, flat cans with the ends removed, or canning jar lid rings under it. You can also improvise a rack by turning a disposable pie pan upside down and punching 10 to 12 holes in the bottom. Be careful that whatever rack arrangement you use doesn't have sharp edges that will scrape the pan's nonstick surface.

Pot Roasting or Braising. There's plenty of room in an electric fry pan to cook large pieces of meat, and the domed lid allows air to circulate for even doneness. But you must add some liquid to the pan to prevent the meat drippings from burning and smoking. So technically speaking, you can't use the pan for dry-heat roasting; however, the small amount of moisture required can be a broth, wine, or sauce that will season the meat as it cooks – with wonderful results. The other "must" of electric fry pan meat cookery is that large pieces of meat or poultry must be raised off the bottom of the pan; otherwise, the bottom of the meat will burn. You can place the meat on a rack, on several skewers laid across the bottom of the pan, on several pieces of crumpled aluminum foil, or on canning jar lid rings – it doesn't have to be raised very high, only enough to keep it from touching the bottom.

Baking. You can bake yeast breads, biscuits and other quick breads, pizzas, pastry, cakes, and cookies in the electric fry pan. Breads and cakes baked in baking pans set in the fry pan will get golden brown on the bottom but not on top. So don't judge doneness by the color of the top; follow the doneness test given in the recipe. Whenever necessary, the recipes also include glazes, toppings, or frostings to conceal the paleness of the cake or bread. When you're baking your own recipes, you might want to sprinkle tops with chopped nuts, poppy seeds, toasted sesame seeds, or a simple icing.

Even if you choose to bake yeast breads in a conventional oven, you may want to proof the dough in the electric fry pan, for the even heat and domed lid create ideal rising conditions. Set the bowl or pan of dough on a rack in the fry pan and cover with the lid. Heat the fry pan at Warm for one minute; then turn it to Off. Let the dough stand, covered, until double in bulk, or as directed in the recipe you're following.

Reheating. Set the electric fry pan at Warm to reheat foods evenly. Use the lid if you want the food to stay moist; remove the lid if the food should be crisp.

Cooking Frozen Dinners. To heat frozen dinners in the electric fry pan, place them on a rack and cook, covered, at 400° for the amount of time indicated on the package.

To Flambé. This dazzling technique is used to burn off the harsh alcoholic taste of brandy, rum, or other liquor used in many kinds of sauces, especially for desserts. To use the fry pan for flambéing, detach power cord from outlet first and then remove the heat control from the fry pan. Be careful to position the pan safely away from the bottoms of cabinets and flammable materials, such as curtains, drapes, and clothing. Step back from the fry pan and ignite with a long kitchen match. It is important to adhere strictly to the indicated amount of alcohol contained within each recipe and not to flambé for more than 2-3 minutes at any given time.

Appetizers

Whether your partying mood is easygoing or elegant, you'll find that an electric fry pan is a great social asset. Guests can't resist dipping crackers or chips into a bubbling panful of creamy Dilled Beef Dip of spicy Chilies Con Queso. And nobody can stop at just one simmering Spiced Meatball or Smoked Sausage Bite. Because these appetizers are served.right from the pan, they stay temptingly hot—and the host can stay out of the kitchen.

The speedy convenience of the fry pan allows you to cook while guests gather 'round, adding the tantalizing aromas of Chicken Teriyaki or Deviled Cheese Burgers to the party scene. Stuffed Mushrooms, and Sautéed Cheese Wedges will entice all appetites. Crisp Oriental Spring Rolls or Spanish Empanadas—those luscious little turnovers filled with chicken or beef—can create international flair. French Onion Tarts offer the double allure of flaky pastry and pizzalike toppings. And Mexican Cheese Squares or Artichoke Frittata provide the creamy satisfaction of a quiche without the fuss of a crust.

Use the fry pan's versatility to schedule maximum flexibility into your party plans. Prepare ingredients or whole recipes in advance if you wish, leaving the final cooking or reheating until everyone has arrived. For a large crowd, this strategy might mean having double or triple amounts of ingredients ready to cook in successive batches as the party progresses. For small groups, it can mean sharing the cooking tableside while savoring the fun.

Chicken Wings Teriyaki

2/3 cup teriyaki sauce	1 clove garlic, minced
1/2 cup water	2 pounds chicken wings, tips cut off
1/3 cup dry sherry	2 tablespoons vegetable oil
2 tablespoons rice wine vinegar	1 1/2 tablespoons cornstarch
1/3 cup light brown sugar	3 tablespoons cold water
1 1/2 teaspoons minced fresh or canned gingerroot	

Mix teriyaki sauce, 1/2 cup water, sherry, vinegar, sugar, gingerroot and garlic in shallow glass baking dish; add chicken. Refrigerate, covered, 1 to 4 hours, turning chicken occasionally. Drain chicken. Strain marinade and reserve; discard gingerroot and garlic.

Heat fry pan at 325°. Add oil and chicken; cook, covered, until tender and golden, 5 to 8 minutes, turning once. Remove chicken; keep warm.

Add reserved marinade to fry pan; cook at 400° until boiling. Mix cornstarch and 3 tablespoons water; stir into marinade. Reduce heat to 225°; cook until thickened, stirring constantly. Spoon sauce over chicken or serve in a bowl as a dipping sauce.

8 servings.

TIP: Rice wine vinegar can be purchased in specialty food stores or large supermarkets. Distilled white vinegar can be substituted.

Deviled Cheeseburgers

1 pound lean ground beef	1/2 teaspoon chopped drained capers
1 tablespoon minced onion	1/2 teaspoon salt
1 tablespoon finely chopped green pepper	1/2 teaspoon pepper
2 tablespoons chili sauce	24 slices cocktail rye bread
1 tablespoon sour cream or sour half-and-half	Melted butter or margarine
2 teaspoons Dijon-style mustard	1/2 cup shredded cheddar or crumbled blue cheese
1 teaspoon Worcestershire sauce	

Mix beef, onion, green pepper, chili sauce, sour cream, mustard, Worcestershire sauce, capers, salt and pepper until well blended. Spread heaping tablespoon meat mixture on each bread slice, spreading to edges.

Heat fry pan at 325°. Place half the bread slices, meat sides down, in fry pan; cook, uncovered, until meat is browned, about 2 minutes. Brush bread lightly with melted butter; turn bread slices over. Sprinkle teaspoon cheese on each; cook, covered, until cheese is soft, but not melted, about 2 minutes. Repeat with remaining bread slices. Serve hot.

2 dozen appetizers.

Oriental Spring Rolls

2 tablespoons vegetable oil	3/4 cup sliced green onions and tops
4 ounces lean pork, finely chopped	1/4 cup water chestnuts, cut into 1/8-inch strips
1/4 cup chopped mushrooms	1 1/4 cups fresh or canned drained bean sprouts
1/2 teaspoon minced fresh or canned gingerroot	6 spring roll or egg roll wrappers
3 tablespoons soy sauce	1 egg white, beaten
1 tablespoon dry sherry	Vegetable oil
1/2 teaspoon sugar	Sweet-sour sauce
1 cup shredded Chinese or green cabbage	

Heat fry pan at 250°. Add 2 tablespoons oil and pork; cook until lightly browned, about 1 minute. Add mushrooms and gingerroot; cook 30 seconds. Stir in combined soy sauce, sherry and sugar; cook 2 minutes, stirring constantly. Add cabbage, onions and water chestnuts; cook until heated through, about 1 minute. Stir in bean sprouts; cook 15 seconds. Spoon mixture into strainer and let drain.

Divide pork mixture on wrappers, spooning mixture into lower corners of wrappers. Fold lower corner of each wrapper over filling; fold in sides so that they overlap in center. Moisten remaining edges of wrappers with beaten egg white; roll up tightly, sealing moistened corners onto rolls.

Heat 1 inch oil in fry pan at 350°. Cook spring rolls until golden, about 3 minutes. Drain on paper toweling. Serve warm with sweet-sour sauce.

6 spring rolls.

TIP: Gingerroot, Chinese cabbage, fresh bean sprouts and spring roll or egg roll wrappers may be purchased in specialty food stores or large supermarkets.

Frittata Squares

7 eggs	1/16 teaspoon ground nutmeg
1 3/4 cups shredded Swiss cheese	2 dashes red pepper sauce
1 3/4 cups shredded cheddar cheese	1/2 teaspoon salt
1 14-ounce can artichoke hearts, drained, sliced	1/16 teaspoon white pepper
10 whole wheat crackers, finely crushed	3 tablespoons butter or margarine
1 teaspoon dried basil leaves	1 cup sliced mushrooms
1/2 teaspoon grated lemon rind	1/4 cup sliced green onions and tops
1/4 teaspoon Worcestershire sauce	

Beat eggs in large bowl until foamy; mix in remaining ingredients except butter, mushrooms, and onions. Heat butter in fry pan at Warm until melted. Add mushrooms and onions; cook at 250° until onions are tender, about 2 minutes. Pour egg mixture into fry pan, stirring gently to distribute mixture evenly over bottom of fry pan; cook, covered, until egg mixture is set and feels firm when touched, 10 to 12 minutes. Cut into squares with plastic or wooden utensil. Serve warm.

3 dozen squares.

Velvet Paté

2 tablespoons butter or margarine	1 3-ounce package cream cheese, softened
1 pound chicken livers, cleaned	1/8 teaspoon ground allspice
1/4 cup finely chopped onion	1/8 teaspoon ground nutmeg
2 tablespoons brandy	1/4 teaspoon salt
2 tablespoons whipping cream or half-and-half	1/8 teaspoon pepper
1/2 cup butter or margarine, softened	French bread, thinly sliced

Heat 2 tablespoons butter in fry pan at Warm until melted. Add chicken livers; cook at 325° for 2 minutes. Add onion; cook until livers are no longer pink in the center, about 3 minutes. Stir in brandy. Turn fry pan to Off, unplug cord from outlet; flame brandy.

Process liver mixture and cream in food processor or blender until smooth; refrigerate, covered, until chilled, about 1 hour. Return mixture to food processor; process, adding 1/2 cup butter and cream cheese, 1 tablespoon at a time. Mix in allspice, nutmeg, salt and pepper. Refrigerate, covered, until chilled. Let stand until room temperature before serving; spread on bread slices.

About 2 cups.

Dilled Beef Dip

2 cups water	1 8-ounce package cream cheese, cubed
1 2 1/2-ounce jar dried beef	1 cup shredded brick cheese
2 tablespoons butter or margarine	1 cup sour cream or sour half-and-half
1/2 cup chopped pecans	1/4 cup mayonnaise or salad dressing
1/2 cup chopped almonds	1/2 teaspoon dried dillweed
1/4 cup chopped onion	Assorted crackers

Heat water in fry pan at 400° until boiling. Add beef; cook 30 seconds. Drain beef well; cut into strips.

Heat butter in fry pan at Warm until melted. Add nuts; cook at 250° for 2 minutes. Stir in onion; cook 2 minutes. Reduce heat to 200°; add remaining ingredients, except beef and crackers, stirring until cheeses are melted and mixture is heated. Stir in beef; cook 1 minute. Reduce heat to Warm; serve from fry pan, with crackers as dippers.

About 2 3/4 cups.

Stuffed Mushroom Appetizers

3 dozen mushrooms
  Spinach or Cheese Stuffing

Dry bread crumbs

Remove stems from mushrooms; reserve 3 tablespoons finely chopped stems for stuffing (refrigerate remaining stems for other use). Make desired stuffing. Fill each mushroom with teaspoon of stuffing. Dip mushrooms, stuffing sides down, in bread crumbs to coat stuffing. Arrange mushrooms, stuffing sides down, in fry pan; cook, covered, at 200°, for 5 minutes. Turn mushrooms over; cook, covered, until heated, about 5 minutes. Serve warm.

3 dozen mushroom caps.

Spinach Stuffing

3/4 cup frozen, thawed, drained, chopped spinach
  3 tablespoons butter or margarine
  3 tablespoons finely chopped onion
  3 tablespoons finely chopped mushroom stems

  3 tablespoons dry bread crumbs
3/4 cup shredded sharp cheddar cheese
  1 slice bacon, fried crisp, crumbled
1/8 teaspoon ground nutmeg
1/4 teaspoon salt

Squeeze excess moisture from spinach. Heat butter in fry pan at Warm until melted. Add onion and mushroom stems; cook at 225°, 2 minutes. Stir in spinach; cook until heated, 1 to 2 minutes. Stir in bread crumbs; cook 1 minute. Turn fry pan to Off; stir in cheese, bacon, nutmeg and salt.

About 3/4 cup.

Cheese Stuffing

  1 3-ounce package cream cheese, softened
1/2 cup shredded Swiss cheese
  2 tablespoons crumbled blue cheese

  3 tablespoons finely chopped mushroom stems
  2 tablespoons finely chopped walnuts

Beat cream cheese until softened; mix in remaining ingredients.

About 3/4 cup.

Chili Con Queso

  4 slices bacon
  1 small onion, finely chopped
  1 medium green pepper, finely chopped
  1 3-ounce can mild or hot chopped chilies, undrained
  1 tomato, chopped
  1 tablespoon dried coriander leaves
  2 teaspoons Worcestershire sauce

1 to 2 teaspoons red pepper sauce (optional)
  2 cups shredded brick cheese
  2 cups shredded processed American cheese
1/2 cup whipping cream or half-and-half
  Tortilla chips

Cook bacon in fry pan at 300° until crisp; remove bacon and crumble. Drain excess fat, reserving 1 tablespoon. Add onion, green pepper and chilies to drippings in fry pan; cook at 225° until tender, 2 to 3 minutes. Stir in tomato, coriander, Worcestershire sauce and red pepper sauce; cook, covered, 5 minutes. Reduce heat to Warm. Stir in cheeses and cream; cook, covered, until cheeses are melted, stirring occasionally. Sprinkle with bacon. Serve from fry pan, with tortilla chips as dippers.

About 3 cups.

French Onion Tart

1 sheet frozen puff pastry, thawed	1/4 teaspoon salt
3 tablespoons olive or vegetable oil	1/16 teaspoon pepper
2 1/2 cups sliced or chopped onions	1 1/2 teaspoons olive or vegetable oil
1 clove garlic, minced	1 tablespoon grated Parmesan cheese
1 teaspoon cornstarch	1 2-ounce can anchovy fillets, well drained (optional)
1 1/2 cups chopped tomatoes	Minced parsley
1/2 cup sliced black olives	

Heat fry pan at 225°. Unfold sheet of puff pastry and fit into fry pan; cook, covered, 30 minutes, or until golden on the bottom. Turn pastry over; cook, covered, 30 minutes. Carefully transfer pastry to wire rack.

Add 3 tablespoons olive oil, onions and garlic to fry pan; cook at 225° until onions are transparent. Reduce heat to 200°. Sprinkle onion mixture with cornstarch; stir well. Stir tomatoes, olives, salt and pepper into onion mixture; cook 3 minutes, stirring occasionally. Spoon onion mixture evenly over pastry; drizzle with 1 1/2 teaspoons oil and sprinkle with cheese. Decorate with anchovies.

Clean fry pan. Place onion tart on rack in fry pan; cook, covered, at 400°, 10 minutes. Transfer tart to serving plate; sprinkle with parsley. Cut into squares to serve.

6 servings.

Sautéed Cheese Wedges

9 ounces camembert or brie cheese, well chilled	1 green onion and top, sliced
1 egg, beaten	1/2 cup chopped chutney
Dry bread crumbs	1/2 teaspoon prepared mustard
2 tablespoons butter or margarine	

Cut cheese into 8 wedges. Dip cheese wedges in egg; coat generously with bread crumbs. Heat butter in fry pan at Warm until melted. Add cheese; cook at 225° until cheese wedges are golden on all sides, turning carefully with tongs (cheese will become soft, but should not melt). Arrange cheese on serving plate.

Add green onion to fry pan; cook 2 to 3 minutes. Stir in chutney and mustard; cook until bubbly, about 2 minutes. Spoon chutney mixture over cheese. Serve warm.

4 servings.

TIP: Chilled cheddar, brick, or mozzarella cheese may be substituted for the camembert or brie cheese; cut into 1-inch cubes or wedges.

Cheese Crisps

1/2 cup shredded cheddar cheese	1/4 teaspoon salt
1/2 cup shredded Swiss cheese	1/3 cup all-purpose flour
1/4 cup butter or margarine, softened	1/2 cup oven-toasted rice cereal
1/4 teaspoon Worcestershire sauce	

Mix cheeses, butter, Worcestershire sauce and salt. Add flour and cereal; form dough mixture into log 1-inch in diameter. Wrap in plastic wrap; place in freezer 30 minutes, or until ready to cook.

Heat fry pan at 350°. Cut dough into 1/4-inch slices; cook until browned on both sides, turning with plastic or wooden spatula. Serve warm or at room temperature.

2 dozen appetizers.

Meatballs with Chili Sauce

Beef and Sausage Meatballs
1/2 cup chopped onions
1/2 cup chopped green pepper
  2 16-ounce cans tomatoes, undrained, coarsely chopped
1/4 cup chili sauce

1 tablespoon sugar
2 teaspoons Worcestershire sauce
1/2 teaspoon ground cumin
1/4 teaspoon ground oregano
1/2 teaspoon salt

Make Beef and Sausage Meatballs. Arrange meatballs in fry pan; cook at 325° until meatballs are browned on all sides, 5 to 8 minutes. Remove meatballs; drain all but 2 tablespoons drippings.

Add onion and green pepper to drippings in fry pan; cook at 325° until tender, 3 to 4 minutes. Add remaining ingredients; cook at 400° until boiling. Add meatballs; reduce heat to simmer, between Warm and 200°; cook until sauce is thickened, 10 to 15 minutes, stirring occasionally. Reduce heat to Warm; serve meatballs from fry pan with wooden picks or cocktail forks.

8 servings (3 meatballs each).

Beef and Sausage Meatballs

1/2 pound lean ground beef
1/2 pound bulk pork sausage
1/4 cup finely chopped onion
1/2 teaspoon beef flavor instant bouillon

1/2 teaspoon chili powder
  1 small clove garlic, minced
1/2 teaspoon salt
1/8 teaspoon pepper

Mix all ingredients until blended. Roll meat mixture into 24 meatballs.

2 dozen meatballs.

Smoked Sausage Bites

  1 teaspoon vegetable oil
12 ounces smoked sausage, cut into 1/2-inch slices
1/4 cup chopped onion
3/4 cup chili sauce

1/2 cup maple or pancake syrup
1/4 cup bourbon
  1 teaspoon prepared mustard
1/4 teaspoon pepper

Heat fry pan at 300°. Add oil, sausage and onion; cook until sausage is browned, 3 to 4 minutes. Stir in remaining ingredients; cook until hot and bubbly. Reduce heat to Warm. Serve sausage from fry pan with wooden picks or cocktail forks.

6 to 8 servings.

Mexican Cheese Squares

4 cups shredded cheddar cheese
2 cups shredded Monterey Jack cheese
4 eggs, beaten
1 tablespoon chopped seeded canned or fresh jalapeño pepper

1 tablespoon butter or margarine
1/4 cup thinly sliced green onions and tops
1/4 cup finely chopped onion

Mix cheeses, eggs and jalapeño pepper in large bowl. Heat butter in fry pan at Warm until melted. Add onions; cook at 300° until tender, 2 to 3 minutes. Stir in cheese mixture; cook, covered, until mixture is set and bottom is beginning to brown, 25 to 30 minutes. Cut into squares with plastic or wooden utensil. Serve warm.

2 dozen squares.

Empanadas
(Mexican-style Turnovers)

1 1/4	cup all-purpose flour
1/4	teaspoon salt
1/2	cup lard or vegetable shortening
1	large egg
2 to 2 1/2	tablespoons ice water

Beef-Olive or Chicken-Raisin Filling
Water
Vegetable oil

Mix flour and salt in bowl; cut in lard until mixture resembles coarse crumbs. Mix in egg and enough ice water to form dough that is soft but not sticky. Refrigerate, covered, 1 hour.

Make desired filling. Roll pastry on lightly floured surface to 1/16-inch thickness; cut into 3-inch circles. Spoon heaping teaspoon filling on half of each pastry circle. Brush edges of pastries with water; fold in half and crimp edges with fork.

Heat 1-inch oil in fry pan at 350°. Fry empanadas in oil until golden, about 2 minutes on each side. Drain on paper toweling. Serve warm.

2 dozen.

Beef-Olive Filling

1/3	pound lean ground beef
1/4	cup finely chopped onion
1	clove garlic, minced
1/4	cup chopped seeded tomato
1/2	teaspoon ground cumin
	Dash cayenne pepper

1/2	teaspoon salt
1/8	teaspoon black pepper
1/4	cup chopped hard-cooked egg
2	tablespoons chopped pitted green olives

Heat fry pan at 250°. Add beef, onion and garlic; cook until beef is browned, about 5 minutes. Drain excess fat. Add tomato; cook 1 minute. Stir in cumin, cayenne pepper, salt and black pepper. Stir in egg and olives. Cool to room temperature.

About 3/4 cup.

Chicken-Raisin Filling

3	tablespoons vegetable oil
1/4	cup finely chopped onion
1	clove garlic, minced
1/2	teaspoon curry powder
1/8	teaspoon ground cinnamon

1/2	pound boneless skinned chicken breast, finely chopped
3/4	teaspoon salt
	Dash white pepper
1/4	cup raisins, chopped

Heat fry pan at 250°. Add oil, onion, garlic, curry powder and cinnamon; cook until onion is tender, about 3 minutes. Stir in chicken, salt and pepper; cook until chicken is done, about 3 minutes. Stir in raisins. Cool to room temperature.

About 3/4 cup.

Salads and Dressings

A salad prepared in a fry pan? It sounds funny—but it tastes great! Think about a tangy Hot German Potato Salad laden with bits of bacon or Pasta Salad with crisp vegetables, and you'll appreciate the convenience of being able to cook and toss all the ingredients in just one pan. Consider a rich Sweet-Sour Dressing for raw spinach and mushrooms or an airy Fruit Dressing for your favorite fruit salad, and you'll realize that the even, easily controlled heat of an electric fry pan is superb for these delicate blends.

Take advantage of the fry pan to steam and stir-fry, and you'll have perfectly crisp-tender vegetables for Antipasto Vegetable Salad and Hot Bean Sprout Salad, both tossed with warm vinaigrette dressings. Poach chicken in the pan, then quickly stir up a wonderful mix of Oriental seasonings, and the fragrance of Hot Chinese Chicken Salad will arouse all appetites. And if anyone still questions the wisdom of a "fry pan salad," treat them to Hot 'N Cold Taco Salad—an absolutely delectable contrast of hot chili-spiced beef and chilled lettuce topped with avocado and cheese.

Spinach Salad with Sweet-Sour Dressing

6 cups fresh spinach, torn into bite-size
   pieces
1 small red onion, thinly sliced
1 cup sliced mushrooms

   Sweet-Sour Dressing
6 slices bacon, fried crisp, crumbled

Combine spinach, onion and mushrooms in salad bowl; spoon Sweet-Sour Dressing over and toss. Sprinkle with bacon.

6 servings.

Sweet-Sour Dressing

3/4 cup sugar
  1 tablespoon cornstarch
1/4 teaspoon salt
1/4 cup distilled white vinegar

1 tablespoon butter or margarine
1/2 cup half-and-half
1 egg, beaten

Mix sugar, cornstarch and salt in fry pan. Stir in vinegar; cook at 400° until boiling, stirring constantly. Reduce heat to simmer, between Warm and 200°; cook until thickened, stirring constantly. Turn heat to Off; stir in butter until melted. Slowly add half-and-half, stirring constantly. Refrigerate, covered, until chilled, about 1 hour.

Beat egg into dressing mixture. Refrigerate, covered, until serving time.

About 1 1/2 cups.

Pasta Salad in Cream Dressing

2 tablespoons butter or margarine
1/2 cup chopped onions
1 clove garlic, minced
1 large stalk broccoli, flowerets removed, stems sliced diagonally
2 carrots, sliced diagonally

1 cup whipping cream or half-and-half
1/2 teaspoon salt
1/16 teaspoon white pepper
8 ounces rotini or spaghetti, cooked
1/2 cup coarsely chopped pecans, toasted
Grated Parmesan cheese

Heat butter in fry pan at Warm until melted. Add onion and garlic; cook at 225° until tender, about 1 minute. Add broccoli and carrots; cook until crisp-tender, about 3 minutes, stirring frequently. Stir in cream; cook at 250° until cream begins to thicken, 3 to 5 minutes. Stir in 1/2 teaspoon salt and pepper; stir in pasta, coating evenly with cream mixture. Stir in pecans and 1 tablespoon Parmesan cheese. Serve with additional cheese.

4 servings.

Fruit Dressing

1 1/2 tablespoons cornstarch
1 1/2 tablespoons packed light brown sugar
1/8 teaspoon ground mace
1/8 teaspoon salt

1 cup unsweetened pineapple juice
2 egg yolks
2 tablespoons lemon juice
2 tablespoons vegetable oil
1/2 teaspoon prepared mustard

Mix cornstarch, sugar, mace and salt in fry pan; stir in pineapple juice until blended. Stir in egg yolks and lemon juice; cook at Warm until thickened, 3 to 4 minutes, whisking constantly. Turn heat to Off; stir in oil and mustard. Cool to room temperature, stirring occasionally; refrigerate, covered. Serve over fruit salads.

About 1 1/3 cups.

Pineapple Whipped Cream Dressing

Fold 1/2 cup whipped cream and 1/4 cup well-drained crushed pineapple into chilled dressing; serve immediately.

About 1 2/3 cups.

Minted Fruit Dressing

Stir 1/4 to 1/2 teaspoon dried mint leaves into uncooked dressing mixture; cook as above.

About 1 1/3 cups.

Cooked Salad Dressing

1/4 cup sugar
2 tablespoons flour
2 to 3 teaspoons dry mustard
3/4 teaspoon salt
1/8 teaspoon cayenne pepper

1 1/2 cups milk or half-and-half
2 eggs, beaten
2 egg yolks, beaten
1/2 cup cider vinegar
1/4 cup butter or margarine, softened

Mix sugar, flour, mustard, salt and pepper in fry pan. Mix milk, eggs and egg yolks; stir into sugar mixture in fry pan. Gradually stir in vinegar; cook at Warm until thickened, 8 to 10 minutes, stirring constantly. Turn heat to Off; stir in butter, 1 tablespoon at a time, until melted. Cool to room temperature, stirring constantly. Refrigerate covered. Serve over vegetable or green salads.

About 2 1/2 cups.

Mustard Dressing

Stir 1/2 cup Bavarian-style mustard into chilled dressing.

About 3 cups.

Chutney Dressing

Stir 2/3 cup chopped chutney into chilled dressing.

About 3 cups.

Oriental Bean Sprout Salad

1 tablespoon sesame or vegetable oil	3 1/2 cups fresh bean sprouts
2 tablespoons sliced green onion and top	1 cup thinly sliced celery
1 clove, garlic, minced	1/2 cup diagonally sliced carrot
1/4 cup rice wine vinegar	1/4 cup vegetable oil
2 teaspoons soy sauce	Shredded lettuce
2 tablespoons sugar	1 teaspoon sesame seeds, toasted
1/4 teaspoon ground ginger	

Heat fry pan at 200°. Add 1 tablespoon sesame oil, onion and garlic; cook 3 minutes. Stir in vinegar, soy sauce, sugar and ginger; cook until heated, stirring constantly.

Add bean sprouts, celery and carrot; toss with 1/4 cup vegetable oil. Spoon onto lettuce on serving plates; sprinkle with sesame seeds.

6 servings.

TIPS: Sesame oil, rice wine vinegar and fresh bean sprouts may be purchased at specialty food stores or large supermarkets. Distilled white vinegar may be substituted for the rice wine vinegar. Two cans (16 ounces each) bean sprouts may be substituted for the fresh. Drain bean sprouts and soak in ice water 1 hour to crisp.

To toast sesame seeds, cook in fry pan at 225° until golden, stirring frequently.

German Potato Salad

1 1/2 pounds potatoes, peeled, cut into quarters	3/4 cup water
Water	1/4 cup flour
4 slices bacon	3/4 cup cider vinegar
1/4 cup chopped onion	3 to 4 tablespoons sugar
2 tablespoons chopped red or green pepper	1 teaspoon salt
2 tablespoons sliced green onion and top	1/16 teaspoon pepper
1 rib celery, sliced	2 hard-cooked eggs, chopped
	1 tablespoon minced parsley

Arrange potatoes in fry pan. Add 1 inch water; cook, covered, at 400° until boiling. Reduce heat to simmer, between Warm and 200°; cook, covered, until potatoes are fork-tender, 15 to 20 minutes. Drain potatoes; cool until warm and cut into scant 1/2-inch cubes.

Cook bacon in fry pan at 300° until crisp; remove and crumble. Drain excess fat leaving 2 tablespoons. Add onion, red pepper and celery to drippings in fry pan; cook at 300° until onion is tender, about 3 minutes. Shake 3/4 cup water and flour in covered jar until blended. Stir in fry pan with vinegar, sugar, salt and pepper; cook until thickened, stirring constantly. Pour sauce over potatoes, toss. Add bacon, eggs and parsley; toss until blended. Refrigerate several hours for flavors to blend.

6 servings.

Hot 'N' Cold Taco Salad

4 cups coarsely chopped iceberg lettuce

2 cups romaine lettuce, torn into bite-size pieces

2 tablespoons vegetable oil

1 onion, chopped

1 clove garlic, minced

1/2 pound lean ground beef

1/4 cup tomato sauce

2 tablespoons chopped tomato

2 tablespoons chopped red or green pepper

1 1/2 teaspoons chili powder

1/4 teaspoon ground cumin

1/16 teaspoon cayenne pepper

1/4 teaspoon salt

1 small avocado, peeled, pitted, chopped

1/2 cup shredded Monterey Jack or cheddar cheese

Tortilla chips, crushed

Toss greens in salad bowl. Heat fry pan at 250°. Add oil, onion and garlic; cook 2 minutes. Add ground beef; cook until browned, stirring occasionally. Drain excess fat. Stir in tomato sauce, tomato, red pepper, chili powder, cumin, cayenne pepper and salt; cook until mixture is hot and beginning to thicken, about 3 minutes, stirring constantly.

Spoon hot beef mixture over greens and toss. Spoon salad onto serving plates; sprinkle with avocado, cheese and tortilla chips.

4 servings.

Chinese Chicken Salad

2 cups water

1/4 cup dry sherry

2 teaspoons chicken flavor instant bouillon

6 chicken breast halves (about 1/2 pound each)

1 tablespoon Szechwan peppercorns, lightly crushed

1/3 cup vegetable oil

3 tablespoons rice wine vinegar

3 tablespoons soy sauce

3 tablespoons honey

3/4 cup diagonally sliced green onions and tops

3 cloves garlic, minced

1/2 teaspoon ground ginger

3 cups finely sliced Chinese or green cabbage

1 8-ounce can water chestnuts, drained, sliced

1 red or green pepper, cut into thin strips

Heat water, sherry and bouillon in fry pan at 400° until boiling. Add chicken; reduce heat to simmer, between Warm and 200°. Cook, covered, until chicken is no longer pink in the center, about 20 minutes. Remove chicken; cool until warm. Discard cooking liquid. Remove chicken from bones and shred coarsely; keep warm.

Heat fry pan at 225°. Add peppercorns; cook until toasted, about 2 minutes, stirring frequently. Add oil, vinegar, soy sauce, honey, onions, garlic and ginger; cook at Warm, 2 minutes. Stir in chicken, cabbage, water chestnuts, and red pepper; toss. Serve immediately.

4 servings (about 1 1/2 cups each).

Vegetables

Consider your electric fry pan a guardian of good nutrition, for it performs beautifully in all kinds of vegetable cookery. Its versatility suggests hundreds of ways to meet the recommended dietary standard of three to four vegetable servings a day. And the brilliant variety of flavors and colors to choose from can turn vegetable side dishes into everyday meal highlights.

You'll find over 30 recipes in this chapter, but they are just a starting point. Once you become familiar with the cooking methods, you can substitute one vegetable for another, according to what looks freshest and is priced best at the market. These are the most frequently used vegetable cooking techniques and ways to make the most of them:

Steaming. Its domed lid and wide surface make the electric fry pan especially efficient for steaming. Any kind of rack can be used to hold the vegetables above the water, but an inexpensive steamer basket (available at most hardware stores and housewares departments) is the most convenient. You'll find precise steaming direction in the first parts of the recipes for Carrots with Herb Bread Crumbs and Asparagus with Orange Sauce. You can use the same method with any fresh vegetable, cut into any size pieces; adjust cooking time according to the type of vegetable and desired degree of doneness.

Sautéing. Because the electric fry pan heats so effectively, you needn't set it higher than 225°F for perfect results. Nonstick surfaces reduce the amount of butter, oil, or other fat needed. The recipe for Julienne Celery with Walnuts provides guidelines that can be used with any firm vegetable that has been sliced, diced, or julienne—cut into small pieces.

Deep Frying. The key to crisp vegetable fritters, onion rings, and other fried foods is keeping the oil at the proper temperature—usually 350° to 375°F. So keep a deep-fat thermometer (preferably the type atttached to a flat metal plate) in the fry pan while you're cooking, since the temperature of the food, as well as other factors, can lower the temperature of the oil. The thermometer will let you know when to raise the fry pan setting to maintain the temperature of the oil.

Baking. Many vegetable dishes that you'd otherwise bake in the oven can be made in the fry pan with even better results, because the fry pan keeps the food moist. Try Baked Corn Custard or Waldorf Baked Squash and you'll appreciate the difference.

Casseroles. Nothing could be easier than fry pan vegetable combinations. Everything is done in one pan in two or three easy steps—all you need to do is turn the heat up or down as you add various ingredients. The recipe for Green Bean and Mushroom Casserole is just one example of a tempting combination that can be made in minutes and varied with other frozen cut-up vegetables.

The simplicity of the basic techniques belies the range of sauced, glazed, and creamed vegetables, as well as stuffings and accompaniments, in this chapter. All of them demonstrate just how good "good-for-you" foods can taste!

Pecan Succotash

2	tablespoons butter or margarine
3/4	cup coarsely chopped pecans
3/4	cup chopped onions
1	16-ounce can whole-kernel corn, drained
1	10-ounce package frozen baby lima beans, thawed

3/4	cup half-and-half
1/2	teaspoon sugar
1/2	teaspoon salt
1/16	teaspoon white pepper

Heat butter in fry pan at Warm until melted. Add pecans; cook at 225° until toasted. Remove pecans and reserve. Add onion; cook 2 minutes. Add remaining ingredients; cook at 400° until boiling. Reduce heat to simmer, between Warm and 200°; cook until half-and-half is absorbed, about 5 minutes. Stir in reserved pecans.

4 to 6 servings.

Sugar-Glazed Brussels Sprouts and Onions

1	10-ounce package frozen Brussels sprouts	1	16-ounce jar boiled whole onions
1	cup water	1/4	cup coarsely chopped walnuts
1/4	teaspoon salt		Salt
2	tablespoons butter or margarine		White pepper
2	tablespoons sugar		

Heat Brussels sprouts, water and 1/4 teaspoon salt in fry pan at 400° until boiling. Reduce heat to simmer, between Warm and 200°; cook, covered, until sprouts are tender, about 10 minutes. Remove sprouts from fry pan; discard cooking liquid. Heat butter in fry pan until melted. Add sugar; cook at 250° for 1 minute. Add onions; cook at 400° until onions are glazed, about 3 minutes, stirring frequently. Stir in sprouts and walnuts; cook 2 minutes. Season to taste with salt and pepper.

6 servings.

Waldorf Baked Squash

2	medium acorn squash	1/2	cup coarsely chopped walnuts
	Water	1/2	teaspoon ground cinnamon
1	cup coarsely chopped mixed dried fruit	1/16	teaspoon ground nutmeg
1/2	cup chopped, unpared, cored apple	1/4	cup maple or pancake syrup

Cut squash into halves; remove seeds and discard. Place squash halves, cut sides down, on rack in fry pan. Add 1 inch water; cook at 400° until boiling. Reduce heat to simmer, between Warm and 200°; cook, covered, until squash are tender, 35 to 40 minutes.

Mix dried fruit, apple, walnuts, cinnamon and nutmeg. Turn squash halves over, cut sides up, on rack; fill cavities with fruit mixture. Drizzle syrup over fruit mixture; cook, covered, until apple is tender, about 10 minutes.

4 servings.

Shredded Potato Pancake

1	pound potatoes, peeled, shredded	1/2	teaspoon salt
1	small onion, finely chopped	1/8	teaspoon white pepper
1/4	cup finely chopped green pepper	2	tablespoons vegetable oil
1/4	cup all-purpose flour		Grated Parmesan cheese
2	eggs, beaten		Ground nutmeg

Mix potatoes, onion, green pepper, flour, eggs, salt and pepper. Heat fry pan at 225°. Add oil and potato mixture to fry pan, shaping into flat pancake with spatula; cook until pancake is golden brown on bottom, 10 to 12 minutes. Slide potato pancake onto dinner plate; invert into fry pan; cook until bottom of pancake is brown and crisp, 10 to 15 minutes. Slide onto serving plate; sprinkle lightly with cheese and nutmeg. Cut into wedges to serve.

4 to 6 servings.

Waldorf Baked Squash, Sugar-Glazed Brussels Sprouts and Onions, Shredded Potato Pancakes

Beer-Battered Onion Rings

1 large Bermuda onion, thinly sliced	Vegetable Oil
1 12-ounce can beer	Powdered Salt (see recipe page 26)
Flour	

Separate onion slices into rings in shallow bowl; pour beer over. Let stand 1 hour, stirring occasionally.

Drain onions, reserving beer. Coat onions lightly with flour; dip into beer and coat with flour again. Arrange into single layer on paper toweling.

Heat 1 inch oil in fry pan at 375°. Add onions; cook until golden, 2 to 3 minutes. Drain on paper toweling; sprinkle very lightly with Powdered Salt. Serve immediately.

4 servings.

Beets in Orange Sauce

Orange Sauce (See recipe, page 73)	1 small orange, peeled, sliced, seeded
2 16-ounce cans sliced beets, drained	1/2 cup coarsely chopped pecans

Make Orange Sauce in fry pan; stir in beets. Cut orange slices into fourths. Stir in orange pieces and pecans; cook, covered, at 200° until beets are heated, about 3 minutes.

4 to 6 servings.

All-Seasons Vegetable Fritters

1 2/3 cups all-purpose flour	1/2 cup shredded cheddar cheese
2 teaspoons baking powder	1 teaspoon paprika
1 1/2 teaspoons salt	Dash cayenne pepper
2 eggs, beaten	Vegetable oil
2/3 cup milk	Powdered Salt (See recipe, page 26)
1 cup coarsely chopped onions	
1 cup coarsely chopped red or green pepper	

Mix flour, baking powder and 1 1/2 teaspoons salt in bowl; mix in eggs and half of the milk. Mix in remaining milk until batter is smooth. Stir in onion, red pepper, cheese, paprika and cayenne pepper.

Heat 1 inch oil in fry pan at 375°. Drop batter into oil, using 1/2 tablespoon batter for each fritter; cook until golden, 3 to 4 minutes, turning so that fritters cook evenly. Drain on paper toweling; sprinkle lightly with Powdered Salt.

8 servings (about 5 fritters each).

Zucchini-Carrot Fritters

Substitute 1 cup shredded zucchini and 1 cup shredded carrots for the chopped onion and pepper. Substitute 2 tablespoons grated Parmesan cheese and 1/8 teaspoon garlic powder for the cheddar cheese, paprika and cayenne pepper.

Corn-Pecan Fritters

Substitute 2 cups canned, drained whole-kernel corn and 2 tablespoons finely chopped pecans for the chopped onion and pepper. Add 1/8 teaspoon curry powder; omit cheddar cheese, paprika and cayenne pepper.

Ratatouille

1 eggplant (about 1 pound), pared, cut crosswise into scant 1/2-inch slices
Salt
Cold water
3 tablespoons olive or vegetable oil
1 large onion, sliced
2 cloves garlic, minced
1 large green pepper, cut into 1/4-inch strips

1 medium zucchini, sliced into scant 1/2-inch slices
1 28-ounce can Italian plum tomatoes, undrained, coarsely chopped
1/4 cup sliced black olives
1 1/2 teaspoons dried basil leaves
1 teaspoon dried tarragon leaves
1/4 teaspoon dried oregano leaves
1/2 teaspoon salt

Cut eggplant slices into quarters; sprinkle lightly with salt and let stand 30 minutes. Rinse well with cold water; drain thoroughly.

Heat fry pan at 225°. Add oil, onion and garlic; cook 2 minutes. Add green pepper; cook 1 minute. Add eggplant and remaining ingredients; cook at 400° until boiling. Reduce heat to simmer, between Warm and 200°; cook, covered, until eggplant is tender and mixture is desired consistency, 1 to 1 1/2 hours.

6 to 8 servings.

Green Bean and Almond Casserole

2 tablespoons butter or margarine
1/4 cup slivered almonds
3/4 cup chopped onions
1 10-ounce package frozen French-style green beans, thawed
1 10 3/4-ounce can cream of celery soup

1 4-ounce can sliced mushrooms, drained
1/4 cup sliced water chestnuts
2 tablespoons grated Parmesan cheese
Paprika

Heat 2 tablespoons butter in fry pan at 200° until melted. Add almonds, cook at 225° until golden. Stir in onion; cook 2 minutes. Stir in beans; cook, covered, until crisp-tender, about 4 minutes. Stir in soup, mushrooms and water chestnuts; cook at 400° until boiling, stirring constantly. Reduce heat to simmer, between Warm and 200°; cook until beans are tender, 10 to 12 minutes, stirring occasionally. Stir in cheese; sprinkle with paprika.

4 to 6 servings.

Cauliflower Polonaise

1 head cauliflower (about 1 pound)
1 egg
Warm water
1/4 cup butter or margarine

1/4 cup dry bread crumbs
1 teaspoon minced parsley
1/8 teaspoon garlic powder

Place cauliflower and egg on rack in fry pan. Add 1 inch warm water; heat at 400° until boiling. Reduce heat to simmer, between Warm and 200°; cook, covered, until cauliflower is tender, about 12 minutes. Remove cauliflower to serving plate; keep warm. Cool egg under cold running water; peel egg and chop finely. Discard water in fry pan.

Heat butter in fry pan at 200° until browned. Stir in bread crumbs, parsley and garlic powder; cook until crumbs are golden, 3 to 5 minutes, stirring frequently. Stir in egg; cook 1 minute. Spoon mixture over cauliflower; cut into wedges to serve.

4 to 6 servings.

New England Bean Bake

3/4	pound bacon	1/2	cup maple syrup or light molasses
2	cups chopped onions	1/2	cup light brown sugar, packed
4	16-ounce cans Great Northern beans, drained	3/4	teaspoon dry mustard
3 1/2	cups water	1	teaspoon salt

Cook bacon in fry pan at 300° until crisp; remove bacon and crumble. Drain excess fat, reserving 3 tablespoons. Add onion to drippings in fry pan; cook at 225° until tender, stirring occasionally. Stir in bacon and remaining ingredients; cook at 400° until boiling. Reduce heat to simmer, between Warm and 200°; cook, covered, until beans are golden and most of liquid is absorbed, about 1 3/4 hours, stirring occasionally.

10 to 12 servings.

Julienne Celery with Walnuts

4	ribs celery, cut crosswise into 3-inch pieces	1	teaspoon grated lemon rind
1	tablespoon butter or margarine	1	teaspoon lemon juice
1	tablespoon vegetable oil	1/4	teaspoon salt
1/2	cup coarsely chopped walnuts	1/8	teaspoon white pepper

Cut celery pieces lengthwise into strips 1/4 inch wide. Heat butter and oil in fry pan at Warm until butter is melted. Add walnuts; cook at 225° until browned, stirring frequently. Add celery and lemon rind; cook until crisp-tender, about 4 minutes, stirring occasionally. Sprinkle with lemon juice, salt and pepper; toss.

4 servings.

Asparagus with Orange Sauce

1 1/2	pounds fresh or frozen asparagus	Orange Sauce (see recipe, page 73)
	Water	

Place asparagus in vegetable steamer in fry pan. Add 1 inch water; heat at 400° until boiling. Reduce heat to simmer, between Warm and 200°; cook, covered, until asparagus is crisp-tender, 8 to 12 minutes. Arrange asparagus on serving plate; keep warm. Discard cooking liquid.

Make Orange Sauce in fry pan; spoon over asparagus.

6 servings.

Wilted Spinach

12	slices bacon	1	tablespoon Worcestershire sauce
3/4	cup tarragon vinegar	1 1/2	teaspoons prepared mustard
1/3	cup brandy	2	10-ounce packages fresh spinach, washed, torn into bite-size pieces
1/3	cup sugar		

Cook bacon in fry pan at 300° until crisp; drain bacon and crumble. Add vinegar, brandy, sugar, Worcestershire sauce and mustard to drippings in fry pan; cook until mixture begins to boil. Stir in spinach; cook, covered, just until spinach is wilted, about 2 minutes. Serve immediately.

4 servings.

Sour Cream Rice and Mushrooms

1/4 cup butter or margarine	2 1/2 cups water
1/2 cup sliced celery	1 teaspoon salt
1/2 cup slivered almonds	1 cup white long grain rice
1/2 cup sliced mushrooms	1 tablespoon butter or margarine
1/4 teaspoon crushed dried rosemary leaves	2/3 cup sour cream
1/4 teaspoon salt	1/2 cup shredded brick or Swiss cheese
1/16 teaspoon white pepper	

Heat 1/4 cup butter in fry pan at Warm until melted. Add celery and almonds; cook at 225° until celery is tender, about 2 minutes. Add mushrooms, rosemary, 1/4 teaspoon salt and pepper; cook 1 minute. Remove vegetable mixture from fry pan and reserve.

Add water and 1 teaspoon salt to fry pan; cook at 400° until water is boiling. Stir in rice and 1 tablespoon butter. Reduce heat to simmer, between Warm and 200°; cook according to time on package. Stir in reserved vegetable mixture; cook until heated, about 2 minutes. Reduce heat to Warm; stir in sour cream and cheese, stirring until cheese is melted.

4 to 6 servings.

Bean Potpourri

6 slices bacon	2 tablespoons dark molasses
1 medium onion, sliced	2 teaspoons Worcestershire sauce
1 medium green pepper, sliced	2 teaspoons prepared mustard
1 10-ounce package frozen green beans	2 to 3 drops red pepper sauce
1 10-ounce package frozen baby lima beans	Salt
1 16-ounce can kidney beans, drained	Pepper
1 16-ounce can tomatoes, undrained, coarsely chopped	

Cook bacon in fry pan at 300° until crisp; remove bacon and crumble. Drain excess fat, reserving 1 tablespoon. Add onion and green pepper to drippings in fry pan; cook at 225° until tender, about 8 minutes. Stir in beans; cook, covered, 3 minutes, stirring occasionally. Stir in tomatoes, molasses, Worcestershire sauce, mustard and red pepper sauce; cook at 400° until boiling. Reduce heat to simmer, between Warm and 200°; cook, covered, until lima beans are tender, 25 to 30 minutes. Season to taste with salt and pepper.

6 servings.

Cheesy Hash Browns

2/3 cup vegetable oil	Seasoned salt
1 cup sliced green onions and tops	Pepper
1 8-ounce can sliced mushrooms, drained	1/2 cup shredded cheddar cheese
1 pound frozen hash brown potatoes	

Heat fry pan at 225°. Add oil and onion; cook 2 minutes. Stir in mushrooms; cook 1 to 2 minutes. Stir in potatoes; cook, covered, at 300° for 15 minutes, stirring occasionally. Season to taste with salt and pepper; cook, uncovered, until potatoes are golden, 15 to 20 minutes. Sprinkle with cheese; cook, covered, until cheese melts, about 2 minutes.

4 to 6 servings.

Whole Wheat Stuffing

8 tablespoons butter or margarine	2 tablespoons minced parsley
1 pound loaf firm whole wheat bread, cut into scant 1-inch cubes	1 1/2 to 2 teaspoons dried sage leaves
2 cups sliced mushrooms	3/4 teaspoon dried thyme leaves
3/4 cup chopped onions	3/4 teaspoon dried rosemary leaves
1 cup thinly sliced celery	1/2 teaspoon salt
1 3/4 to 2 cups chicken broth	1/4 teaspoon pepper
1 egg, beaten	

Heat 3 tablespoons butter in fry pan at Warm until melted. Add half the bread cubes; cook at 300° until golden, stirring occasionally. Remove to large bowl. Add 3 tablespoons butter to fry pan; cook remaining bread cubes. Remove to bowl.

Add remaining 2 tablespoons butter, mushrooms, onion and celery to fry pan; cook at 250° until onion is tender, about 4 minutes. Add vegetable mixture to bread cubes in bowl. Mix 1 3/4 cup of the chicken broth and egg; stir into bread cube mixture. Mix in parsley, sage, thyme, rosemary, salt, pepper and remaining broth if desired for consistency. Spoon stuffing into fry pan; cook, covered, at 200° about 15 minutes, stirring occasionally. Serve hot.

8 servings.

Squash-Nut Stuffing

Heat 2 tablespoons butter in fry pan at Warm until melted. Add 2 cups coarsely chopped peeled acorn squash and 1/2 cup coarsely chopped pecans or walnuts; cook, covered, at 200°, 10 minutes, or until crisp-tender. Remove from fry pan and reserve. Make Whole Wheat Stuffing as above, substituting 1/2 teaspoon ground cinnamon and 1/4 teaspoon ground nutmeg for the sage, thyme and rosemary; stir into squash mixture. Cook, covered, at 200° until squash is tender, about 15 minutes.

10 servings.

Fruit and Sausage Stuffing

Cook 1/2 pound sausage in fry pan at 250° until browned, breaking into pieces with a fork. Remove from fry pan and reserve. Discard drippings. Make Whole Wheat Stuffing as above; stir in cooked sausage and 1 cup coarsely chopped mixed dried fruit. Cook, covered, at 200° until fruit is tender, 15 to 20 minutes.

8 to 10 servings.

Broccoli-Mushroom Casserole

1/2 cup butter or margarine	1 teaspoon Worcestershire sauce
2 cups coarsely chopped broccoli	1/2 cup cottage cheese
1 1/2 cups sliced mushrooms	1/2 cup shredded cheddar cheese
1 cup chopped onions	1/4 cup dry bread crumbs
1 cup thinly sliced carrot	1 egg
1/2 cup sliced water chestnuts	Salt
3/4 cup half-and-half	Pepper
1/4 cup mayonnaise or salad dressing	

Heat butter in fry pan at Warm until melted. Add broccoli, mushrooms, onion, carrot and water chestnuts; cook at 225° until vegetables are tender, 12 to 15 minutes. Mix half-and-half, mayonnaise and Worcestershire sauce; stir into broccoli mixture. Mix cottage cheese, cheddar cheese, bread crumbs and egg; stir into broccoli mixture. Cook until heated, about 5 minutes, stirring frequently. Season to taste with salt and pepper.

8 servings.

Baked Corn Custard

3 eggs, beaten
2 cups half-and-half
2 tablespoons melted butter or margarine
1/4 cup all-purpose flour
1 teaspoon sugar
1/2 teaspoon dried savory leaves
   Dash ground nutmeg

1/2 teaspoon salt
1/4 teaspoon white pepper
1 17-ounce can whole-kernel corn, drained
1 cup shredded cheddar cheese
1/4 cup thinly sliced green onions and tops
1 tablespoon butter or margarine

Combine eggs, half-and-half and melted butter. Stir in flour, sugar, savory, nutmeg, salt and pepper. Mix in corn, cheese and onion.

Heat 1 tablespoon butter in fry pan at Warm until melted. Pour in corn mixture; cook, covered, at 250° until set, about 30 minutes. Cut into squares with plastic or wooden utensil. Serve immediately.

8 servings.

Tomato Pudding

1/4 cup butter or margarine
4 tablespoons vegetable oil
4 3/4-inch thick slices Italian bread, cut into 3/4-inch cubes
1 1/2 cups chopped onions
1 clove garlic, minced
1 1/2 teaspoons curry powder
1/2 teaspoon ground ginger

1/8 teaspoon ground cinnamon
3 28-ounce cans whole tomatoes, undrained, coarsely chopped
3/4 cup chopped chutney
1 1/2 tablespoons light brown sugar
1 1/2 teaspoons chicken-flavor instant bouillon
1/16 teaspoon cayenne pepper

Heat butter and 2 tablespoons of the oil in fry pan at Warm until butter is melted. Add bread cubes; cook at 325° until golden, stirring frequently. Remove bread cubes from fry pan and reserve.

Heat remaining 2 tablespoons oil in fry pan at 225°. Add onion and garlic; cook 2 minutes. Stir in curry powder, ginger and cinnamon; cook 1 minute. Stir in tomatoes and 3 cups of liquid, reserved bread cubes, chutney, brown sugar, bouillon and cayenne pepper; cook at 400° until boiling. Reduce heat to simmer, between Warm and 200°; cook, covered, until liquid is absorbed, about 15 minutes. Serve hot.

6 to 8 servings.

Southern Fried Okra

Vegetable oil
1 pound fresh okra, cleaned, caps removed
2 eggs, beaten

1 cup self-rising white cornmeal
   Powdered Salt (see recipe page 26)

Heat 1 inch oil in fry pan at 375°. Cut okra into 1/2-inch pieces; dip in beaten eggs and coat generously with cornmeal. Cook okra in hot oil until golden, 1 to 2 minutes. Drain on paper toweling; sprinkle lightly with Powdered Salt.

4 to 6 servings.

Fried Spaghetti Wedges

3 eggs
1/2 cup grated Parmesan cheese
1 clove garlic, minced
1 teaspoon minced parsley
1/4 teaspoon dried basil leaves

1/2 teaspoon salt
1/4 teaspoon white pepper
8 ounces spaghetti, cooked
1 tablespoon olive or vegetable oil

Mix eggs, cheese, garlic, parsley, basil, salt and pepper until blended; stir into spaghetti. Heat fry pan at 250°. Spread oil evenly over bottom of fry pan. Add spaghetti mixture, pressing evenly in bottom with pancake turner; cook, with cover 1/2 inch ajar, until spaghetti is golden and crisp on the bottom, 5 to 7 minutes. Slide spaghetti onto dinner plate. Invert into fry pan; cook, with cover 1/2 inch ajar, until golden and crisp on the bottom, about 5 minutes. Slide onto serving plate; cut into wedges to serve.

4 to 6 servings.

Saratoga Potato Chips

1 pound Idaho potatoes, unpared
Vegetable oil

Powdered Salt

Cut potatoes into scant 1/4-inch slices; heat 1 inch oil in fry pan at 275°. Cook potatoes, a few slices at a time, until limp, 3 to 5 minutes (potatoes will not brown). Drain on paper toweling; reserve oil for later use.

Make Powdered Salt. Heat oil at 350°; cook potatoes, a few slices at a time, until golden. Drain on paper toweling; sprinkle lightly with Powdered Salt. Serve immediately.

4 servings.

TIPS: Potatoes are crisper when cooked twice. After cooking at 275°, the potatoes can stand at room temperature for several hours. Regular salt can be substituted for the Powdered Salt.

Powdered Salt

1/4 cup salt

Process salt in blender (do not use food processor) until finely powdered, about 1 minute. Spoon into shaker container.

1/4 cup.

TIP: Powdered Salt is excellent on all fried food as it adheres to the food nicely.

Potatoes Gratin

2 pounds potatoes, peeled, cut into 1/2-inch cubes
Salt
White pepper

2 cups half-and-half
1 tablespoon grated Parmesan cheese
Nutmeg

Arrange potatoes in fry pan; sprinkle lightly with salt and pepper. Pour half-and-half over potatoes; cook, covered, at 250° for 10 minutes, stirring frequently. Reduce heat to Warm; cook, covered, until potatoes are tender and half-and-half is almost absorbed, about 25 minutes, stirring every 10 minutes. Sprinkle potatoes with cheese and nutmeg.

6 to 8 servings.

Mixed Squash Sauté

6 slices bacon
1/2 cup chopped onions
1 clove garlic, minced
1 yellow squash, peeled and sliced

1 zucchini squash, sliced
1 cup sliced mushrooms
2 to 3 teaspoons Worcestershire sauce
1/4 teaspoon salt

Cook bacon in fry pan at 300° until crisp; remove bacon and crumble. Drain drippings and reserve 2 tablespoons. Add onion and garlic; cook at 225° until tender, about 2 minutes. Stir in squash and mushrooms; cook until squash is tender, about 5 minutes, stirring frequently. Sprinkle with Worcestershire sauce and salt; toss. Sprinkle with crumbled bacon.

6 servings.

Greek-Style Green Beans

3 tablespoons olive or vegetable oil
1 pound fresh green beans, ends trimmed
3/4 cup chopped onion

2 cloves garlic, minced
2 16-ounce cans tomatoes, undrained, coarsely chopped
Water

Heat fry pan at 225°. Add oil, beans, onion and garlic; cook 10 minutes, stirring occasionally. Add tomatoes with liquid; cook, covered, until beans are tender, about 1 hour, stirring every 15 minutes. Add water, 1/4 cup at a time, if mixture becomes extremely dry.

6 to 8 servings.

Artichokes Italian-Style

4 artichokes
2 tablespoons olive or vegetable oil

Salt
Water

Cut stems off artichokes; cut pointed tips off leaves with scissors. Stand artichokes in fry pan; drizzle olive oil over artichokes and sprinkle with salt. Add 1/2 inch water to fry pan; cook at 400° until boiling. Reduce heat to simmer, between Warm and 200°; cook, covered, until artichokes are tender (leaf will pull easily from base of artichoke), about 35 minutes. Cook, uncovered, until water has evaporated from fry pan and artichokes are deep golden brown on the bottom, about 10 minutes.

4 servings.

Sweet Potatoes with Nut Butter

2 sweet potatoes
Vegetable oil
1/4 cup butter or margarine-butter blend
1/16 teaspoon ground cinnamon

2 dashes ground nutmeg
1/2 teaspoon grated orange rind
1 tablespoon finely chopped pecans, toasted

Pierce potatoes in several places with fork; rub lightly with oil. Place potatoes on rack in fry pan; cook, covered, at 375° until tender, about 45 minutes. Remove from fry pan.

Beat butter, cinnamon and nutmeg in small bowl until fluffy; mix in orange rind and pecans. Serve on potatoes.

2 servings.

Sautéed Asparagus with Garlic

1 pound fresh asparagus, ends trimmed
1 clove garlic, crushed
3 tablespoons olive or vegetable oil
2 tablespoons water
Salt

Place asparagus and garlic in fry pan. Drizzle with oil and water; cook, covered at 225°, 5 minutes. Reduce heat to 200°; cook until water has evaporated and asparagus is browned on all sides, 8 to 10 minutes, turning frequently with tongs. Season to taste with salt.

4 servings.

Carrots with Herb Bread Crumbs

2 pounds carrots, cut into sticks
  4" × 1/4" × 1/4"
  Water
1/2 cup butter or margarine
3/4 cup dry bread crumbs
1 tablespoon minced parsley
1/2 teaspoon dried basil leaves
1/4 teaspoon dried tarragon leaves

Place carrots in vegetable steamer in fry pan; add 1/2 inch water. Cook at 400° until water is boiling. Reduce heat to simmer, between Warm and 200°; cook, covered, until carrots are crisp-tender. Remove to serving bowl; keep warm. Discard water.

Heat butter in fry pan at Warm until melted. Stir in remaining ingredients; cook at 200° until crumbs are browned, 2 to 3 minutes, stirring frequently. Spoon crumb mixture over carrots and toss.

8 servings.

Creamed Spinach with Nutmeg

1 1/2 cups half-and-half
3 egg yolks
2 10-ounce packages frozen spinach,
  thawed, well-drained
3/4 teaspoon salt
1/8 teaspoon white pepper
  Ground nutmeg

Mix half-and-half and egg yolks in fry pan until thoroughly blended; cook at 225° until thickened, stirring constantly. Stir in spinach, salt and pepper; cook, covered, until spinach is tender, about 5 minutes, stirring occasionally. Spoon spinach mixture into serving bowl; sprinkle generously with nutmeg.

4 to 6 servings.

Bourbon-Glazed Sweet Potatoes

1/3 cup butter or margarine
1/2 cup light brown sugar
2 tablespoons bourbon
1 tablespoon grated orange rind
2 16-ounce cans sweet potatoes, drained
1/4 cup coarsely chopped pecans, toasted

Heat butter in fry pan at Warm until melted. Add sugar, bourbon and orange rind, stirring until sugar is melted. Add potatoes, tossing to coat evenly with sugar syrup; cook, covered, at 250° until heated, about 8 minutes, stirring occasionally. Stir in pecans.

6 servings.

TIP: Brandy or orange juice may be substituted for the bourbon.

Meats

When choosing a meat dish to serve, every cook has to juggle many factors—not only individual tastes but also cooking time, cost, occasion, and number of diners. So this chapter has been planned to suit all circumstances.

The electric fry pan can be counted on for meals in minutes, plain or fancy, when time is of the essence. Pork Chop 'N Yam Casserole, Swedish Meatballs with Mushroom Gravy, Country-Fried Steak, and Lamb Chops with Mint Sauce are just a few of the family style favorites that can be made in less than an hour. But it takes no longer to prepare Veal Cutlets Normandy or Rib Steaks Bearnaise when you want a luxurious meal.

A large group for dinner? The fry pan can hold Beer Glazed Ham to feed a dozen or Braised Beef Roast and Vegetables for eight to ten. You can serve spice-fragrant Greek-Style Lamb Roast or Chinese-Style Roast Pork Loin with Sweet-Sour Fruit. Not only does the fry pan easily hold five-pound roasts, but it conveniently doubles as a big saucepan for making stuffings and gravies to go with the meat. Two techniques ensure success with large cuts of meat: Use a rack when necessary, as directed in the recipe, to lift long-cooking pieces off the bottom of the pan and prevent them from burning. And insert a meat thermometer, as you would for oven-roasting, to ensure proper degree of doneness.

Looking for an easy change of pace? Fast and economical Southwestern Beef and Cornbread Pie will delight any casual gathering with its rich, spicy Tex-Mex flavors. Steaks Wellington with Bordelaise Sauce is as elegant as you could wish. And if the occasion is brunch, everyone will enjoy the meaty goodness of Savory Homemade Sausage Patties or Country Roast Beef Hash.

Sauerbraten

3   **pounds beef blade or round bone chuck roast**
    Vinegar Marinade
3   **slices bacon**
1   **large onion, sliced**

2   **whole cloves**
1   **bay leaf**
1/2 **cup raisins**
10 **gingersnaps, crushed (optional)**

Place beef in glass baking dish; make Vinegar Marinade and pour over meat. Refrigerate, covered, 2 to 3 days, turning meat over twice each day.

Remove meat from marinade; strain marinade, reserving liquid. Dry meat well with paper toweling. Cook bacon in fry pan at 300°; drain and crumble. Reserve 2 tablespoons bacon drippings in fry pan. Add meat; cook, covered, at 325° until browned, about 5 minutes on each side. Remove meat. Add onion; cook at 225° for 10 minutes, stirring occasionally. Add meat, reserved marinade liquid, cloves and bay leaf; cook at 400° until boiling. Reduce heat to simmer, between Warm and 200°; cook, covered, until meat is tender, 1 to 1 1/2 hours. Stir in bacon, raisins and gingersnap crumbs during last 30 minutes of cooking time.

4 to 6 servings.

Vinegar Marinade

2   **cups water**
1   **cup white wine vinegar**
2   **medium onions, sliced**

2   **tablespoons pickling spice**
1   **bay leaf**
12 **juniper berries, lightly crushed (optional)**

Combine all ingredients in fry pan; cook at 400° until boiling. Turn heat to Off; cool to room temperature.

About 4 cups.

TIP: Juniper berries can be purchased in specialty food stores or the spice department of large supermarkets. There is no substitute. If not available, omit from recipe.

Home-Style Pot Roast

3 1/2 pounds beef blade or round bone
      chuck roast
2 tablespoons flour
1/2 teaspoon dry mustard
1/2 teaspoon salt
1/4 teaspoon pepper
2 tablespoons vegetable oil
1 cup beer
1 teaspoon beef-flavor instant bouillon

8 small potatoes, unpeeled
6 carrots, cut crosswise into halves
4 small whole onions
2 tablespoons flour
1/4 cup cold water or milk
  Salt
  Pepper

Coat meat with mixture of 2 tablespoons flour, mustard, 1/2 teaspoon salt and 1/4 teaspoon pepper. Heat fry pan at 325°. Add oil and meat; cook until well browned on both sides. Add beer and bouillon; cook at 400° until boiling. Reduce heat to simmer, between Warm and 200°; cook, covered, 1 hour. Peel strip from centers of potatoes. Add potatoes, carrots and onions; cook, covered, until meat is fork-tender, about 1 hour.

Arrange meat and vegetables on serving platter; cover with aluminum foil. Stir 2 tablespoons flour and cold water into pan juices; cook at 250°, until thickened, about 2 minutes, stirring constantly. Season to taste with salt and pepper. Serve gravy over meat.

6 to 8 servings.

Vegetable-Stuffed Flank Steak

2 pounds beef flank steak, excess fat trimmed
1 8-ounce bottle Italian salad dressing
  Vegetable Stuffing

1 tablespoon vegetable oil
2 cups water

Pound flank steak with mallet until even in thickness (scant 3/4 inch thick). Score steak diagonally in diamond pattern on both sides, using sharp knife. Place steak in shallow glass baking dish; pour dressing over. Refrigerate, covered, 1 1/2 to 2 hours, turning steak occasionally.

Make Vegetable Stuffing. Remove steak from marinade; reserve marinade. Spread Vegetable Stuffing on steak, leaving 2-inch margin along sides. Roll up lengthwise, jelly-roll style; secure edge with wooden picks.

Heat fry pan at 325°. Add oil and steak; cook until well browned, 7 to 8 minutes on each side. Remove meat. Add water to fry pan, scraping drippings from bottom of fry pan with wooden or plastic utensil. Add reserved marinade and steak; cook at 400° until boiling. Reduce heat to simmer, between Warm and 200°; cook, covered, until meat is tender, about 45 minutes. Remove meat to serving platter; let stand, loosely covered with aluminum foil, 10 minutes before slicing.

6 servings.

Vegetable Stuffing

1 tablespoon butter or margarine
1 tablespoon olive or vegetable oil
1 4-ounce can sliced mushrooms, drained
1/2 cup chopped carrot
1/4 cup thinly sliced celery
1/4 cup thinly sliced green onions and tops

1 small clove garlic, minced
1/4 cup dry bread crumbs
1/2 teaspoon dried basil leaves
1/4 teaspoon salt
1/16 teaspoon white pepper

Heat butter and oil in fry pan at Warm until butter is melted. Add mushrooms, carrot, celery, onion and garlic; cook at 225°, 2 minutes. Stir in bread crumbs, basil, salt and pepper; cook until crumbs are browned, 2 to 3 minutes.

About 1 1/4 cups stuffing.

Braised Beef Roast and Vegetables

3 tablespoons vegetable oil	3/4 cup strong coffee
4 1/2 pounds beef eye of round roast	3/4 cup water
1 cup broccoli flowerets	1/2 teaspoon beef-flavor instant bouillon
1 red pepper, cut into 1-inch pieces	1 1/2 pounds small potatoes, peeled
1 small zucchini, cut into 3/4-inch pieces	3 carrots, cut into 1/2-inch pieces
1 cup chopped onions	2 ribs celery, cut into 2-inch pieces
1 clove garlic, minced	4 whole green onions, tops removed
1/2 teaspoon dried marjoram leaves	1 cup small whole mushrooms
1/2 teaspoon dried savory leaves	2 tablespoons cornstarch
1/8 teaspoon dried thyme leaves	1/4 cup cold water
1/4 teaspoon salt	Salt
1/4 teaspoon pepper	Pepper

Heat fry pan at 325°. Add oil and roast; cook until well browned on all sides. Remove roast; drain all but 2 tablespoons drippings. Add broccoli, red pepper and zucchini; cook at 225° until crisp-tender, about 3 minutes. Remove vegetables; reserve. Add chopped onions and garlic; cook 2 minutes. Stir in marjoram, savory, thyme, 1/4 teaspoon salt and 1/4 teaspoon pepper; cook 1 minute. Add coffee, 3/4 cup water and bouillon, scraping drippings from bottom of fry pan with plastic or wooden utensil. Add roast; cook at 400° until boiling. Reduce heat to simmer, between Warm and 200°; cook, covered, until roast is tender, 2 1/2 to 3 hours. Add potatoes, carrots, celery and green onions during last 45 minutes of cooking time. Add reserved vegetables and mushrooms during last 15 minutes of cooking time.

Arrange roast and vegetables on serving platter; let stand, covered with aluminum foil, 10 minutes before slicing. Strain pan juices and return to fry pan; heat at 400° until boiling. Mix cornstarch and cold water; stir into pan juices. Cook at 225° until thickened, about 2 minutes, stirring constantly. Season to taste with salt and pepper. Serve gravy with roast and vegetables.

8 to 10 servings.

Braised Beef Roast and Vegetables

Italian Pot Roast

3 1/2 pounds beef blade or round bone
chuck roast
1/2 teaspoon salt
1/2 teaspoon pepper
2 tablespoons vegetable oil
1 16-ounce can tomatoes, undrained,
coarsely chopped
1 cup dry red wine

1 6-ounce can tomato paste
3/4 teaspoon ground basil leaves
1/2 cup sliced celery
1/2 cup coarsely chopped carrot
1/2 cup sliced mushrooms
8 small potatoes
6 small onions

Sprinkle both sides of meat with salt and pepper. Heat fry pan at 325°. Add oil and meat; cook until browned on both sides. Add tomatoes with liquid, wine, tomato paste and basil; cook at 400° until boiling. Reduce heat to simmer, between Warm and 200°; cook, covered, 1 3/4 to 2 hours, or until meat is fork-tender. Add celery, carrot, mushrooms, potatoes and onions during last 45 minutes of cooking time.

6 to 8 servings.

Steaks Wellington with Bordelaise Sauce

1 sheet frozen puff pastry, thawed
1 tablespoon butter or margarine
1 tablespoon vegetable oil
4 beef tenderloin or rib eye steaks,
3/4 inch thick

Salt
Pepper
Bordelaise Sauce
1 2-ounce can liver pâté or high quality
liverwurst (optional)

Cut 4 rounds from puff pastry using cutter approximately 1 inch smaller in diameter than the steaks. Cut piece of parchment or brown paper grocery bag to fit rack; place on rack in fry pan. Heat fry pan at 350°. Place pastry rounds on paper; cook, covered, until puffed and crisp, about 25 minutes. Remove and cool pastry rounds.

Heat butter and oil in fry pan at Warm until butter is melted. Lightly sprinkle steaks with salt and pepper. Place in fry pan; cook at 325° to desired degree of doneness (3 minutes on each side for medium). Remove from fry pan; keep warm. Reserve pan drippings.

Make Bordelaise Sauce. Place steaks on serving plates. Cut pâté into 4 slices; place on steaks. Spoon sauce over; top with pastry rounds.

4 servings.

Bordelaise Sauce

Reserved pan drippings (from above
Steak Wellington recipe)
2 tablespoons finely chopped onion
1/2 cup red wine
1/4 teaspoon dried thyme leaves
1 bay leaf

2 whole peppercorns
1 cup water
1 teaspoon beef flavor instant bouillon
1 tablespoon cornstarch
2 tablespoons cold water

Heat fry pan at 225°. Add reserved drippings and onion; cook 1 minute. Stir in wine, thyme, bay leaf and peppercorns; cook 3 minutes, stirring frequently. Stir in 1 cup water and bouillon scraping drippings from bottom of fry pan with plastic or wooden utensil. Heat at 400° until boiling. Mix cornstarch and cold water; stir into sauce; cook until thickened, stirring constantly. Strain, discard herbs.

About 1 1/2 cups.

Italian Pot Roast

Swedish Meatballs with Mushroom Sauce

3/4 pound lean ground beef
1/2 pound ground pork
3/4 cup instant potato flakes
1/2 cup milk
1/3 cup finely chopped onion
1 egg
1 tablespoon grated lemon rind
1 tablespoon minced parsley

1/4 teaspoon ground nutmeg
1/4 teaspoon paprika
1/2 teaspoon salt
1/2 teaspoon pepper
2 tablespoons butter or margarine
2 tablespoons vegetable oil
Mushroom Sauce (see recipe, page 72)

Mix all ingredients except butter, oil and Mushroom Sauce; shape into 16 meatballs. Heat butter and oil in fry pan at 200° until butter is melted. Add meatballs; cook at 275° until browned on all sides and no longer pink in the center, 10 to 12 minutes. Remove meatballs; discard drippings. Clean fry pan. Make Mushroom Sauce. Add meatballs to sauce; cook, covered, at 200°, until heated through, 3 to 4 minutes.

4 servings (4 meatballs each).

Rib Eye Steaks Stroganoff

1 tablespoon butter or margarine
2 tablespoons vegetable oil
4 beef rib eye steaks, 3/4-inch thick
Salt
Pepper
3 cups sliced mushrooms
3/4 cup chopped red or green pepper

1/2 teaspoon dried marjoram leaves
1/4 teaspoon dried thyme leaves
1/4 teaspoon salt
1/8 teaspoon pepper
3 tablespoons cream cheese, softened
1/3 cup half-and-half

Heat butter and oil in fry pan at 325° until butter is melted. Add steaks; cook to desired degree of doneness (about 3 minutes on each side for medium). Sprinkle lightly with salt and pepper; remove to serving platter and keep warm.

Add mushrooms and red pepper; cook at 225°, 2 minutes, scraping drippings from bottom of fry pan with plastic or wooden utensil. Stir in marjoram, thyme, 1/4 teaspoon salt and 1/8 teaspoon pepper; cook 2 minutes. Mix cream cheese and half-and-half until smooth. Add to fry pan; cook until heated through, stirring constantly. Spoon vegetable mixture over steaks and serve immediately.

4 servings.

TIP: Any tender beef steaks may be used in this recipe.

Hearty Roast Beef Hash

1/4 cup vegetable oil
1 cup finely chopped onions
2 tablespoons sliced green onion and top
1 small clove garlic, minced
2 1/2 cups finely chopped roast beef
2 cups coarsely chopped, cooked potatoes

1/2 cup chopped, cooked carrot
1/3 cup water
1/4 teaspoon beef flavor instant bouillon
1/2 teaspoon dried tarragon leaves
1 teaspoon salt
1/4 teaspoon pepper

Heat fry pan at 225°. Add oil, onion and garlic; cook until golden, about 8 minutes. Stir in remaining ingredients; pat mixture evenly in bottom of fry pan with pancake turner. Reduce heat to between Warm and 200°; cook until bottom of hash is brown and crisp, 30 to 40 minutes.

4 to 6 servings.

Calves Liver with Onions and Apples

3 slices bacon	1 pound calves liver
1/4 cup butter or margarine	1/3 cup all-purpose flour
1 large onion, sliced 1/4 inch thick	1/4 teaspoon ground allspice
1 teaspoon sugar	1/4 teaspoon salt
2 tart apples, cored, cut into 1/2-inch wedges	1/8 teaspoon pepper

Cook bacon in fry pan at 300° until crisp; remove and crumble. Add 2 tablespoons butter, onion and sugar; cook at 225° until onion begins to brown, about 5 minutes. Stir in apples; cook until tender, 3 to 4 minutes. Remove onion mixture and reserve.

Coat liver slices lightly with mixture of flour, allspice, salt and pepper. Heat fry pan at 325°. Add remaining 2 tablespoons butter; cook until butter melts and browns. Add liver; cook until no longer pink in the center, about 2 minutes on each side. Return reserved onion mixture to fry pan; cook, covered, about 2 minutes, or until heated through.

4 servings.

Southwestern Beef and Corn Bread Pie

2 tablespoons vegetable oil	1/4 teaspoon salt
2 pounds lean ground beef	1/4 teaspoon pepper
3/4 cup chopped onions	2 8½-ounce packages corn muffin mix
1 clove garlic	2 eggs
1 8-ounce can mild or hot chili salsa	2/3 cup milk
1/3 cup sliced black olives	2 to 3 teaspoons chili powder
1/2 teaspoon dried oregano leaves	1 cup shredded cheddar cheese
1/4 teaspoon ground cumin	

Heat fry pan at 300°. Add oil, beef, onion and garlic; cook until beef is browned, stirring occasionally. Drain excess fat. Stir in salsa, olives, oregano, cumin, salt and pepper; cook, covered, at 200°, 5 minutes.

Make corn muffin mix according to package directions, using eggs, milk and chili powder; fold in cheese. Spoon batter over beef mixture in fry pan; cook at 225°, with cover ajar 1 inch, until batter is cooked through, 20 to 25 minutes.

8 servings.

Rib Steaks Bearnaise

4 3/4-inch thick slices French bread	4 3/4-inch thick beef rib eye steaks
Butter or margarine, softened	Salt
2 tablespoons butter or margarine	Pepper
2 tablespoons vegetable oil	Creamy Béarnaise Sauce (see recipe page 71)

Heat fry pan at 325°. Spread bread slices on both sides with softened butter; cook in fry pan until toasted on both sides. Remove toast.

Heat 2 tablespoons butter and oil in fry pan at Warm until butter is melted. Add steaks; cook at 325° to desired degree of doneness (about 3 minutes on each side for medium-rare). Remove steaks; sprinkle lightly with salt and pepper.

Make Creamy Béarnaise Sauce. To serve, arrange steaks on toast slices; spoon sauce over.

4 servings.

Country Fried Steak

1 pound beef round steak, excess fat trimmed, pounded to 1/4-inch thickness
1/4 cup all-purpose flour
2 tablespoons dry bread crumbs
1/4 teaspoon paprika
1/4 teaspoon garlic powder
1/2 teaspoon salt
1/8 teaspoon pepper

1/4 cup vegetable oil
1 large onion, sliced
2/3 cup water
1/2 teaspoon beef flavor instant bouillon
2/3 cup milk
2 tablespoons flour
Salt
Pepper

Cut round steak into 4 serving pieces; coat generously with mixture of 1/4 cup flour, bread crumbs, paprika, garlic powder, 1/2 teaspoon salt and 1/8 teaspoon pepper. Heat fry pan at 300°. Add oil and steak; cook until well browned, about 2 minutes on each side. Remove steaks. Add onion; cook, covered, at 225°, until tender, about 5 minutes, stirring occasionally. Remove onion.

Stir in water and bouillon, scraping drippings from bottom of fry pan with plastic or wooden utensil. Shake milk and 2 tablespoons flour in covered jar. Stir mixture into fry pan; cook at 400° until mixture boils and thickens, stirring constantly. Add meat and onion, coating with gravy; cook at Warm, covered, until heated through, about 5 minutes.

4 servings.

Savory Cheese Meat Loaf

1 pound lean ground beef
1 pound ground pork
1/2 cup uncooked oats
1/3 cup chopped green pepper
1/4 cup chopped onion
1/2 cup catsup
2 tablespoons Worcestershire sauce

1 3-ounce package cream cheese, softened
2 tablespoons milk
2 eggs
1/2 teaspoon salt
1/4 teaspoon pepper
1 cup shredded cheddar cheese

Mix all ingredients, except 1/4 cup catsup and 1/4 cup cheddar cheese; form into round or oval loaf in fry pan. Spread remaining 1/4 cup catsup on top; cook, covered, at 200° until meat is no longer pink in the center, 55 to 60 minutes. Sprinkle top of loaf with remaining 1/4 cup cheese; cook, covered, until cheese is melted, about 3 minutes. Remove to serving platter; let stand 10 minutes before slicing.

8 servings.

Chutney-Peanut Meat Loaf

Substitute 3/4 cup chopped chutney for the catsup, mixing 1/2 cup chutney into meat mixture. Mix in 1/2 cup chopped peanuts, 1/2 teaspoon curry powder and 1/4 teaspoon ground ginger. Cook as above. Spoon remaining chutney over cooked loaf and sprinkle with 2 tablespoons chopped peanuts.

8 servings.

Veal Marsala

1 1/2 pounds veal scallops	3 tablespoons vegetable oil
1/2 cup all-purpose flour	2/3 cup Marsala wine
1/4 teaspoon salt	4 tablespoons butter or margarine
1/8 teaspoon white pepper	1 teaspoon dried chives

Pound veal with flat side of mallet until 1/8 inch thick; cut into serving-size pieces. Coat veal lightly with mixture of flour, salt and pepper. Heat fry pan at 325°. Add oil and veal; cook until browned, about 1 minute on each side. Remove veal. Stir wine into fry pan, scraping drippings from bottom of fry pan with plastic or wooden utensil. Stir in butter, 1 tablespoon at a time, stirring until sauce is thickened, about 3 minutes. Stir in chives. Return veal to fry pan; cook at Warm until heated, turning to coat with sauce. Arrange veal on serving platter; spoon sauce over.

6 to 8 servings.

Veal Cutlets Normandy

1 1/2 tablespoons butter or margarine	2 medium apples, cored, cut into 1/4-inch rings
1 1/2 tablespoons vegetable oil	3/4 cup whipping cream or half-and-half
6 veal cutlets or chops, about 1/2 inch thick	1/4 cup sour cream or sour half-and-half
1/2 cup finely chopped onions	1 teaspoon flour
3/4 teaspoon ground cinnamon	Salt
1/8 teaspoon ground nutmeg	White pepper
3/4 cup apple juice	

Heat butter and oil in fry pan at Warm until butter is melted. Add veal; cook at 325° until browned and no longer pink in the center, about 3 minutes on each side. Remove veal. Add onion, cinnamon and nutmeg; cook at 225°, 1 minute. Stir in apple juice, scraping drippings from bottom of fry pan with plastic or wooden utensil. Add apples; cook until tender, 1 to 2 minutes. Remove apple mixture and reserve. Stir in whipping cream; cook 1 minute. Stir sour cream and flour into sauce; cook 1 minute. Season to taste with salt and pepper. Add reserved veal and apples, spooning sauce over veal; cook, covered, until heated through, 1 to 2 minutes.

4 to 6 servings.

Osso Bucco

4 pound veal shanks (6 pieces)	1/3 cup dry white wine or chicken broth
Flour	1 teaspoon grated lemon rind
2 tablespoons olive or vegetable oil	1/2 teaspoon dried basil leaves
2 medium carrots, finely chopped	Salt
2 ribs celery, thinly sliced	Pepper
1 medium red onion, chopped	Hot cooked rice
1 clove garlic, minced	
1 28-ounce can Italian plum tomatoes, undrained, coarsely chopped	

Coat veal shanks lightly with flour. Heat fry pan at 350°. Add oil and veal; cook until browned on all sides, about 10 minutes. Stir in carrots, celery, onion and garlic; cook until tender, 3 to 5 minutes, stirring frequently. Add tomatoes with liquid, wine, lemon rind and basil; cook at 400° until boiling. Reduce heat to simmer, between Warm and 200°; cook, covered, until tender, 1 1/2 to 2 hours. Season to taste with salt and pepper. Serve veal with rice.

6 servings.

Veal Scallops Parmesan

1 pound veal scallops or cutlets	1/4 teaspoon black pepper
1/4 cup all-purpose flour	2 tablespoons olive or vegetable oil
1/4 teaspoon salt	1 16-ounce can Italian plum tomatoes, drained, coarsely chopped
1/8 teaspoon white pepper	1 cup tomato sauce
2 eggs	1 clove garlic, minced
1/4 cup dry bread crumbs	1/2 teaspoon sugar
2 tablespoons grated Parmesan cheese	1 teaspoon dried basil leaves
1/4 teaspoon dried basil leaves	1/4 teaspoon dried oregano leaves
1/8 teaspoon dried oregano leaves	2 cups shredded mozzarella cheese
1/2 teaspoon salt	

Pound veal with flat side of mallet until 1/4 inch thick; cut into serving-size pieces. Mix flour, 1/4 teaspoon salt and white pepper in shallow bowl. Beat eggs until foamy. Mix bread crumbs, Parmesan cheese, 1/4 teaspoon basil, 1/8 teaspoon oregano, 1/2 teaspoon salt and black pepper in shallow bowl. Coat veal pieces lightly with flour mixture; dip into beaten egg; coat generously with crumb mixture.

Heat fry pan at 325°. Add oil and veal; cook until golden, about 1 1/2 minutes on each side. Remove veal from fry pan; drain on paper toweling. Discard excess oil. Return veal to fry pan. Combine remaining ingredients, except mozzarella cheese; pour over veal and sprinkle with cheese. Cook, covered, until cheese melts, about 5 minutes.

4 to 6 servings.

Moroccan Lamb Stew

2 tablespoons butter or margarine	2 whole cloves
1/2 cup blanched whole almonds	1 bay leaf
1/2 cup raisins	1 teaspoon salt
1/4 cup olive or vegetable oil	1/4 teaspoon pepper
2 1/2 pounds lamb cubes for stew	1 16-ounce can tomatoes, undrained, coarsely chopped
3/4 cup coarsely chopped onions	1/2 cup tomato juice
2 cloves garlic, minced	3 hard-cooked eggs, cut into wedges
1/2 teaspoon ground cinnamon	Hot cooked rice
1/4 teaspoon ground ginger	

Heat butter in fry pan at Warm until melted. Add almonds; cook at 225° until golden. Stir in raisins; cook 1 minute. Remove almond mixture and reserve.

Heat fry pan at 300°. Add oil and lamb; cook until browned, about 8 minutes. Remove meat. Add onion and garlic, cook 1 minute. Stir in cinnamon, ginger, cloves, bay leaf, salt and pepper; cook 1 minute. Return lamb to fry pan. Add tomatoes with liquid and tomato juice; cook at 400° until boiling. Reduce heat to simmer, between Warm and 200°; cook, covered, until lamb is tender, 1 to 1 1/2 hours. Cook, uncovered, until sauce is thickened to desired consistency, 5 to 10 minutes.

Mound hot rice in center of rimmed serving platter; spoon stew onto rice. Arrange egg wedges around edge of platter; sprinkle reserved almond mixture over stew.

6 servings.

Lamb Chops with Mint Sauce

6   lamb loin or rib chops, 3/4 inch thick
    Salt
    Pepper
2   tablespoons vegetable oil

1/4   cup water
1/4   cup mint jelly
1/4   cup peach preserves
1/2   teaspoon dried mint leaves

Heat fry pan at 325°. Sprinkle chops lightly with salt and pepper. Add oil and chops; cook until browned and no longer pink in the center, about 3 minutes on each side. Remove chops and keep warm. Discard fat.

Reduce temperature to 200°; add water to fry pan, scraping drippings from bottom of fry pan with plastic or wooden utensil. Add jelly, preserves and mint; cook until jelly and preserves are melted, stirring constantly. Serve sauce with lamb.

4 to 6 servings.

Greek-Style Lamb Roast

1/4   cup butter or margarine
1   cup pine nuts or slivered almonds
1/2   cup finely chopped onions
2   cloves garlic, minced
2   cups white long grain rice
2   teaspoons ground cinnamon
1/4   teaspoon ground nutmeg
1/2   teaspoon ground allspice
1/4   teaspoon ground cloves
1   small bay leaf
5   cups water

2   teaspoons chicken flavor instant bouillon
    Salt
    White pepper
4   pounds boned rolled tied leg of lamb
2   large cloves garlic, cut into slivers
1   teaspoon dried mint leaves
    Salt
    Black pepper
1   egg
2   tablespoons olive or vegetable oil
2   cups water

Heat butter in fry pan at Warm until melted. Add pine nuts; cook at 225° until golden. Remove pine nuts and reserve. Add onion and minced garlic; cook 2 minutes. Add rice, cinnamon, nutmeg, allspice, cloves and bay leaf; cook 1 minute, stirring constantly. Stir in 5 cups water and bouillon; heat at 400° until boiling. Reduce heat to simmer, between Warm and 200°; cook, covered, until rice is tender and water absorbed, about 20 minutes. Remove bay leaf. Stir reserved pine nuts into rice mixture; season to taste with salt and white pepper. Remove rice mixture and reserve. Clean fry pan.

Unroll lamb. Make small incisions in meat, using sharp knife, and insert garlic slivers. Sprinkle meat lightly with mint, salt and black pepper. Mix 1 1/2 cups of the rice mixture with egg; spoon onto meat, leaving 1 1/2-inch margin around edges of meat. Roll up and tie.

Heat fry pan at 325°. Add oil; cook roast until browned on all sides. Remove roast. Insert meat thermometer so that tip is in center of meat, away from fat. Place meat on rack in fry pan. Add 2 cups water; heat at 400° until boiling. Reduce heat to simmer, between Warm and 200°; cook, covered, 1 hour, or until thermometer registers 160°.

Spoon remaining rice mixture into covered heat-proof casserole or dish; place on rack with meat during last 20 minutes of cooking time. Remove roast to serving platter; let stand, loosely covered with foil, 15 minutes before slicing. Spoon extra rice around roast.

10 to 12 servings.

Roast Pork Loin with Sweet-Sour Fruit

5   pounds pork loin roast
1   tablespoon soy sauce
1   cup water
1   tablespoon vegetable oil
1   medium green pepper, cut into strips
1   medium red or green pepper, cut into chunks
3   green onions, sliced diagonally
1   clove garlic, minced
1   20-ounce can sliced pineapple, drained, syrup reserved

1   10-ounce can Mandarin orange segments, drained, syrup reserved
1/2   cup water
1/2   teaspoon chicken flavor instant bouillon
1/4   cup cider vinegar
3   tablespoons soy sauce
3   tablespoons tomato sauce
2   tablespoons cornstarch
1   tablespoon sugar
1/8   teaspoon ground ginger

Place roast on rack in fry pan; brush with 1 tablespoon soy sauce. Insert meat thermometer in roast, with tip of thermometer in center of meat, away from fat and bone. Add 1 cup water to fry pan; cook at 400° until boiling. Reduce heat to simmer, between Warm and 200°; cook, covered, 2 3/4 to 3 hours, or until thermometer registers 170°. Remove roast to serving platter; let stand, loosely covered with aluminum foil, 15 minutes before slicing. Clean fry pan.

Heat fry pan at 250°. Add oil, peppers, onions and garlic; cook until peppers are crisp-tender, about 3 minutes. Mix reserved fruit syrups and remaining ingredients, except fruit. Stir into pepper mixture; cook, until thickened, stirring constantly. Add pineapple slices and orange segments; cook until heated through, about 3 minutes. Serve fruit mixture with roast.

8 servings.

Cinnamon Fruit Pork Roast

1   11-ounce package mixed dried fruit
2   cups apricot nectar
1/2   cup almond flavor liqueur or peach nectar
1   cinnamon stick
1   whole clove
1   small bay leaf

1   cardamom pod
1/16   teaspoon ground nutmeg
2 1/2   pounds boned, rolled, tied pork loin roast
Salt
Pepper
1   tablespoon vegetable oil
1   cup water

Pit prunes. Place fruit, apricot nectar, liqueur, cinnamon, clove, bay leaf, cardamom and nutmeg in fry pan; cook at 400° until boiling. Reduce heat to simmer, between Warm and 200°; cook, covered, 20 minutes. Remove fruit mixture, cool. Clean fry pan.

Unroll roast; sprinkle lightly with salt and pepper. Spread half the fruit mixture on roast; roll up and tie. Heat fry pan at 325°. Add oil and roast; cook until browned on all sides, about 10 minutes. Remove roast. Add water to fry pan; heat at 400° until boiling. Reduce heat to simmer, between Warm and 200°. Insert meat thermometer in roast, with tip of thermometer in center of meat, away from fat. Place roast on rack in fry pan; cook, covered, 2 hours, or until thermometer registers 170°. Place remaining fruit mixture in covered heat-proof casserole or dish; place on rack with roast during last 10 minutes of cooking time.

Remove roast to serving platter; let stand 15 minutes before slicing. Serve fruit as accompaniment.

6 to 8 servings.

Roast Pork Loin with Sweet-Sour Fruit

Saucy Barbecued Spareribs

Hot Chili Barbecue Sauce
(see recipe, page 72)

4 pounds pork spareribs, cut into
serving-size pieces

4 cups water

1 cup cider vinegar

Make Hot Chili Barbecue Sauce. Arrange ribs in fry pan, meat sides down. Add water and vinegar; heat at 400° until boiling. Reduce heat to simmer, between Warm and 200°; cook, with cover ajar 1/2 inch, 30 minutes, or until pork is tender. Remove meat; pour off liquid.

Replace meat in fry pan and pour barbecue sauce over ribs; cook, covered, at Warm 10 minutes. Turn ribs over; cook, covered, 10 minutes. Uncover and cook at 200°, 2 minutes on each side.

4 servings.

TIP: Any desired barbecue sauce may be substituted for the Hot Chili Barbecue Sauce.

Beer-Glazed Ham

5 pounds fully cooked boneless ham
Whole cloves

3/4 cup light brown sugar

3 tablespoons spicy brown mustard

1 12-ounce can beer or ginger ale

2 to 3 cups water

Score fat on top of ham; stud with cloves. Place ham on rack in fry pan; insert meat thermometer in ham, with tip of thermometer in center of meat, away from fat.

Mix brown sugar, mustard and 2 tablespoons beer; spoon mixture over ham. Add remaining beer and 2 cups water to fry pan; heat at 400° until boiling. Reduce heat to simmer, between Warm and 200°; cook, covered, 1 1/2 hours, or until thermometer registers 130°. Baste ham with pan juices every 15 minutes; add remaining water if juices become too thick. Remove ham to serving platter; spoon pan juices over ham. Let stand, loosely covered with aluminum foil, 15 minutes before slicing.

12 to 14 servings.

Spiced Cherry Ham Slice

3 tablespoons butter or margarine

3 tablespoons light brown sugar

1 tablespoon lemon juice

1 teaspoon Bavarian-style mustard

1/8 teaspoon ground ginger

1/16 teaspoon ground cinnamon

Dash ground cloves

1/16 teaspoon white pepper

1 16-ounce can pitted Queen Anne
cherries, drained

1 1/2 pounds center-cut ham steak
(3/4 inch thick)

Heat butter in fry pan at Warm until melted. Stir in sugar; cook at 200°, 1 minute. Stir in lemon juice, mustard, ginger, cinnamon, cloves and pepper; cook 1 minute. Stir in cherries; cook 1 minute. Add ham steak; cook until ham is glazed and heated, about 3 minutes on each side.

6 servings.

Smoked Sausage and Potatoes Casserole

1 tablespoon vegetable oil	2/3 cup milk
8 ounces smoked sausage, cut into 1/4-inch slices	2 tablespoons butter or margarine
1/3 cup chopped onion	1 teaspoon dried basil leaves
1 5.25-ounce package scalloped potatoes	5 slices deluxe processed American cheese, cut diagonally into halves
2 1/2 cups water	

Heat fry pan at 250°. Add oil, sausage and onion; cook until onion is tender, about 4 minutes. Remove sausage mixture and reserve. Clean fry pan.

Mix potatoes in fry pan according to package directions, using water, milk, butter and basil; cook at 400° until boiling. Reduce heat to simmer, between Warm and 200°; cook, covered, 30 minutes or until potatoes are tender. Stir in reserved sausage mixture; cook until heated, about 3 minutes. Arrange cheese slices decoratively on potatoes; cook, covered until cheese begins to melt, about 2 minutes.

4 to 6 servings.

Pork Chop 'N' Yam Casserole

4 to 6 pork loin chops (1/2 inch thick)	3 tablespoons dark molasses
Poultry seasoning	1 tablespoon lemon juice
Salt	1/4 cup light brown sugar
Pepper	1/4 teaspoon anise seeds, crushed
2 tablespoons vegetable oil	1 17-ounce can sweet potatoes, drained
1 16-ounce can sliced peaches, undrained	

Sprinkle chops lightly with poultry seasoning, salt and pepper. Heat fry pan at 300°. Add oil and chops; cook until browned on both sides. Drain peaches, adding syrup to fry pan. Stir in molasses, lemon juice, brown sugar and anise seeds; cook at 400° until boiling. Reduce heat to simmer, between Warm and 200°; cook, covered, 20 minutes. Add sweet potatoes and peaches, spooning syrup over; cook, covered, 10 minutes, or until pork chops are fork-tender.

4 to 6 servings.

Savory Homemade Sausage Patties

1 pound ground pork	1/4 teaspoon fennel seeds, crushed
1/2 teaspoon dried sage leaves	1/8 teaspoon dried thyme leaves
1/4 teaspoon dried marjoram leaves	1/2 teaspoon salt
1/4 teaspoon dried rosemary leaves	1/4 teaspoon pepper

Mix all ingredients until well blended. Form mixture into 8 patties. Heat fry pan at 325°; cook sausage patties until brown and no longer pink in the center, about 5 minutes on each side.

4 servings.

Poultry

Is there anything better than golden Country Fried Chicken with old-fashioned Cream Gravy? Well, it's a matter of taste. Maybe your first choice is spicy Mexican Chicken with Green Sauce, tempting Curried Chicken, or juicy Roast Chicken with Garden Vegetables. If you favor the most delicate fare, you'll love Chicken Piccata, sauced with lemon and sherry. But if you prefer a luscious Italian tomato-wine sauce, you'll want second helpings of Chicken Cacciatore.

The many guises of chicken showcase the capabilities of the electric fry pan, which can just as easily deep fry Peanut Butter Drumsticks to crispy perfection or bake whole, moist Mustard Baked Chicken. In a most unusual twist, the pan is used to poach Chicken Breasts with Asparagus—extremely attractive chicken rolls shaped and cooked in plastic wrap. If you want to vary the chicken selections even more, you can substitute an equal weight of any type of chicken parts for the legs, unboned breasts, or cut-up chicken used in many of the recipes. Often, you can save money or please white- or dark-meat devotees in this way, but do keep in mind that smaller pieces, such as drumsticks, will cook faster than meatier breast halves.

You don't have to wait for a holiday to feature Duckling with Sweet-Sour Cabbage or Baked Turkey Breast with Stuffing. Though festive and delectable, the recipes for these entrées are easy enough for everyday. And if you have turkey left over, don't hesitate to substitute it in Chicken Creole, a New Orleans-style melange that makes any plain poultry taste wonderful the second time around.

Almond Chicken Casserole

4	boned skinned chicken breast halves (about 1 1/2 pounds)
2	tablespoons butter or margarine
2	tablespoons vegetable oil
1	cup chopped onions
1	cup sliced mushrooms
1/2	cup chopped green pepper
1/4	cup sliced carrot
1/4	cup sliced celery
1	clove garlic, minced
1/4	cup all-purpose flour

1	teaspoon minced parsley
1/4	teaspoon dried thyme leaves
2	cups water
1 1/2	teaspoons chicken-flavor instant bouillon
1/2	cup frozen peas, thawed
6	ounces egg noodles, cooked
1/2	cup slivered almonds, toasted
2	dashes cayenne pepper
	Salt
	White pepper

Cut chicken into 1/2-inch pieces. Heat butter and oil in fry pan at Warm until butter is melted. Add chicken; cook at 225° until chicken is no longer pink in the center, about 5 minutes. Remove chicken and reserve. Stir in onion, mushrooms, green pepper, carrot, celery, and garlic; cook at 225° for 3 minutes, stirring frequently. Stir in flour, parsley, and thyme; cook 2 minutes, stirring constantly. Stir in water and bouillon; cook at 400° until boiling. Reduce heat to simmer, between Warm and 200°; cook, covered, 5 minutes; uncovered, 3 minutes. Stir in reserved chicken and peas; cook 2 minutes. Stir in noodles and almonds; cook until heated through, about 5 minutes. Stir in cayenne pepper; season to taste with salt and white pepper.

4 servings.

Peanut Butter Chicken Legs

1/2   cup all-purpose flour

1/4   teaspoon salt

1/8   teaspoon white pepper

1/4   cup peanut butter

1/4   cup milk

  1   egg, beaten

  2   cups oven-toasted rice cereal, lightly crushed

1/2   cup coarsely chopped unsalted peanuts

1/2   teaspoon chili powder

1/4   teaspoon curry powder

  6   chicken drumsticks

      Vegetable oil

Mix flour, salt, and pepper in shallow bowl. Mix peanut butter, milk, and egg in shallow bowl. Mix cereal, peanuts, chili powder, and curry powder in shallow bowl. Coat chicken lightly with flour mixture; dip into peanut butter mixture; coat generously with cereal mixture.

Heat 1 inch oil in fry pan at 300°. Add chicken; cook, covered, until crisp and juices are clear when thickest parts are pierced with a fork, about 15 minutes, turning chicken every 5 minutes.

4 to 6 servings.

Chicken Piccata

4   boned skinned chicken breast halves (about 1 pound)

     Flour

4   tablespoons butter or margarine

2   tablespoons vegetable oil

       Salt

       Pepper

2 to 4   tablespoons dry sherry

2 to 3   tablespoons lemon juice

Pound chicken with flat side of mallet until scant 1/4 inch thick; cut into serving-size pieces. Coat chicken lightly with flour. Heat 2 tablespoons butter and oil in fry pan at Warm until butter is melted. Add chicken; cook at 300° until browned, 3 to 4 minutes on each side. Remove chicken, sprinkle lightly with salt and pepper.

Add remaining 2 tablespoons butter, sherry and lemon juice; cook at 225° until sauce is thickened, scraping drippings from bottom of fry pan with plastic or wooden utensil. Return chicken to fry pan; cook 2 minutes, turning chicken to coat with sauce. Arrange chicken on serving platter; spoon remaining sauce over.

4 servings.

Chicken Creole

  3   tablespoons bacon drippings or vegetable oil

1/2   cup chopped onions

1/2   cup chopped celery

2/3   cup chopped green pepper

  2   cloves garlic, minced

1/2   cup all-purpose flour

  1   teaspoon salt

  1   teaspoon black pepper

  2   16-ounce cans tomatoes, undrained, coarsely chopped

1 1/2   cups water

  2   teaspoons chicken flavor instant bouillon

  4   cups cubed cooked chicken

  1   tablespoon minced parsley

1/2 to 1   teaspoon crushed red pepper

      Hot cooked rice

Heat fry pan at 225°. Add bacon drippings, onion, celery, green pepper and garlic; cook until vegetables are tender, about 4 minutes. Stir in flour, salt and black pepper; cook until flour is light brown, about 5 minutes, stirring frequently. Stir in tomatoes with liquid, water and bouillon; cook at 400° until boiling. Reduce heat to simmer, between Warm and 200°; cook until slightly thickened, 10 to 15 minutes, stirring occasionally. Stir in chicken, parsley and red pepper; cook, covered, 5 minutes. Serve with rice.

4 servings.

Country Fried Chicken with Cream Gravy

3 pounds chicken pieces
1/2 cup self-rising flour
1/2 teaspoon paprika
1/4 teaspoon poultry seasoning
1/4 teaspoon pepper

Vegetable oil
2 tablespoons all-purpose flour
1 1/2 cups whipping cream or half-and-half
Salt
Pepper

Coat chicken pieces generously with mixture of self-rising flour, paprika, poultry seasoning and 1/4 teaspoon pepper. Heat 1 inch oil in fry pan at 300°. Add chicken; cook, covered, until browned on all sides, about 15 minutes. Turn chicken; cook, covered, until chicken is tender and juices are clear when thickest pieces are pierced with a fork, 15 to 20 minutes. Remove chicken to serving platter; keep warm. Drain all but 2 tablespoons drippings from fry pan.

Stir flour into drippings; cook at 225°, 2 minutes, scraping drippings from bottom of fry pan with plastic or wooden utensil. Gradually stir in cream; cook at 300° until thickened, 2 to 3 minutes, stirring constantly. Season with salt and pepper. Serve chicken with gravy.

4 servings.

Mexican Chicken with Green Sauce

2 tablespoons vegetable oil
6 chicken breast halves (about 2 1/2 pounds)
Salt
1/4 cup coarsely chopped onion
1 large clove garlic, minced
2 8-ounce cans mild or hot green salsa
3 cups packed romaine leaves
1/2 cup water

1/2 teaspoon chicken flavor instant bouillon
1 teaspoon dried coriander leaves
1/4 cup sour cream or sour half-and-half
1 teaspoon flour
2 16-ounce cans refried beans, heated
Hot cooked rice

Heat fry pan at 300°. Add oil and chicken; cook until lightly browned, about 5 minutes on each side. Remove chicken; sprinkle lightly with salt. Drain all but 1 tablespoon fat from fry pan.

Add onion and garlic; cook at 225° for 2 minutes. Process salsa and romaine in food processor or blender until mixture is almost smooth. Add salsa mixture to fry pan, scraping drippings from bottom of fry pan with plastic or wooden utensil. Stir in water, bouillon and coriander; cook 5 minutes, stirring occasionally. Add chicken pieces, skin sides down, spooning sauce over; cook, covered, until chicken is tender and juices are clear when thickest parts are pierced with a fork, 35 to 40 minutes. Mix sour cream with flour and stir into sauce; cook 1 minute. Arrange chicken on serving platter; spoon sauce over. Serve chicken with refried beans and rice.

4 to 6 servings.

Roast Chicken with Garden Vegetables

3 tablespoons vegetable oil

4 ounces green beans, ends trimmed

4 ounces small mushrooms

1 small zucchini, sliced diagonally into 1/2-inch pieces

1 medium red or green pepper, cut into 1-inch pieces

3 pound roasting chicken
  Salt
  Pepper

1 tablespoon vegetable oil

1 medium onion, sliced

1 clove garlic, minced

1/4 teaspoon dried basil leaves

1/4 teaspoon dried marjoram leaves

1/4 teaspoon dried rosemary leaves

1/4 teaspoon dried thyme leaves

1/2 cup dry white wine

1 to 1 1/2 cups water

1/2 teaspoon chicken flavor instant bouillon
  Salt
  Pepper

Heat fry pan at 225°. Add oil, beans, mushrooms, zucchini and red pepper; cook 2 to 3 minutes, stirring occasionally. Remove vegetables and reserve.

Sprinkle cavity of chicken lightly with salt and pepper. Add 1 tablespoon oil and chicken; cook at 300° until well browned, turning every 2 to 3 minutes. Remove chicken. Add onion and garlic; cook at 225° for 2 minutes. Stir in basil, marjoram, rosemary and thyme; cook 2 minutes. Return chicken to fry pan. Add wine, 1 cup water and bouillon; cook at 400° until boiling. Reduce heat to simmer, between Warm and 200°; cook, covered, 40 minutes, adding more water if necessary. Add reserved vegetables to fry pan; cook, covered, until vegetables are tender and juices in chicken are clear when inside of thigh is pierced with a fork, about 10 minutes. Season vegetables to taste with salt and pepper.

4 servings.

Curried Chicken Breasts

2 tablespoons vegetable oil

6 boned chicken breast halves (about 1 1/2 pounds)

1 cup chopped onions

1 clove garlic, minced

1 teaspoon minced fresh or canned gingerroot

1 tablespoon curry powder

1/4 teaspoon ground cinnamon

1/4 teaspoon dried coriander leaves

1/8 teaspoon ground cumin

1/16 teaspoon crushed red pepper

3 tablespoons flour

1 16-ounce can tomatoes, drained, coarsely chopped

1 1/2 cups water

3/4 teaspoon chicken flavor instant bouillon

1 medium apple, peeled, cored, cut into 16 slices

1/4 cup golden raisins
  Salt
  Hot cooked rice
  Plain yogurt

Heat fry pan at 300°. Add oil and chicken; cook until browned, about 2 minutes on each side. Remove chicken. Add onions, garlic and gingerroot; cook at 225° until onions are tender, about 2 minutes. Stir in curry powder, cinnamon, coriander, cumin and red pepper; cook 1 minute. Stir in flour; cook 1 minute. Stir in tomatoes, water and bouillon. Return chicken to fry pan; cook at 400° until boiling. Reduce heat to simmer, between Warm and 200°; cook, covered, until chicken is tender and juices are clear when thickest parts are pierced with a fork, about 45 minutes. Stir in apple and raisins during last 10 minutes of cooking time. Season to taste with salt. Serve chicken with rice; pass yogurt as an accompaniment.

4 to 6 servings.

Chicken Hawaiian

6	chicken legs with thighs attached	1 1/2	tablespoons soy sauce
1/2	cup all-purpose flour	1/4	cup cider vinegar
1	teaspoon salt	1/4	cup sugar
1/4	teaspoon white pepper	1	small clove garlic, minced
3	tablespoons vegetable oil	1	tablespoon cornstarch
1	cup water	2	tablespoons cold water
1/2	teaspoon chicken flavor instant bouillon	1	large tomato, cut into wedges
2	tablespoons vegetable oil		Salt
2	cups sliced mushrooms		White pepper
1/2	cup unsweetened pineapple juice		Hot cooked rice
1/2	cup water		

Coat chicken with mixture of flour, 1 teaspoon salt and 1/4 teaspoon white pepper. Heat fry pan at 300°. Add oil and chicken; cook until golden, about 5 minutes on each side. Drain excess fat. Add 1 cup water and bouillon; cook at 400° until boiling. Reduce heat to simmer, between Warm and 200°; cook, covered, until chicken is tender and juices are clear when thickest parts are pierced with a fork, about 30 minutes. Remove chicken; keep warm. Clean fry pan.

Heat fry pan at 225°. Add oil and mushrooms; cook 1 minute. Stir in pineapple juice, 1/2 cup water, soy sauce, vinegar, sugar and garlic; cook at 400° until boiling. Reduce heat to simmer, between Warm and 200°. Mix cornstarch and cold water. Stir into pineapple juice mixture; cook until thickened, about 1 minute, stirring constantly. Stir in tomato; cook 1 minute. Season to taste with salt and white pepper.

Spoon rice onto serving platter; arrange chicken on rice. Spoon sauce with vegetables over.

6 servings.

Poached Chicken Breasts with Asparagus

6	boned chicken breast halves	8	cups water
1 1/2	teaspoons dried tarragon leaves	6	teaspoons chicken flavor instant bouillon
	Salt	1/4	teaspoon dried thyme leaves
	White pepper	1	small bay leaf
1	10-ounce package frozen asparagus spears, thawed		Sherry Newberg Sauce (see recipe, page 70)

Pound chicken with flat side of mallet until even in thickness (almost 1/4 inch thick); sprinkle lightly with tarragon, salt and pepper. Lay each piece chicken on piece of plastic wrap, 8 × 8 inches. Press asparagus lightly with paper toweling to remove excess moisture. Trim asparagus into lengths to fit chicken pieces. Arrange 3 or 4 spears lengthwise on each piece chicken; fold each breast lengthwise in half and roll up in plastic wrap. Twist ends of plastic wrap to seal (chicken packets will resemble small sausages); tie each end with piece of string.

Heat water, bouillon, thyme and bay leaf in fry pan at 400° until boiling. Reduce heat to simmer, between Warm and 200°. Add chicken packets; cook, covered, 10 minutes. Turn chicken over; cook, covered, 10 minutes. Remove chicken to shallow baking dish; pour cooking liquid over.

Make Sherry Newberg Sauce. Remove chicken from cooking liquid and unwrap; remove skin and discard. Slice diagonally into scant 1/2-inch slices. Arrange chicken on serving plate; serve with sauce.

4 to 6 servings.

TIP: Poached chicken is also delicious cold. Let cool in cooking liquid; drain and refrigerate until chilled. Unwrap and slice, as above.

Chicken Hawaiian

Chicken Cacciatore

2 tablespoons olive or vegetable oil
3 pounds chicken pieces
1 large onion, coarsely chopped
1 cup halved mushrooms
2 cloves garlic, minced
1 16-ounce can tomatoes, undrained, coarsely chopped
1 8-ounce can tomato sauce
1/4 cup sliced black olives

1 teaspoon sugar
2 teaspoons dried oregano leaves
2 bay leaves
1 cup dry red wine
Salt
Pepper
Italian bread, sliced, heated

Heat fry pan at 300°. Add oil and chicken; cook until browned on all sides, about 10 minutes. Remove chicken. Add onion, mushrooms and garlic; cook at 225° until onion is tender, about 3 minutes. Return chicken to fry pan. Add tomatoes with liquid, tomato sauce, olives, sugar, oregano and bay leaves; cook at 400° until boiling. Reduce heat to simmer, between Warm and 200°; cook, covered, 30 minutes. Stir in wine; season to taste with salt and pepper; cook, covered, 10 minutes, or until chicken is tender. Serve chicken and sauce in shallow bowls with warm bread.

4 servings.

Mustard Baked Chicken

3 pound roasting chicken
Salt
Pepper
2 tablespoons vegetable oil
1/2 cup Dijon-style mustard
1 tablespoon melted butter or margarine

2 teaspoons dried chives
1 teaspoon dried tarragon leaves
1/2 cup dry white wine or chicken broth
1 tablespoon flour
1 cup half-and-half

Sprinkle cavity of chicken lightly with salt and pepper. Heat fry pan at 300°. Add oil and chicken; cook until well browned, turning every 2 to 3 minutes. Place chicken on rack in fry pan. Mix mustard, butter, chives and tarragon; brush 2 tablespoons of mixture on chicken. Pour wine into fry pan; cook, covered, at 225°, until chicken is tender and juices are clear when inside of thigh is pierced with a fork, 45 to 50 minutes. Remove chicken to serving platter; keep warm.

Stir in remaining mustard mixture, flour and half-and-half into pan juices; cook at 200° until sauce is thickened, about 5 minutes, stirring constantly.

4 servings.

Braised Turkey Legs

3 tablespoons vegetable oil
2 turkey legs
Salt
Pepper

2 cups water
1 1/2 teaspoons chicken flavor instant bouillon
1/2 teaspoon dried sage leaves
1/2 teaspoon dried rosemary leaves

Heat fry pan at 325°, add oil and turkey legs; cook, covered, until well browned, 10 to 12 minutes. Remove turkey legs; sprinkle lightly with salt and pepper. Add water, bouillon, sage and rosemary to fry pan; heat at 400° until boiling. Reduce heat to simmer, between Warm and 200°. Place turkey legs on rack in fry pan; cook, covered, until turkey legs are tender and juices are clear when thickest parts are pierced with a fork, 1 1/4 to 1 1/2 hours.

Arrange turkey legs on serving platter; keep warm.

2 servings.

Baked Turkey Breast with Stuffing

Whole Wheat Stuffing or Variations (see recipe, page 24)
4 1/2 to 5 **pound frozen turkey breast, thawed**
Vegetable oil
Salt

Pepper
2 **cups water**
1 **teaspoon chicken flavor instant bouillon**

Make Whole Wheat Stuffing or desired variation; do not cook. Loosen skin on top of turkey breast with sharp knife; spoon half the stuffing evenly under skin. Lightly brush turkey breast with oil; sprinkle cavity of turkey lightly with salt and pepper. Insert meat thermometer so that tip is in center of thickest part of breast, away from bone. Place turkey breast on rack in fry pan. Add water and bouillon; heat at 400° until boiling. Reduce heat to 325°; cook, covered, 30 minutes. Reduce heat to 275°; cook, covered, 1 1/4 hours, or until thermometer registers 175°.

Place remaining stuffing in covered casserole or aluminum foil packet; place on rack with turkey breast during last 30 minutes of cooking time.

Remove turkey breast to serving platter; let stand, loosely covered with aluminum foil, for 15 minutes. Slice and serve with stuffing.

8 to 10 servings.

Duckling with Sweet-Sour Cabbage

4 **pound frozen duckling, thawed, cut into quarters**
Salt
Pepper

1 **cup water**
1/2 **cup chicken flavor instant bouillon**
Sweet-Sour Cabbage

Pierce skin of ducking pieces generously with fork. Heat fry pan at 300°; cook duckling, covered, until well-browned, about 8 minutes on each side. Remove duckling from fry pan; sprinkle lightly with salt and pepper. Drain fat from fry pan and discard. Place duckling pieces, skin side up, on rack in fry pan; add water and bouillon; heat at 400° until boiling. Reduce heat to simmer, between Warm and 200°; cook, covered, until duckling is tender and juices are clear when thickest parts are pierced with a fork, 1 to 1 1/4 hours. Remove duckling from fry pan. Clean fry pan.

Make Sweet-Sour Cabbage. Arrange duckling pieces on cabbage mixture; cook, covered, at 200° until cabbage is tender and duckling is heated through, about 10 minutes.

4 servings.

Sweet-Sour Cabbage

2 **tablespoons olive or vegetable oil**
1/4 **cup chopped onion**
1 **pound cabbage, thinly sliced**
1 **16-ounce can tomatoes, undrained, coarsely chopped**
2 **tablespoons white wine vinegar**

2 **tablespoons light brown sugar**
1/4 **cup sliced almonds**
1/4 **cup raisins**
Salt
Pepper

Heat fry pan at 225°. Add oil and onion, cook 2 minutes. Stir in remaining ingredients, except almonds, raisins, salt, and pepper; cook at 400° until boiling. Reduce heat to simmer, between Warm and 200°; cook, covered, until cabbage is crisp-tender, about 10 minutes. Stir in almonds and raisins; season to taste with salt and pepper.

4 servings.

Fish and Seafood

The trend toward lighter dining, prompted by concern for fitness and good health, has made fish an increasingly popular choice. Almost all types of fish provide fewer calories and less cholesterol than equivalent portions of meat. Just as importantly, the many ways to prepare fish yield a spectrum of mouthwatering fare. And because fish is naturally tender, it never takes more than minutes to cook.

All fishermen know that nothing tastes better than pan-fried fresh fish. Sprinkle the fish lightly with seasoned flour or cornmeal (or a bit of both), sizzle it in a hot pan, and you have the makings of a feast. The electric fry pan is always ready for any day's catch, and its nonstick surface reduces the amount of cooking oil needed. Southern-Style Fried Catfish offers a classic preparation that can be applied to any small freshwater fish. Trout with Garlic Sauce is a tantalizing variation for those who like a mild garlic flavor; it can be adapted to almost any whole fish or fillet if you adjust the cooking time according to the size and thickness of the fish.

Steaming and poaching are excellent ways to highlight the delicacy of seafood. The electric fry pan not only takes the guesswork out of these techniques but also makes fast work of the light sauces that go so well with the simply prepared fish. In this chapter you'll find salmon steaks very briefly sautéed, then steamed and served with Cucumber-Dill Butter Sauce; whole trout steamed in parchment paper (or aluminum foil) to seal in the delicious juices; and sole fillets poached in a sherry-lemon blend that is then used to make a delectable Mornay sauce. Most refined of all is Rolled Turbot Fillets filled with Shrimp Mousse and served with Drawn Butter Sauce—a real show-stopper when company's coming.

For downhome suppers, keep canned seafood on hand to turn into Crab Cakes, Tuna-Mushroom Casserole, or Salmon Loaf with Sour Cream-Cucumber Sauce. And you needn't worry about substituting frozen fish for fresh in the other recipes, but be careful not to over-defrost it, or it may become dry or mushy. Thaw the fish in the refrigerator or in a bowl of cold water until it's not quite completely defrosted—it should still be cold and firm. Then rinse off any remaining ice crystals and pat dry with paper toweling.

Red Snapper with Tomato-Jalapeño Sauce

2 **pound whole dressed red snapper**	1/2 **cup sliced black olives**
Salt	1 **tablespoon chopped seeded jalapeño pepper**
Pepper	
1/4 **cup lime juice**	2 **teaspoons drained capers**
2 **tablespoons vegetable oil**	1 **teaspoon dried cilantro leaves**
2 **cups sliced onions**	1/2 **teaspoon salt**
2 **cloves garlic, minced**	2 **tablespoons olive or vegetable oil**
2 **16-ounce cans tomatoes, undrained, coarsely choppped**	

Score skin on both sides of fish diagonally, using sharp knife. Sprinkle fish lightly with salt and pepper; place in shallow baking dish. Pour lime juice over fish; let stand 30 minutes, turning fish occasionally.

Heat fry pan at 225°. Add oil, onion and garlic; cook until tender, about 3 minutes. Drain tomatoes reserving 1/2 cup liquid. Stir in tomatoes, 1/2 cup liquid and remaining ingredients, except olive oil; cook at 400° until boiling. Reduce heat to simmer, between Warm and 200°; cook 3 minutes stirring frequently. Add fish to fry pan, spooning sauce over. Drizzle with olive oil; cook with cover 1/2 inch ajar, basting with sauce occasionally. Turn fish over; continue cooking with cover 1/2 inch ajar, until fish is tender and flakes with a fork, 20 to 30 minutes.

4 to 6 servings.

Sole Florentine with Mornay Sauce

2 10-ounce packages frozen chopped spinach, thawed
1/4 cup butter or margarine
2 tablespoons finely chopped onion
1/8 teaspoon ground nutmeg
1/4 teaspoon salt
1/16 teaspoon white pepper
1 pound sole fillets

Salt
White pepper
1/2 cup dry sherry
3 tablespoons lemon juice
1 tablespoon butter or margarine
Mornay Sauce
Paprika
Lemon slices

Squeeze excess moisture from spinach. Heat 1/4 cup butter in fry pan at Warm until melted. Stir in spinach and onion; cook at 225° for 2 minutes. Stir in nutmeg, 1/4 teaspoon salt and 1/16 teaspoon pepper. Spoon spinach mixture on serving platter and keep warm. Clean fry pan.

Fold fish fillets lengthwise in half; sprinkle with salt and pepper. Heat sherry, lemon juice and 1 tablespoon butter in fry pan at 400° until boiling. Reduce heat to simmer, between Warm and 200°. Add fish; cook, covered, until fish is tender and flakes with a fork, about 5 minutes. Arrange fish on spinach mixture; keep warm. Reserve cooking liquid for Mornay Sauce.

Make Mornay Sauce; spoon over fish. Sprinkle with paprika; garnish with lemon slices.

4 servings.

Mornay Sauce

2 tablespoons butter or margarine
2 tablespoons flour
2/3 cup water
Reserved cooking liquid (from Sole Florentine recipe)
1/4 cup whipping cream or half-and-half

1 teaspoon Dijon-style mustard
1/16 teaspoon ground nutmeg
1/2 cup shredded Swiss cheese
Salt
White pepper

Heat butter in fry pan at Warm until melted. Stir in flour; cook 1 minute. Stir in water and reserved cooking liquid; cook at 400° until boiling, stirring constantly. Reduce heat to 200°; stir in cream, mustard and nutmeg. Add cheese, stirring until melted. Season to taste with salt and pepper.

About 1 1/2 cups.

Trout with Garlic Sauce

1/2 cup butter or margarine
25 cloves garlic, peeled, crushed
2 tablespoons finely chopped onion
2 tablespoons finely chopped green onion and top
4 5-ounce fresh or frozen thawed whole dressed Rocky Mountain or other fresh water trout

1/4 cup all-purpose flour
1/4 teaspoon salt
1/8 teaspoon white pepper
1/4 cup vegetable oil

Heat butter in fry pan at Warm until melted. Add garlic, onion and green onion; cook between Warm and 200° until garlic cloves are golden, about 30 minutes, stirring occasionally. Remove garlic mixture. Clean fry pan.

Coat fish lightly with mixture of flour, salt and pepper. Heat oil in fry pan at 300°. Add fish; cook, covered, until fish is tender and flakes with a fork, about 3 minutes on each side. Spoon garlic mixture over fish; cook, covered, until heated through, about 1 minute.

4 servings.

Rolled Sole Fillets with Shrimp Mousse and Drawn Butter Sauce

8 ounces uncooked peeled deveined shrimp	2 cups dry white wine
1 tablespoon minced parsley	1 cup sliced onion
1/4 teaspoon paprika	4 lemon slices
1/4 teaspoon salt	1/4 teaspoon anise seed
1/8 teaspoon white pepper	1 whole clove
1 egg white	1 teaspoon salt
1/4 cup whipping cream or half-and-half	3 whole black peppercorns
2 8-ounce sole or other white fish fillets	Drawn Butter Sauce (see recipe Page 72)
2 cups water	

Process shrimp, parsley, paprika, salt and white pepper in food processor or blender until shrimp is finely ground. Add egg white, process 1 minute. With machine running, slowly add cream, process until cream is thoroughly incorporated.

Cut sole fillets lengthwise in half; spread shrimp mousse mixture on fillets, leaving 1/2 inch margin along sides of fish. Roll up fish, jelly-roll style; secure ends with wooden picks.

Place remaining ingredients, except Drawn Butter Sauce in fry pan; cook at 400° until boiling. Reduce heat to simmer, between Warm and 200°. Add fish rolls; cook until fish is tender and flakes with a fork, about 8 minutes. Remove fish, keep warm. Discard cooking liquid. Clean fry pan. Make Drawn Butter Sauce. Arrange fish on serving platter. Pass sauce to spoon over fish.

4 servings.

Crab Cakes

6 ounces fresh, frozen, or canned snow crab meat	1/4 teaspoon salt
1 egg	1/4 teaspoon white pepper
2 tablespoons finely chopped celery	1/8 to 1/4 teaspoon cayenne pepper
1 tablespoon finely chopped onion	1/3 cup crushed saltines
1 tablespoon mayonnaise or salad dressing	Vegetable oil
3 drops red pepper sauce	Tartar sauce

Mix all ingredients, except saltine crumbs, oil and tartar sauce. Mix in half the saltine crumbs. Form crab mixture into 4 patties; coat with remaining saltine crumbs. Refrigerate crab cakes 1 hour. Heat 1/4 inch oil in fry pan at 325°. Add crab cakes; cook until golden, 2 to 3 minutes on each side. Serve hot with tartar sauce.

2 servings.

Southern-Style Fried Catfish

1 1/4 pound whole dressed skinned catfish	1/4 teaspoon white pepper
1/4 cup white self-rising cornmeal	1 egg, beaten
1/4 cup all-purpose flour	2 tablespoons milk
1/16 teaspoon cayenne pepper	1/2 cup vegetable oil
1/2 teaspoon salt	

Coat catfish with mixture of cornmeal, flour, cayenne pepper, salt and white pepper. Dip fish in mixture of egg and milk; coat again with cornmeal mixture. Heat fry pan at 300°. Add 1/4 cup oil and fish; cook, covered, until golden and no longer pink in the center, 10 to 12 minutes on each side, adding more oil if necessary.

2 servings.

TIP: Any whole dressed fish can be substituted for the catfish; less cooking time will be required for smaller fish.

Trout in Parchment with Tarragon-Chive Butter Sauce

1   green onion and top, cut in half
2   5-ounce fresh or frozen thawed whole dressed Rocky Mountain or other fresh-water trout
    Salt

White pepper
Butter
Tarragon-Chive Butter Sauce (see recipe page 72)

Place half green onion in cavity of each fish; sprinkle cavities lightly with salt and pepper. Butter 2 pieces of parchment paper or aluminum foil, 11 × 8 inches; place each fish on piece of parchment. Fold parchment paper lengthwise in half; fold edges down 2 or 3 times to seal tightly. Place parchment packets on rack in fry pan; cook, covered, at 350° for 10 minutes. Remove from fry pan.

Make Tarragon-Chive Butter Sauce in fry pan. Place fish on serving plates, allowing each person to open parchment packets. Pass sauce to spoon over fish.

2 servings.

Seafood and Shrimp Newburg

1/2 cup butter or margarine
1/2 cup sliced mushrooms
1/4 cup chopped onion
1/2 cup all-purpose flour
4   cups milk
1   tablespoon dry sherry
1/8 teaspoon ground nutmeg

1   teaspoon salt
1/4 teaspoon white pepper
2   pounds fresh or frozen thawed skinless cod or other white fish fillets, cut into 3/4-inch pieces
4   ounces peeled deveined shrimp, cooked, cut into half lengthwise
     Hot cooked rice

Heat butter in fry pan at Warm until melted. Add mushrooms and onion; cook at 225° until tender, about 4 minutes. Stir in flour; cook 1 minute, stirring frequently. Gradually stir in milk; cook at 400° until boiling and thickened, stirring constantly. Stir in sherry, nutmeg, salt and white pepper; reduce heat to 250°. Stir in fish and shrimp; cook, covered, until fish is tender and flakes with a fork, 3 to 5 minutes. Serve with hot rice.

6 servings.

Tuna-Mushroom Casserole

2   tablespoons butter or margarine
1   tablespoon vegetable oil
1 1/2 cups sliced mushrooms
1/2 cup chopped red or green pepper
1/2 cup sliced water chestnuts
1   rib celery, thinly sliced
1/4 cup chopped green onions and tops
1   10 1/2-ounce can condensed mushroom soup
1/2 cup milk

1   10-ounce package frozen peas, thawed
1   pound spaghetti, cooked
1   6 1/2-ounce can tuna in water, drained
2   tablespoons soy sauce
1/2 teaspoon dried coriander leaves
1   clove garlic, minced
     Salt
     White pepper

Heat butter and oil in fry pan at Warm until butter is melted. Add mushrooms, red or green pepper, water chestnuts, celery and onions; cook at 225° until vegetables are tender, about 8 minutes. Stir in soup, milk and peas; cook at 325°, 5 minutes, stirring occasionally. Stir in spaghetti, tuna, soy sauce, coriander and garlic; cook until heated through, 5 to 8 minutes, stirring occasionally. Season to taste with salt and pepper.

4 to 6 servings.

Salmon Loaf
with Sour Cream-Cucumber Sauce

2 15 1/2-ounce cans salmon, drained
1 cup crushed whole wheat crackers
1/3 cup thinly sliced green onions and tops
1/4 cup sliced black olives
1/4 cup chopped celery
1/4 cup chopped green pepper
1/2 cup milk
1 tablespoon tomato paste

1 tablespoon lemon juice
1 teaspoon grated lemon rind
1 teaspoon Worcestershire sauce
1/16 teaspoon ground nutmeg
1/2 teaspoon salt
1/8 teaspoon pepper
    Sour Cream-Cucumber Sauce

Remove bones and skin from salmon; flake salmon with a fork. Mix salmon and remaining ingredients, except Sour Cream-Cucumber Sauce, in large bowl until blended; shape into loaf in greased 8 1/2 × 4 1/2 × 2 1/2 inch loaf pan. Heat fry pan at 325°. Place pan on rack in fry pan; cook, covered, at 325° until loaf is set and top is browned, about 1 1/4 hours.

Make Sour Cream-Cucumber Sauce. Remove salmon loaf from fry pan; invert onto serving platter and slice. Pass sauce to spoon over salmon.

6 to 8 servings.

Sour Cream-Cucumber Sauce

1/2 cup sour cream or sour half-and-half
1/2 cup finely chopped seeded cucumber
1/4 cup half-and-half or milk
2 tablespoons mayonnaise or salad dressing

1 teaspoon dried dillweed
1/8 teaspoon garlic powder
1/8 teaspoon salt

Mix all ingredients; refrigerate, covered, until serving time.

About 1 1/4 cups.

Cioppino
(Fish Stew)

3 tablespoons olive or vegetable oil
1 cup chopped onions
2 cloves garlic, minced
1 1/2 cups chopped green pepper
1 teaspoon dried basil leaves
1/4 teaspoon dried oregano leaves
1/16 teaspoon cayenne pepper
1 star anise (optional)
1 small bay leaf
2 16- ounce cans tomatoes, drained, coarsely chopped

1 8-ounce can tomato sauce
1 cup dry white wine
1 teaspoon sugar
3 tablespoons minced parsley
1/4 teaspoon salt
1/4 teaspoon pepper
6 cherrystone clams (optional)
8 ounces peeled deveined shrimp
1 pound fresh or frozen thawed cod or other white fish fillets, cut into 2-inch pieces

Heat fry pan at 225°. Add oil, onion and garlic; cook 2 minutes. Add green pepper; cook 2 minutes. Stir in basil, oregano, cayenne pepper, anise and bay leaf; cook 1 minute. Add tomatoes, tomato sauce, wine, sugar, parsley, salt and pepper; cook at 400° until boiling. Reduce heat to simmer, between Warm and 200°; cook, covered, 30 minutes. Stir in clams; cook, covered, 5 minutes. Add shrimp and cod; cook, covered, until cod is tender and flakes with a fork, about 5 minutes. Serve in bowls.

6 servings.

Salmon Steaks
with Cucumber-Dill Butter Sauce

1	tablespoon butter or margarine	1/4	teaspoon salt
1	tablespoon vegetable oil	1/4	teaspoon white pepper
4	6-ounce salmon or white fish steaks, 1-inch thick		Cucumber-Dill Butter Sauce (see recipe page 72)
1/4	cup all-purpose flour		Dill or parsley sprigs

Heat butter and oil in fry pan at Warm until butter is melted. Coat salmon steaks lightly with mixture of flour, salt, and pepper. Heat fry pan at 325°. Add salmon; cook, 1 minute on each side. Remove salmon. Clean fry pan.

Place salmon on rack in fry pan; cook, covered, at 325° until fish is tender and flakes with a fork, about 14 minutes. Remove salmon from fry pan; keep warm.

Make Cucumber-Dill Butter Sauce in fry pan. Arrange salmon on serving platter; garnish with dill. Pass sauce to spoon over salmon.

4 servings.

Salmon Steaks with Cucumber-Dill Butter Sauce

Pasta and Rice

Think of all the times when a pasta or rice entrée would hit the spot ... like after a show or a football game, for supper on a blustery day, or for a special luncheon. Think of the convenience of these dishes for buffet tables, the low cost per serving, and the wise nutrition of eating more grains.

And now think about the sensational tastes ... like Fettuccine with Ham and Walnuts in a creamy Parmesan cheese sauce, or Sausage Lasagna with savory Marinara Sauce, or Bayou Jambalaya, a jazzy combo of rice, sausage, ham, and shrimp. You can make easy, all-in-one-pan Fry Pan Spaghetti for a quick supper or create a wonderful evening around Greek Islands Casserole, a classic cinnamon- and mint-scented com-

bination of macaroni, meat sauce, and rich egg custard. Pork Risotto, a famous Northern Italian tradition, features an unusually good way to prepare rice—neither steamed nor boiled but gently stirred with chicken broth until it becomes tender. Beef and Brown Rice Casserole enhances the naturally nutlike flavor of brown rice with both fresh and dried mushrooms. Best Chicken Tetrazzini stands out simply because it's a terrific version of a favorite dish—as well as a great way to use leftover chicken or turkey.

With these and the other recipes in this chapter, the only things you need to round out a meal are a tossed salad, a plain steamed vegetable, perhaps fruit or ice cream for dessert—and a hearty appetite!

Greek Islands Casserole

8	cups water	1/4	teaspoon black pepper
7	ounces elbow macaroni	1	15-ounce can tomato sauce
2	teaspoons salt	1/4	cup water
1/2	pound ground lamb	1/4	cup butter or margarine
1/2	pound lean ground beef	1/3	cup all-purpose flour
1	cup chopped onions	2 1/2	cups half-and-half or milk
1	clove garlic, minced	2	eggs
1/2	teaspoon dried oregano leaves	1/16	teaspoon ground nutmeg
1/2	teaspoon dried mint leaves	3/4	teaspoon salt
1/4	teaspoon ground cinnamon	1/8	teaspoon white pepper
1/2	teaspoon salt	2	tablespoons grated Parmesan cheese

Bring 8 cups water to a boil in fry pan at 400°. Add macaroni and 2 teaspoons salt; cook according to macaroni package directions. Drain macaroni and reserve. Heat fry pan to 325°. Add meats; cook until browned, 3 to 4 minutes, stirring occasionally; drain excess fat. Add onion and garlic; cook 2 minutes.

Stir in oregano, mint, cinnamon, 1/2 teaspoon salt and black pepper; cook 2 minutes. Stir in tomato sauce and 1/4 cup water; cook at 400° until boiling. Reduce heat to simmer, between Warm and 200°; cook 3 minutes. Remove meat mixture and reserve. Clean fry pan.

Heat butter in fry pan at Warm until melted. Stir in flour; cook at 200°, 2 minutes, stirring constantly. Stir in half-and-half; cook until thickened, about 2 minutes, stirring constantly. Stir 1/2 cup half-and-half mixture into eggs; stir egg mixture into half-and-half mixture. Stir in nutmeg, 3/4 teaspoon salt and white pepper; cook 1 minute, stirring constantly. Remove custard mixture from fry pan. Clean fry pan.

Spread half the reserved meat mixture in bottom of fry pan; spoon reserved macaroni evenly over meat mixture. Spread remaining meat mixture over macaroni. Pour custard mixture over all. Sprinkle with cheese; cook, covered, between Warm and 200°, until custard mixture is set, 25 to 30 minutes. Turn heat to Off; let stand, covered, 5 minutes. Cut into squares to serve.

4 to 6 servings.

Sausage Lasagna

Marinara Sauce (see recipe page 71)
- 1 pound mild or hot Italian sausage, casing removed, crumbled
- 1 pound ricotta cheese
- 3/4 cup grated Parmesan cheese
- 2 eggs, beaten
- 1/2 cup chopped black olives
- 1 tablespoon minced parsley
- 1/8 teaspoon garlic powder
- 1/8 teaspoon ground nutmeg
- 1/8 teaspoon white pepper
- 9 ounces lasagna noodles, cooked
- 3 cups shredded mozzarella cheese

Make Marinara Sauce in fry pan; remove from fry pan and reserve. Clean fry pan.

Cook sausage in fry pan at 325° until brown, 5 to 7 minutes, stirring frequently. Drain excess fat. Remove sausage from fry pan and reserve. Mix ricotta and Parmesan cheese, eggs, olives, parsley, garlic powder, nutmeg and pepper. Spread a thin layer of Marinara Sauce in bottom of fry pan. Arrange half of the noodles, slightly overlapping, on sauce. Spoon half the remaining sauce over noodles; sprinkle with half the sausage, half the ricotta mixture, and half the mozzarella cheese. Repeat layers; cook, covered, between Warm and 200°, until lasagna is heated through, about 30 minutes. Cook, covered, at 200°, 15 minutes. Turn heat to Off and let stand, uncovered, 5 minutes. Cut into squares to serve.

4 servings.

Best Chicken Tetrazzini

Sherry Newberg Sauce (see recipe, page 70)
- 1/2 cup milk
- 1 teaspoon chicken flavor instant bouillon
- 1 teaspoon minced parsley
- 1/4 teaspoon ground nutmeg
- 2 cups cubed cooked chicken (about 1 pound)
- 8 ounces spaghetti, cooked
- 1 4-ounce can sliced mushrooms, drained
- 1/4 cup grated Parmesan cheese
- Ground nutmeg

Make Sherry Newberg Sauce in fry pan. Stir in all ingredients, except nutmeg; cook at 200° until heated through, about 5 minutes, stirring occasionally. Sprinkle lightly with ground nutmeg.

4 servings.

Spaghetti with Chicken Cutlets and Marinara Sauce

Marinara Sauce (see recipe page 71)
- 6 boned skinned chicken breast halves (about 2 1/2 pounds)
- 1/2 cup all-purpose flour
- 1/2 teaspoon salt
- 1/4 teaspoon white pepper
- 2 tablespoons olive or vegetable oil
- 1 tablespoon vegetable oil
- 1 pound spaghetti, cooked
- Grated Parmesan cheese

Make Marinara Sauce in fry pan. Remove sauce and reserve. Clean fry pan.

Pound chicken with flat side of mallet until scant 1/2 inch thick; coat lightly with mixture of flour, salt and pepper. Heat fry pan at 300°. Add oils and chicken; cook until brown, 3 to 4 minutes on each side. Remove chicken and keep warm.

Add spaghetti; cook at 225°, 1 minute. Stir in reserved Marinara Sauce. Arrange chicken on spaghetti mixture. Sprinkle generously with cheese; cook, covered, until heated through, about 2 minutes.

4 to 6 servings.

Fry Pan Spaghetti

3/4 pound lean ground beef	1 cup tomato juice
1/2 cup sliced green onions and tops	1/2 teaspoon dried basil leaves
1/2 cup chopped green pepper	1/4 teaspoon dried oregano leaves
3 cups water	8 ounces spaghetti
1 16-ounce can tomatoes, undrained, coarsely chopped	Grated Parmesan cheese

Heat fry pan at 300°. Add ground beef, onions and green pepper; cook until beef is brown, about 5 minutes. Drain excess fat. Add remaining ingredients, except cheese; cook at 400° until boiling. Reduce heat to simmer, between Warm and 200°; cook, covered, until spaghetti is al dente (tender, but firm to the bite), about 15 minutes, stirring occasionally. Sprinkle generously with cheese.

2 to 4 servings.

Fettuccine with Ham and Walnuts

3 cups water	3/4 cup coarsely chopped walnuts
10 ounces egg noodles	2 cups whipping cream or half-and-half
1 1/2 teaspoons salt	1/2 cup grated Parmesan cheese
4 tablespoons butter or margarine	1/16 teaspoon white pepper
1/2 pound baked ham, cubed	Ground nutmeg

Bring 3 cups water to a boil in fry pan at 400°. Add noodles and salt; cook according to noodle package directions. Drain noodles and reserve.

Heat 2 tablespoons butter in fry pan at Warm until melted. Add ham and walnuts; cook at 225° until walnuts are toasted, about 4 minutes. Add remaining 2 tablespoons butter, reserved noodles and cream; cook at 400° until cream begins to boil, stirring constantly. Reduce heat to Warm. Stir in cheese; cook until cheese is melted and creamy. Season to taste with pepper; sprinkle lightly with nutmeg.

4 servings.

Beef and Brown Rice Casserole

4 Chinese dried mushrooms	1/2 teaspoon dried savory leaves
1/2 cup hot water	1/4 teaspoon dried chervil leaves
3 tablespoons vegetable oil	1 1/2 cups brown rice
1 pound lean beef top round steak, cut into 3/4-inch pieces	3 cups water
3/4 cup sliced mushrooms	1 teaspoon beef flavor instant bouillon
1/2 cup thinly sliced celery	1 cup sour cream or sour half-and-half
2 green onions and tops, sliced	Salt
1 teaspoon minced parsley	Pepper

Let dried mushrooms stand in hot water until softened, about 10 minutes. Drain mushrooms, reserving liquid. Slice mushrooms, discarding tough centers; reserve mushrooms.

Heat fry pan at 325°. Add oil and beef; cook until browned on all sides, about 5 minutes. Stir in mushrooms, celery, onions, parsley, savory and chervil; cook at 225° until vegetables are tender, about 4 minutes, stirring occasionally. Stir in rice; cook 2 minutes, stirring occasionally. Stir in water, bouillon and mushroom liquid; cook at 400° until boiling. Reduce heat to simmer, between Warm and 200°; cook, covered, until rice is tender and liquid absorbed, 60 to 65 minutes, stirring occasionally. Reduce heat to Warm. Stir in sour cream; season to taste with salt and pepper.

4 servings.

Tex-Mex Mac and Cheese

2 tablespoons vegetable oil	1/4 cup mild or hot red salsa
1 pound lean ground beef	2 to 3 teaspoons chili powder
1/4 cup sliced green onions and tops	3 cups elbow macaroni, cooked
1 clove garlic, minced	1/3 cup sliced black olives
1/4 cup butter or margarine	1/4 cup grated Parmesan cheese
1/4 cup all-purpose flour	Salt
2 cups half-and-half or milk	Pepper
3 cups shredded Monterey Jack cheese	Tomato Wedges
1 3-ounce package cream cheese, cut into cubes	Minced parsley or coriander

Heat fry pan at 250°. Add oil and ground beef, onion and garlic; cook until beef is browned. Remove beef mixture and drain excess fat. Reserve beef mixture. Clean fry pan.

Heat butter in fry pan at Warm until melted. Stir in flour; cook at 225° until flour is lightly brown, about 3 minutes, stirring occasionally. Stir in half-and-half; cook until thickened, stirring constantly. Stir in cheeses, salsa and chili powder; cook until cheeses are melted, stirring constantly. Stir in reserved beef mixture, macaroni and olives; cook, covered, until heated, 4 to 5 minutes. Stir in Parmesan cheese; season to taste with salt and pepper. Spoon mixture into serving bowl; garnish with tomato wedges and sprinkle with parsley.

4 to 6 servings.

Bayou Jambalaya

1 tablespoon bacon drippings or vegetable oil	1/2 teaspoon dried thyme leaves
1/2 cup chopped onion	1/4 teaspoon cayenne pepper
1 green pepper, chopped	1/16 teaspoon ground cloves
1 clove garlic, minced	1/16 teaspoon ground nutmeg
1 tablespoon flour	3 to 4 drops red pepper sauce
1/2 pound pork link sausages, cut into 1-inch pieces	1/2 teaspoon salt
1/2 pound baked ham, cubed	3 cups cooked rice
1 16-ounce can tomatoes, undrained, coarsely chopped	8 ounces uncooked peeled deveined shrimp
1 cup water	Minced parsley
1 teaspoon chicken flavor instant bouillon	

Heat bacon drippings in fry pan at 225°. Add onion, green pepper and garlic; cook until tender. Stir in flour; cook 1 minute. Stir in sausage and ham; cook at 250° until sausage is brown and no longer pink in the center, 7 to 8 minutes, stirring occasionally. Stir in tomatoes with liquid, water, bouillon, thyme, cayenne pepper, cloves, nutmeg, red pepper sauce and salt; cook at 400° until boiling. Reduce heat to simmer, between Warm and 200°; cook, covered, 15 minutes. Stir in rice and shrimp; cook, uncovered, until heated, 8 to 10 minutes, stirring occasionally. Spoon into serving bowl; sprinkle with parsley.

4 servings.

Pork Risotto

1 tablespoon olive or vegetable oil	1 tablespoon butter or margarine
1 pound coarsely chopped lean pork	1 cup long grain white rice
1/4 cup sliced green onions and tops	3 1/2 to 4 cups hot chicken broth
1 clove garlic, minced	1/4 cup grated Parmesan cheese
2 tablespoons olive or vegetable oil	1/8 teaspoon pepper

Heat fry pan at 325°. Add 1 tablespoon oil, pork, onions and garlic; cook until pork is brown, about 5 minutes. Drain excess fat. Remove meat mixture from fry pan and reserve.

Add 2 tablespoons oil and butter to fry pan; reduce heat to 250°. Add rice; cook until rice is golden, 3 to 4 minutes, stirring frequently. Add reserved meat mixture. Stir in 1/2 cup of the broth; cook until broth is absorbed, stirring constantly. Continue adding broth, 1/2 cup at a time, cooking until broth is absorbed before adding more; stir constantly. Taste rice after 3 1/2 cups of broth have been added; if rice is al dente (tender, but firm to the bite), cooking is completed. If rice is not tender, add remaining 1/2 cup broth and cook until absorbed. (Risotto requires about 25 minutes cooking time.) Stir in 2 tablespoons of cheese and pepper. Garnish with remaining cheese.

2 servings.

Fruit and Nut Rice

2 tablespoons butter or margarine	3/4 cup water
1/4 cup chopped celery	1/2 teaspoon chicken flavor instant bouillon
1 tablespoon golden raisins	3/4 cup enriched precooked rice
1 tablespoon slivered almonds	
1/16 teaspoon ground cinnamon	1/4 cup mandarin orange segments, drained
1/8 teaspoon salt	

Heat butter in fry pan at Warm until melted. Add celery; cook at 225° for 2 minutes. Stir in raisins, almonds, cinnamon and salt; cook 2 minutes. Remove celery mixture from fry pan. Stir water and bouillon into fry pan; heat at 400° until boiling. Stir in rice; turn heat to Off and let stand, covered, until liquid is absorbed, about 5 minutes. Stir in celery mixture and orange segments; cook at 200° until heated, about 2 minutes.

2 servings.

Poppy Seed Noodles

3 tablespoons butter or margarine-butter blend	1 teaspoon poppy seed
2 cups cooked egg noodles	White pepper

Heat butter in fry pan at Warm until melted; cook at 200° until butter is browned. Add noodles, stirring to coat with butter; cook, covered, until heated, about 3 minutes. Stir in poppy seed; season to taste with pepper.

2 servings.

Sandwiches and Snacks

The best kind of sandwich is a real bonanza—and that's the kind you'll find in this chapter! Awaiting all hearty appetites are such satisfying combos as Philly Beef Sandwiches, with lots of hot beef, peppers, and cheese; Italian Sausage with plenty of sautéed peppers and onion; and Very Best Beef Barbecue—the meatiest, the spiciest, and the best you've ever tasted! If you like Mexican food, you'll crave Acapulco Tostados—crisp tortillas heaped with homemade refried beans, well-seasoned beef, shredded lettuce, cheese, avocado, and tomato. If you'd rather stick with burgers, you'll savor the surprise of the pickle spear or cheese stick wrapped in each Burger Dog. And if you want an "all good things

in every mouthful" treat, you'll discover it in French Toasted Ham Salad sandwiches, a treasury of almond-crunched ham salad and Swiss cheese fried in an egg-milk batter.

There are two ways to approach a snack, and they're both included here. You can appease appetites quickly, with sauce and cheese-laden Pizza Bread, crispy Fried Won Tons with Sweet-Sour Sauce, or fried tortilla Quesadillas. Or you can prudently fill a container with crunchy Curried Snack Mix or Fried Pecans to keep on hand. And yes, you can also use the electric fry pan to pop popcorn, that great all-American snack—and to blend the seasoned butter for Popcorn Snack Mix, too.

Italian Sausage with Pepperonata

1 to 1 1/4 **pounds mild or hot Italian sausage, cut into 5-inch pieces**
1/3 **cup butter or margarine**
1 **large red onion, sliced**
3 **medium green peppers, sliced**
3 **medium red or green peppers, sliced**

Water
Salt
Pepper
4 **hoagie or French rolls**

Cook sausage in fry pan at 200° until browned and no longer pink in the center, about 10 minutes. Remove from fry pan; reserve. Heat butter in fry pan at Warm until melted. Add onion; cook at 200° until onion is golden, about 20 minutes, stirring occasionally. Add green and red peppers; cook, covered, until very soft, about 30 minutes, adding water, 1/4 cup at a time if mixture becomes too dry. Add reserved sausage; cook, covered, until heated through, 2 to 3 minutes. Spoon sausage-pepper mixture into rolls.

4 servings.

Pizza Bread

1 **loaf French bread, 10 inches long**
   Olive or vegetable oil
2 **tablespoons butter or margarine**
1 **tablespoon olive or vegetable oil**
1 **cup chopped onions**
1 **cup sliced mushrooms**

1/2 **cup chopped green pepper**
1/2 **cup tomato sauce**
1 1/4 **teaspoons dried basil leaves**
3/4 **teaspoon dried oregano leaves**
1 **cup shredded mozzarella cheese**

Cut bread lengthwise in half; brush cut sides of bread lightly with olive oil. Heat fry pan at 300°. Place bread, cut sides down, in fry pan; cook until toasted. Remove from fry pan. Heat butter and 1 tablespoon oil in fry pan at Warm until butter is melted. Add onion, mushrooms and green pepper; cook at 225° until onion is tender, about 5 minutes. Remove onion mixture from fry pan and reserve. Clean fry pan.

Mix tomato sauce, basil and oregano; spread on bread halves. Top with onion mixture; sprinkle with cheese. Place bread on rack in fry pan; cook, covered, at 300° until cheese is melted, about 5 minutes. Cut into slices; serve hot.

6 servings.

Greek-Style Pitas

1/3 cup olive or vegetable oil

3 tablespoons white wine vinegar

1 teaspoon sugar

1 teaspoon dried oregano leaves

1/2 teaspoon dried dillweed

1 large clove garlic, minced

1/2 teaspoon salt

1/2 pound thinly sliced medium-rare roast beef

2 pita breads, cut into halves

1/4 cup chopped seeded cucumber

1/4 cup chopped onion

2 tablespoons sliced Greek or black olives

Mix oil, vinegar, sugar, oregano, dillweed, garlic and salt; pour over beef in shallow glass baking dish. Let stand 20 minutes, stirring occasionally. Transfer beef and marinade to fry pan; cook at 200° until heated through, about 5 minutes. Spoon beef mixture into pita breads; sprinkle with cucumber, onion and olives.

4 servings.

Shrimp Rolls

1 loaf Italian bread, cut into 1 1/2-inch slices
Softened butter or margarine

1 pound peeled deveined cooked shrimp, chopped

1/2 cup finely chopped celery

2 tablespoons thinly sliced green onion and top

1/2 cup mayonnaise or salad dressing

1 teaspoon Dijon-style mustard

1 teaspoon lemon juice

1/4 teaspoon cayenne pepper

Cut bread slices vertically to form rolls, slicing to, but not through, bottom of bread (shape will resemble hot dog buns or rolls). Spread outsides of rolls lightly with butter. Heat fry pan at 275°. Add rolls; cook until golden on both sides. Remove.

Combine shrimp, celery, and onion in small bowl; mix in remaining ingredients. Spoon shrimp mixture into buns.

4 servings.

Very Best Beef Barbecue

2 tablespoons vegetable oil

3 pounds beef cubes for stew

1 cup chopped onions

2 cups water

2 teaspoons beef flavor instant bouillon

1 cup chili sauce

1 cup catsup

3 tablespoons cider vinegar

1 tablespoon Worcestershire sauce

1/3 cup light brown sugar

2 teaspoons dry mustard

1 teaspoon ground allspice

1/2 teaspoon salt

1/2 teaspoon pepper

8 hamburger buns, toasted

Heat fry pan at 325°. Add oil, beef cubes and onion; cook until beef is brown and onion is tender, about 5 minutes. Add water and bouillon; cook at 400° until boiling. Reduce heat to simmer between Warm and 200°; cook, covered, until beef is tender, about 2 hours. Shred beef in fry pan, using 2 forks. Stir in remaining ingredients, except buns; cook at 400° until boiling. Reduce heat to simmer between Warm and 200°; cook, covered, 15 minutes, stirring occasionally. Spoon hot beef mixture into buns.

8 servings.

Shrimp Rolls, Greek-Style Pitas

Burger Dogs

4   hot dog buns, cut in half
    Butter or margarine
1   pound lean ground beef
1/4 cup chopped onion
2   tablespoons dry bread crumbs

1   egg, beaten
1   tablespoon soy sauce
1/2 teaspoon salt
1/4 teaspoon pepper
    Dill pickle quarters or cheddar cheese sticks

Spread cut sides of buns lightly with butter. Heat fry pan at 300°. Place buns buttered side down, in fry pan; cook until toasted. Remove from fry pan.

Mix ground beef, onion, bread crumbs, egg, soy sauce, salt and pepper. Divide beef mixture into 4 equal parts; form each part around pickle, making hot dog shapes that will fit buns. Heat fry pan at 250°. Place meat in fry pan; cook, covered, to desired degree of doneness, about 8 minutes for medium. Serve in toasted buns.

4 servings.

Philly Beef Sandwiches

3   tablespoons butter or margarine
4   hoagie or small French rolls, cut in half
2   tablespoons vegetable oil
1   medium onion, sliced
1   medium green pepper, cut into thin strips
1/2 cup water
1/2 teaspoon beef flavor instant bouillon

1/4 teaspoon dried basil leaves
1/8 teaspoon pepper
1/2 pound thinly sliced medium-rare roast beef
4   1-ounce slices processed American cheese, cut diagonally into halves

Heat butter in fry pan at Warm until melted. Place rolls, cut sides down, in fry pan; cook at 250° until toasted, 4 to 5 minutes. Remove rolls from fry pan.

Heat fry pan at 225°. Add oil, onion and green pepper; cook until tender, about 5 minutes. Stir in water, bouillon, basil and pepper; cook 2 minutes. Stir in beef; cook until heated, 2 to 3 minutes.

To assemble sandwich place 1/2 cheese slice on bottom half of each roll. Top each with beef mixture, 1/2 cheese slice and half roll. Clean fry pan. Place sandwiches on rack in fry pan; cook, covered, at 350° until cheese is melted, 4 to 5 minutes. Serve hot.

4 sandwiches.

Triple Cheese Grill

2   tablespoons mayonnaise or salad dressing
1/8 teaspoon dried basil leaves
1/8 teaspoon dried oregano leaves
4   slices white or whole wheat bread
2   1-ounce slices cheddar cheese

2   1-ounce slices brick or Monterey Jack cheese
2   thin slices tomato
2   1-ounce slices provolone cheese
    Softened butter or margarine

Mix mayonnaise, basil and oregano; spread mixture on 1 side of bread slices. Top each of 2 slices bread with 1 slice Cheddar, 1 slice brick cheese, tomato, provolone cheese and bread slice. Lightly butter bread on outsides of sandwiches. Heat fry pan at 275°. Add sandwiches; cook until golden on bottom. Turn sandwiches over; cook until bread is golden and cheese is melted. Serve hot.

2 servings.

French Toasted Ham Salad Sandwiches

	Ham Salad	1/8	teaspoon paprika
8	1-ounce slices Swiss cheese	1/4	teaspoon salt
8	slices firm-textured white sandwich bread	1/16	teaspoon white pepper
1/4	cup milk	1	tablespoon butter or margarine
1	egg	1	tablespoon vegetable oil
1	tablespoon grated Parmesan cheese		

Make Ham Salad. Place 1 slice Swiss cheese on each of four slices of bread; spread Ham Salad on the slices of cheese. Top with remaining Swiss cheese and bread slices.

Beat milk, egg, Parmesan cheese, paprika, salt and pepper in shallow bowl. Heat butter and oil in fry pan at Warm until butter is melted. Dip each sandwich in milk mixture, coating both sides generously; cook, covered, in fry pan at 250° until golden, about 4 minutes on each side. Serve hot.

4 servings.

Ham Salad

1	cup coarsely chopped baked ham	1/4	cup chopped black olives
1/4	cup chopped green onions and tops	1/4	cup chopped almonds, toasted
1/4	cup chopped green pepper	1/4	cup mayonnaise or salad dressing
1/4	cup chopped celery	2	teaspoons Dijon-style mustard

Combine all ingredients.

About 2 cups.

Cheese Melts

4	slices whole wheat bread	4	1-ounce slices sharp cheddar cheese
	Dijon-style mustard	1	tablespoon butter or margarine
4	slices onion, 1/4 inch thick	1	tablespoon vegetable oil

Spread bread slices lightly with mustard; top each with slice of onion and cheese. Heat butter and oil in fry pan at Warm until butter is melted. Add bread slices; cook, covered, at 275° until bread is golden and cheese is melted, about 3 minutes.

4 servings.

Curried Snack Mix

3	tablespoons butter or margarine	1	cup cashews
1 1/2	tablespoons light brown sugar	1	cup cocktail peanuts
1 1/2	teaspoons curry powder	1/2	cup shredded coconut
2	cups toasted wheat cereal squares	1	cup raisins

Heat butter in fry pan at Warm until melted. Stir in sugar and curry powder; cook at 250° for 1 minute. Stir in cereal, cashews and peanuts; cook at 275°, 5 minutes, stirring frequently. Add coconut; cook until mixture is golden, about 5 minutes, stirring frequently. Stir in raisins. Spread mixture on jelly roll pan to cool; store in airtight containers.

About 5 cups.

Acapulco Tostadas

Refried Beans
Mexican Beef
Vegetable oil
8 corn tortillas
2 cups shredded iceberg lettuce
1 medium tomato, chopped

1 avocado, peeled, pitted, chopped
1/4 cup sliced black olives
2 green onions and tops, sliced
Taco sauce
3/4 cup shredded cheddar cheese
1/2 cup sour cream or sour half-and-half

Make Refried Beans; remove from fry pan and keep warm. Clean fry pan. Make Mexican Beef; remove from fry pan and keep warm. Clean fry pan.

Heat 1/2 inch oil in fry pan at 350°. Add tortillas; cook until crisp, 2 to 3 minutes. Drain on paper toweling. Combine lettuce, tomato, avocado, olives and onions in bowl. Spread each tortilla with about 2 tablespoons Refried Beans. Spoon Mexican Beef evenly over beans. Top each tortilla with 1/4 cup lettuce mixture; drizzle with taco sauce. Sprinkle with cheese; top with dollop of sour cream.

8 servings.

Refried Beans

1/4 cup bacon drippings or vegetable oil
1/4 cup finely chopped onion
1 clove garlic, minced
2 16-ounce cans pinto beans, drained, rinsed

1/2 teaspoon dried cilantro or coriander leaves
1/4 teaspoon ground cumin
1 to 2 tablespoons vegetable oil

Heat fry pan at 225°. Add bacon drippings, onion and garlic; cook until onion is tender, about 2 minutes. Add beans; cook, covered, until very tender, about 8 minutes. Stir in cilantro and cumin. Turn heat to Off; mash beans coarsely with fork, adding 1 to 2 tablespoons oil, if necessary, to make spreading consistency.

About 1 cup.

Mexican Beef

1 tablespoon vegetable oil
1 pound lean ground beef
1/2 cup chopped onions
1 clove garlic, minced
1 10-ounce can mild enchilada sauce

1/4 teaspoon dried oregano leaves
1/8 teaspoon dried sage leaves
1/2 teaspoon salt
1/4 teaspoon pepper

Heat fry pan at 300°. Add oil, ground beef, onion and garlic; cook until beef is brown, about 5 minutes, stirring occasionally. Drain excess fat. Stir in remaining ingredients; cook until thickened, about 8 minutes.

About 2 cups.

Popcorn Snack Mix

2 tablespoons vegetable oil
1/3 cup popcorn
1 tablespoon butter or margarine

3/4 teaspoon dried oregano leaves
1 cup mixed nuts
1/2 cup grated Parmesan cheese

Heat fry pan at 350°. Add oil and popcorn; cook, covered, until corn is popped, shaking pan gently after corn begins to pop. Place popped corn in large bowl.

Heat butter in fry pan at Warm until melted. Stir in oregano and nuts; cook at 275° until nuts are golden, about 5 minutes. Combine nuts and popped corn. Sprinkle with cheese; toss.

About 5 cups.

Apple-Peanut Butter Squares

4   slices whole wheat bread
    Butter or margarine
4   tablespoons smooth or chunky
    peanut butter
1   medium apple, cored, cut into 16 slices

4   1-ounce slices processed
    American cheese
1   tablespoon butter or margarine
1   tablespoon vegetable oil

Spread bread slices lightly with butter; spread each with 1 tablespoon peanut butter. Arrange 4 slices apple on each bread slice; top with slice of cheese.

Heat 1 tablespoon butter and oil in fry pan at Warm until butter is melted. Add bread slices; cook, covered, at 250° until bread is golden on the bottom and cheese is melted, 6 to 8 minutes. Serve hot.

4 servings.

Fried Pecans

Vegetable oil
2   cups unsalted pecans

Salt, garlic salt or seasoned salt

Heat 1 inch oil in fry pan at 375°. Add 1/2 cup pecans; cook until light brown, about 30 seconds. Remove pecans from oil with slotted spoon; drain on paper toweling. Repeat with remaining pecans, cooking 1/2 cup at a time. Sprinkle warm pecans lightly with desired seasoned salt. Serve warm or at room temperature.

2 cups.

TIP: Unsalted almonds, cashews or walnuts may be substituted for the pecans.

Quesadillas
(Tortillas with Cheese Filling)

4   flour tortillas
    (about 7 inches in diameter)
1   cup shredded Monterey Jack
    or cheddar cheese
2 to 3   tablespoons chopped seeded
    mild or hot chilies

2   tablespoons chopped black olives
2   tablespoons butter or margarine
    Salsa, green chili sauce or
    taco sauce

Sprinkle each tortilla with 1/4 cup cheese; sprinkle chilies and olives over cheese. Fold tortillas in half. Heat butter in fry pan at Warm until melted. Add 2 tortillas; cook at 300° until lightly browned, about 2 minutes on each side. Remove tortillas from fry pan; cut each tortilla in half. Repeat with remaining tortillas. Serve warm, drizzled with desired sauce.

4 servings.

Sauces

The electric fry pan makes it much easier for cooks to master a wide repertoire of sauces. You can ensure smoothness and avoid scorching just by setting the heat control—a vast improvement over the tricky business of regulating stove-top heat.

You can stir up a little excitement any day with a White Sauce or Drawn Butter Sauce to top plain green vegetables, fish, or poultry. Both of these recipes are accompanied by suggested variations, including Cheese Sauce and Tarragon-Chive Butter Sauce, but you'll no doubt come up with many other seasoning possibilities too. Creamy Bearnaise Sauce or Rich Mushroom Sauce are the finest complements for broiled or roast beef or lamb—as elegant as any restaurant, yet deceptively easy to make. When pork or ham are on the menu, the delicate sweetness of Orange Sauce or Raisin Sauce—either with the meat or with accompanying vegetables—will make the meal memorable.

One of the most satisfying ways to save money is to make your own Marinara Sauce for spaghetti and other Italian favorites, Hot Chili Barbecue Sauce for best-ever grilled meats, and Mexican Salsa for tacos, burritos, and other south-of-the-border treats. The homemade sauces taste incomparably fresher and more delicious than purchased blends, and for everyday convenience they can be refrigerated at least a week or frozen for up to six months.

Cranberry Chutney, studded with raisins and nuts, is a superb holiday trimming for turkey or ham. Ginger Peach Chutney and Cinnamon Spice Apple Butter are wonderful with breakfast breads. Turn to these recipes also for lovely homemade gifts. They keep well in the refrigerator in sterilized jars for up to two months, ready to wrap up for any occasion. To sterilize the jars, stand them in a large kettle, add water to cover, and heat to boiling; boil, covered, for 10 minutes and leave jars immersed in the water until you're ready to fill them.

White Sauce with Variations

1/4 cup butter or margarine	2 dashes ground nutmeg
1/4 cup all-purpose flour	1/4 teaspoon salt
2 cups milk	1/8 teaspoon white pepper

Heat butter in fry pan at Warm until melted. Stir in flour; cook at 200°, 3 minutes, stirring constantly. Whisk in milk, cook at 400° until boiling. Reduce heat to 200°; cook until thickened, whisking constantly. Whisk in nutmeg, salt and pepper.

About 2 cups.

Sherry Newberg Sauce

Make White Sauce as above. Stir in 4 teaspoons dry sherry; cook 1 minute.

About 2 cups.

Minced Onion Sauce

Make White Sauce as above. Stir in 2 tablespoons finely chopped onion; cook 1 minute.

About 2 cups.

Vermouth Sauce

Make White Sauce as above. Stir in 1 tablespoon dry vermouth; cook 1 minute.

About 2 cups.

Cheese Sauce

Make White Sauce as above. Stir in 1/4 cup shredded cheddar cheese and 1/4 cup shredded Swiss cheese; cook, stirring constantly until cheese is melted.

About 2 cups.

Creamy Hollandaise Sauce

1/4 cup butter or margarine
3/4 cup mayonnaise or salad dressing
1/2 cup sour cream or sour half-and-half

2 egg yolks, beaten
2 tablespoons lemon juice
1 teaspoon Dijon-style mustard
1/8 to 1/4 teaspoon cayenne pepper

Heat butter in fry pan at Warm until melted. Whisk in remaining ingredients; cook until warm, but not boiling (110° to 115°), whisking constantly. Serve immediately.

About 1 1/2 cups.

Creamy Bearnaise Sauce

Make Creamy Hollandaise Sauce as above, adding 1 1/2 teaspoons dried tarragon leaves.

About 1 1/2 cups.

Raisin Sauce

1/4 cup currant jelly
3 tablespoons light brown sugar
2 tablespoons butter or margarine
2 cups orange juice
2 tablespoons cornstarch

1/4 cup cold water
3/4 cup golden raisins
2 tablespoons almond flavor liqueur or 1/2 teaspoon almond extract
2 dashes white pepper

Combine jelly, sugar and butter in fry pan; cook at 200° until mixture is melted, about 4 minutes, stirring constantly. Whisk in orange juice; cook at 400° until boiling. Reduce heat to simmer between Warm and 200°. Mix cornstarch and cold water; whisk into orange juice mixture, whisking until sauce thickens. Stir in raisins, liqueur, and pepper; cook 2 minutes. Serve over carrots, beets, poultry, pork or ham.

About 2 1/2 cups.

Marinara Sauce

2 tablespoons olive oil or vegetable oil
1 1/2 cups finely chopped onions
1 cup finely chopped carrots
1/2 cup chopped green pepper
2 cloves garlic, minced
2 16-ounce cans Italian plum tomatoes, undrained, coarsely chopped
3 tablespoons tomato paste
1 cup water
2 teaspoons light brown sugar

1/2 teaspoon chicken flavor instant bouillon
1 teaspoon dried basil leaves
1/2 teaspoon dried oregano leaves
1/4 teaspoon fennel seed, crushed
1 bay leaf
1/2 teaspoon salt
1/4 teaspoon pepper
2 tablespoons grated Parmesan cheese

Heat fry pan at 225°. Add oil, onion, carrots, green pepper and garlic; cook 5 minutes, stirring frequently. Stir in remaining ingredients, except Parmesan cheese; cook at 400° until boiling. Reduce heat to simmer between Warm and 200°; cook, covered, 1 1/4 hours. Stir in cheese.

About 1 quart.

Rich Mushroom Sauce

1/4 cup butter or margarine
1 cup chopped mushrooms
1/4 cup all-purpose flour
2 cups water
1 1/2 teaspoons chicken-flavor instant bouillon

1/4 cup whipping cream or half-and-half
1/16 teaspoon ground nutmeg
Salt
White pepper

Heat butter in fry pan at Warm until melted. Add mushrooms; cook at 200°, 2 minutes. Stir in flour; cook 2 minutes. Whisk in water and bouillon; cook at 400° until boiling. Reduce heat to simmer, between Warm and 200°; cook, whisking constantly until thickened. Whisk in cream and nutmeg; season to taste with salt and pepper.

About 1 3/4 cups.

Clear Mushroom Sauce

Omit flour and cream in above recipe. Cook mushrooms in butter as above. Add water and bouillon; cook at 400° until boiling. Reduce heat to simmer, between Warm and 200°. Mix 2 tablespoons cornstarch and 1/4 cup cold water; whisk into mixture in fry pan, whisking constantly until thickened. Whisk in nutmeg; season to taste with salt and pepper.

About 1 3/4 cups.

Drawn Butter Sauce

1/3 cup butter or margarine-butter blend
2 tablespoons all-purpose flour
1 cup boiling water
1 to 2 tablespoons lemon juice

1/4 teaspoon Dijon-style mustard
1/2 teaspoon salt
1/16 teaspoon white pepper

Heat butter in fry pan at Warm until melted. Stir in flour; cook 1 minute. Whisk in boiling water; cook at 200° until slightly thickened, about 5 minutes, whisking constantly. Whisk in lemon juice, mustard, salt and pepper. Serve over fish or vegetables.

About 1 1/4 cups.

Tarragon-Chive Butter Sauce

Make Drawn Butter Sauce as above. Whisk in 1 teaspoon dried chives and 1/2 teaspoon dried tarragon leaves. Serve over fish, poultry or vegetables.

About 1 1/4 cups.

Cucumber-Dill Butter Sauce

Make Drawn Butter Sauce as above. Whisk in 1/2 cup finely chopped seeded cucumber and 1/2 teaspoon dried dillweed. Serve over fish, poultry or vegetables.

About 1 2/3 cups.

Hot Chili Barbeque Sauce

2 10-ounce jars apricot preserves
1 cup chili sauce
1 clove garlic, minced
2 tablespoons distilled white vinegar

1 tablespoon Worcestershire sauce
3 to 3 1/2 tablespoons chili powder
1/4 teaspoon ground ginger
4 to 6 drops red pepper sauce

Mix all ingredients in fry pan; cook at 400° until boiling. Reduce heat to simmer, between Warm and 200°; cook 10 minutes. Cool to room temperature. Refrigerate, covered, up to 1 month.

About 3 cups.

Cinnamon-Spice Apple Butter

8 cups coarsely chopped, cored, peeled tart apples	1/2 teaspoon ground cinnamon
2/3 cup water	1/2 teaspoon ground allspice
2 tablespoons lemon juice	1/4 teaspoon ground cloves
1 to 1 1/4 cups sugar	

Combine apples, water and lemon juice in fry pan; cook at 400° until boiling. Reduce heat to simmer, between Warm and 200°; cook, covered, until apples are tender, about 20 minutes. Stir in 1 cup sugar, cinnamon, allspice and cloves; cook until thickened to desired consistency, 10 to 15 minutes, stirring frequently. Add remaining 1/4 cup sugar, if necessary, for sweetness; cook, stirring until sugar is dissolved.

Spoon mixture into sterilized jar; cool to room temperature. Refrigerate, covered, up to 1 month.

1 pint.

Orange Sauce

1/2 cup undiluted frozen orange juice concentrate	1/2 teaspoon grated lemon rind
2/3 cup water	1 tablespoon cornstarch
1/4 teaspoon chicken flavor instant bouillon	2 tablespoons cold water
1/2 teaspoon grated orange rind	2 tablespoons butter, softened
	2 dashes white pepper

Mix orange juice concentrate, 2/3 cup water, bouillon, orange rind and lemon rind in fry pan; cook at 400° until boiling. Reduce heat to simmer, between Warm and 200°. Mix cornstarch and cold water; whisk into orange juice mixture until thickened, whisking constantly. Whisk in butter, 1 tablespoon at a time, until melted. Whisk in pepper. Serve with green vegetables, chicken, pork or ham.

1 cup.

TIP: For use as a dessert sauce, make sauce, omitting bouillon and pepper. Serve over poached fruit, rice pudding or cake slices.

Cranberry Chutney

1 cup orange juice	1/8 teaspoon ground ginger
1 cup granulated sugar	1/8 teaspoon cayenne pepper
1 cup light brown sugar	2 10-ounce packages fresh or frozen cranberries
1/4 cup finely chopped onion	2/3 cup raisins
1 clove garlic, minced	1/4 cup cider vinegar
1 tablespoon grated orange rind	1/4 cup orange flavor liqueur
1 teaspoon ground cinnamon	3/4 cup coarsely chopped pecans
1/4 teaspoon ground cloves	
1/8 teaspoon ground cardamom	

Mix orange juice, sugars, onion, garlic, orange rind, cinnamon, cloves, cardamom, ginger and cayenne pepper in fry pan; cook at 400° until boiling, stirring constantly until sugar is dissolved. Reduce heat to simmer, between Warm and 200°. Stir in cranberries, raisins and vinegar; cook 15 minutes, or until thickened to desired consistency, stirring occasionally. Stir in liqueur and pecans; cook 3 to 5 minutes, stirring constantly.

Spoon mixture into sterilized jars; cool to room temperature. Refrigerate, covered, up to 2 months.

About 2 pints.

Ginger Peach Chutney

2	cups apricot nectar	1	teaspoon minced fresh or canned ginger root
1/2	cup cider vinegar		
2 1/2	pounds peaches, peeled, pitted, coarsely chopped	1	teaspoon dry mustard
		1/2	teaspoon ground cinnamon
1	cup raisins	1/4	teaspoon ground mace
1/3	cup finely chopped onion	1/2 to 3/4	cup light brown sugar

Combine all ingredients, except sugar, in fry pan; cook at 400° until boiling, stirring occasionally. Reduce heat to simmer, between Warm and 200°. Stir in sugar to taste, stirring constantly, until sugar is dissolved. Cook until thickened to desired consistency, stirring occasionally.

Spoon mixture into sterilized jars; cool to room temperature. Refrigerate, covered, up to 2 months.

About 1 1/2 pints.

Mexican Salsa

2	tablespoons vegetable oil	2	tablespoons cider vinegar
1/2	cup chopped onions	2	teaspoons sugar
1	clove garlic, minced	1/2	teaspoon dried coriander leaves
2	16-ounce cans tomatoes, drained, coarsely chopped	1/2	teaspoon salt
1	3-ounce can chopped mild or hot chilies		

Heat fry pan at 250°. Add oil, onion and garlic; cook until tender, 3 to 5 minutes. Stir in remaining ingredients; cook at 400° until boiling. Reduce heat to simmer, between Warm and 200°; cook until slightly thickened, 8 to 10 minutes. Spoon into sterilized jar; cool to room temperature. Refrigerate, covered, up to 2 weeks.

About 1 1/4 cups.

Breads

You may be surprised by how many kinds of bread you can make in the electric fry pan. The pan doubles as a baker for traditional yeast loaves just as readily as it turns out a quick batch of biscuits or cornbread.

In fact, even the quick breads—so called because they're made without yeast and don't require rising time—include some unusual choices. There are Parmesan-Dill Biscuits to perk up a stew, casserole, or chicken dinner and Jalapeño Cornbread to enliven soups, pork chops, and other everyday fare. And there are also big, golden rounds of puffy Fry Bread—almost an event in itself!—and moist Ice Cream Muffins for brunch, coffee, or dessert.

For a more substantial loaf that comes together almost as fast, start with packaged hot roll mix and top it with sautéed onions and cheese to make Onion Bread. For the unmatched pride of made-from-scratch yeast breads, try English Muffins, Poppy Seed Pan Rolls, Oatmeal Loaves, or elegant, egg-enriched Individual Brioches. There is no more exquisite brunch treat than either the English Muffins or the classic French Brioche—especially if you serve them with your own Cinnamon-Spice Apple Butter or Ginger-Peach Chutney (see Sauce Chapter for recipes).

Perhaps the biggest surprise of all is how helpful the electric fry pan can be for all yeast baking. Even if you choose to bake your favorite recipes in the oven, you'll still want to proof the dough in the fry pan, for it provides just the right degree of warmth for even rising. Just set the bowl or pan of dough on a rack in the covered fry pan; heat the fry pan at Warm for 1 minute and then turn it to Off. Let the dough stand, covered, until doubled in bulk, or as directed in the recipe.

Oatmeal Loaves

2 1/3	cups unbleached or bread flour	1/4	teaspoon baking soda
1/3	cup quick-cooking oats	1/2	teaspoon salt
1	1/4-ounce package active dry yeast	1 1/4	cups very warm milk (120°)
2	teaspoons light brown sugar		

Mix flour, oats, yeast, sugar, baking soda and salt in bowl. Stir in milk; beat until mixture is smooth. Spoon batter into 2 greased loaf pans, 7 1/2 × 3 1/2 inches.

Place loaf pans on rack in fry pan. Heat, covered, at Warm for 1 minute. Turn heat to Off; let stand, covered, until batter has doubled in size, about 45 minutes. Heat fry pan at 325°. Cook, covered, until bottom of bread is deep golden and loaves sound hollow when tapped, 50 to 60 minutes. Remove loaves from pans; cool on wire rack.

2 loaves.

Ice Cream Muffins

1	cup self-rising flour	1/4	teaspoon ground cinnamon
1	cup vanilla ice cream, slightly softened	1/8	teaspoon ground allspice
1	tablespoon sugar		

Mix flour and ice cream in small bowl until blended. Combine sugar, cinnamon and allspice; stir all but 1 teaspoon sugar mixture into batter. Spoon batter into 12 greased mini-muffin tins, filling each about three-fourths full; sprinkle with 1 teaspoon sugar mixture.

Heat fry pan at 400°. Place muffin pan on rack in fry pan; cook, with cover 1 inch ajar, for 20 to 25 minutes, or until toothpick inserted near centers of muffins comes out clean. Cool muffins on wire rack.

12 mini-muffins.

Onion Bread, Fry Bread, English Muffins, Individual Brioche.

English Muffins

2	cups milk	1	1/4-ounce package active dry yeast
3	tablespoons butter or margarine	4 1/2 to 4 3/4	cups all-purpose flour
2	tablespoons sugar		Vegetable shortening
1 1/2	teaspoons salt	1 1/2	tablespoons cornmeal

Cook milk in fry pan at 400° just until bubbles begin to appear. Turn heat to Off; stir in butter, sugar and salt, stirring until butter is melted. Cool to lukewarm (110°). Stir in yeast until dissolved; let stand 2 minutes. Stir in enough flour to make moderately stiff dough; stirring until smooth, about 5 minutes. Let stand, covered, until dough has doubled in size, about 1 hour.

Remove dough from fry pan. Clean fry pan. Roll dough on lightly floured surface to 1/2-inch thickness; cut into 3-inch rounds with cutter. Let stand, lightly covered, 30 minutes (dough will not double in size).

Heat fry pan at 250°. Grease fry pan lightly with shortening and sprinkle with cornmeal; cook muffins in fry pan until golden on bottom, about 15 minutes. Turn muffins; cook until golden on bottom, 15 to 20 minutes. Cool on wire rack. Split muffins with fork to serve.

12 to 14 muffins.

Individual Brioche

(A roll baked from rich yeast dough)

1	1/4-ounce package active dry yeast	3 to 3 1/4	cups all-purpose flour
1/4	cup warm water (110°)	1 1/2	teaspoons salt
1/3	cup butter or margarine, softened	1/4	cup milk
2	tablespoons sugar	1	egg, beaten
2	eggs		

Stir yeast into warm water in small bowl; let stand 5 minutes. Beat butter and sugar in mixer bowl until fluffy; beat in 2 eggs; 1 at a time. Add 1 cup flour and salt; mix in milk and beat at medium speed 2 minutes. Mix in enough remaining flour to make soft dough. Knead on lightly floured surface until dough is smooth and elastic, about 5 minutes.

Place dough in greased casserole; turn greased side up. Place casserole on rack in fry pan. Heat, covered, at Warm for 1 minute. Turn heat to Off; let stand until dough has doubled in size, 1 to 1 1/2 hours.

Punch dough down. Shape two-thirds of the dough into 12 balls; place in 12 greased 6-ounce custard cups or two 6-cup muffin pans. Shape remaining one-third dough into 12 balls. Make holes in tops of larger balls with finger; place smaller balls in holes. Refrigerate 6 of the custard cups, loosely covered with waxed paper.

Place remaining 6 custard cups on rack in fry pan. Heat, covered, at Warm for 1 minute. Turn heat to Off. Let stand, covered, until dough has doubled in size, about 20 minutes; brush rolls lightly with beaten egg. Heat fry pan at 375°, cook rolls covered, until deep golden brown on bottom, 25 to 30 minutes. Remove rolls; cool on wire rack. Turn heat to Off.

Remove the other 6 custard cups from refrigerator when beginning to cook first rolls; let stand at room temperature. When first rolls are done, place other custard cups on rack in fry pan. If fry pan has cooled, heat, covered, at Warm for 1 minute. Turn heat to Off. Let stand, covered, until dough has doubled in size, 30 to 40 minutes. Cook, covered, as above.

1 dozen.

Onion Bread

1 13 3/4-ounce package hot roll mix	2 cups sliced onions
3/4 cup warm water (110°)	1 cup shredded cheddar cheese
1 egg	1 teaspoon poppy seed
1/4 cup butter or margarine	

Make hot roll mix according to package directions, using hot water and egg; knead on lightly floured surface 5 minutes. Cover with towel; let stand while preparing onions.

Heat butter in fry pan at Warm until melted. Add onion; cook at 200° until beginning to brown, about 10 minutes, stirring occasionally. Remove onion and reserve. Clean fry pan.

Roll dough on lightly floured surface to fit bottom of fry pan; place in fry pan. Spoon reserved onion mixture evenly over dough. Heat fry pan, covered, at Warm for 1 minute. Turn heat to Off; let stand, covered, until dough has almost doubled in size, 20 to 30 minutes. Heat fry pan at 250°; until bottom of dough is deep golden, 20 to 25 minutes. Sprinkle cheese and poppy seed over mixture; cook, covered, until cheese is melted, about 5 minutes. Remove bread from fry pan with plastic or wooden utensil. Cool on wire rack.

1 large loaf.

Fry Bread

2 cups all purpose flour	1 1/2 teaspoons mayonnaise or salad dressing
2 teaspoons baking powder	3/4 cup water
3/4 teaspoon salt	Vegetable oil

Mix flour, baking powder and salt in small bowl; add mayonnaise and rub through flour mixture with fingers until completely blended. Add water gradually, stirring mixture with fork until dough forms. Knead dough on lightly floured surface 5 minutes. Roll dough into log 6 inches long; let stand, uncovered, 40 minutes.

Cut dough into 6 equal pieces. Roll each piece into ball; roll out with floured rolling pin into rounds 1/16 inch thick.

Heat 1 inch oil in fry pan at 375°. Carefully stretch each dough round until about 8 inches in diameter; cook rounds, 1 at a time, until puffed and golden, about 2 minutes on each side. Drain on paper toweling.

6 breads.

Jalapeño Corn Bread

1 1/4 cups all-purpose flour	1 cup milk
3/4 cup cornmeal	1 egg, beaten
2 tablespoons sugar	1/4 cup vegetable oil
1 tablespoon baking powder	1/4 cup chopped, seeded jalapeño peppers
1 tablespoon instant minced onion	1 cup shredded cheddar or Monterey Jack cheese
1/2 teaspoon salt	

Mix flour, cornmeal, sugar, baking powder, onion and salt in medium bowl; mix in combined milk, egg and oil. Spoon mixture into greased 8-inch square baking pan.

Heat fry pan at 400°. Place baking pan on rack in fry pan; cook, covered, until toothpick inserted near center of corn bread comes out clean, about 30 minutes. Sprinkle top of corn bread with peppers and cheese; cook, covered, until cheese is melted, about 5 minutes. Cut into squares; serve warm.

6 servings.

TIP: To make plain corn bread, omit jalapeño peppers and cheese.

Desserts and Candies

What's your favorite dessert? Is it a rich, chocolatey temptation, or a summer-fresh fruit tart? Perhaps it's spicy pumpkin pie or carrot cake, creamy rice pudding or a caramel-topped custard, dazzling crepes Suzette or a dense, moist cheesecake. Can you resist a pan of homemade nut brittle or a piece of meltaway toffee? Is your weakness a matter of just-baked cookies or a gooey ice cream treat?

You'll find all these and many more in this chapter—enough to please every sweet tooth and those who prefer light desserts, too. Browse through and you'll undoubtedly come across one that you'll want to make right away and another for your next big dinner gathering or party. If you look forward to bringing someone a gift, you'll find great inspiration among the candies. If there are children around, they'll surely be eager to help you prepare a big batch of bar cookies or fudge.

Just a few tips:

• To translate your own dessert recipes into fry pan-easy techniques, look for a similar recipe in this chapter—whether for poached fruit, upside-down cake, cheesecake, or candy—and follow the same basic procedure for combining and heating ingredients.

• Use a candy thermometer to ensure proper consistency with the caramels, nut brittle, and toffee.

For safety's sake, be sure that your electric fry pan is positioned away from the bottom of cabinets and flammable materials such as curtains, drapes and clothing when you use it to make flambéed desserts. Remember to detach power cord from outlet first and then remove the heat control from the fry pan. Be sure to ignite the mixture with a long kitchen match and flambé for no more than 2-3 minutes at any one time.

Easiest Fudge

1	**pound semi-sweet chocolate, coarsely chopped**
1	**14-ounce can sweetened condensed milk**
1 1/2	**teaspoons vanilla**

	Dash salt
3/4	**cup chopped walnuts**
1/2	**cup raisins**

Combine chocolate, condensed milk, vanilla and salt in fry pan; cook at Warm until chocolate is melted, stirring frequently. Stir in walnuts and raisins. Pour into aluminum-foil-lined 8 × 8 inch baking pan. Refrigerate until firm, about 15 minutes. Cut into squares. Store in airtight container.

1 1/2 pounds.

Flaming Bananas Foster

1/3	**cup butter or margarine-butter blend**
1/2	**cup light brown sugar**
1/4	**cup coarsely chopped pecans**
1/2	**teaspoon ground cinnamon**

3	**medium bananas, sliced**
1/4	**cup light rum**
	Vanilla ice cream

Heat butter at Warm until melted. Stir in sugar, pecans and cinnamon; cook at 200° until sugar is melted, about 2 minutes, stirring constantly. Stir in bananas; cook until heated, 1 to 2 minutes, stirring occasionally. Stir in rum; turn heat to OFF and unplug cord from wall outlet. Flame banana mixture.

Spoon ice cream into dishes; spoon banana mixture over. Serve immediately.

6 servings.

Pumpkin Spiced Pie

1/3 cup butter or margarine
1 cup graham cracker crumbs
1/2 cup chopped pecans
1/4 cup granulated sugar
1 16-ounce can pumpkin
1/4 cup light brown sugar
1/2 cup sour cream or sour half-and-half
2 eggs

1/4 cup half-and-half or milk
1 tablespoon butter or margarine, melted
1 1/2 teaspoons ground cinnamon
1/2 teaspoon ground nutmeg
1/2 teaspoon ground ginger
1/8 teaspoon ground cloves
1/4 teaspoon salt

Place 1/3 cup butter in bottom of 9-inch spring-form pan. Place pan on rack in fry pan; heat at Warm until butter is melted. Remove spring-form pan from fry pan. Stir in graham cracker crumbs, pecans and sugar until blended. Pat mixture evenly in bottom and scant 1/2 inch up side of spring-form pan.

Beat remaining ingredients in bowl until well blended; pour into crust. Heat fry pan at 350°. Place spring-form pan on rack in fry pan; cook, covered, until filling is set, about 1 3/4 hours. Cool on wire rack; refrigerate until serving time. Remove rim of spring-form pan; cut pie into wedges to serve.

8 to 10 servings.

Fresh Berries in Patty Shells

Pastry cream (see recipe page 83)
1 10-ounce package frozen patty shells
1 1/2 to 2 cups fresh raspberries, blueberries or sliced strawberries.

Whipped cream
Ground nutmeg

Make Pastry Cream in fry pan, using 2 tablespoons flour and 2 egg yolks instead of 3 tablespoons flour and 3 egg yolks. Clean fry pan.

Heat fry pan at 400°. Place rack in fry pan; cover with piece of parchment paper or brown grocery paper. Place frozen patty shells on paper; cook, covered, 1 hour. Remove moist dough from centers of patty shells with fork; cook, covered, 5 minutes. Remove patty shells from fry pan; cool on wire rack.

Place patty shells on serving plates; fill shells with berries. Spoon Pastry Cream over; garnish with whipped cream. Sprinkle lightly with nutmeg.

6 servings.

TIP: Any fresh or canned fruit may be substituted for the berries.

Cherries Jubilee

1 28-ounce can pitted dark sweet cherries
2 tablespoons light brown sugar
1 tablespoon cornstarch
2 tablespoons cold water

2 tablespoons butter or margarine
1/4 cup dark rum or brandy
Vanilla ice cream
Whipped cream

Combine cherries with liquid and sugar in fry pan; cook at 400° until boiling. Mix cornstarch and cold water; stir into cherry mixture until thickened. Reduce heat to simmer, between Warm and 200°; stir in butter until melted. Stir in rum; turn heat to Off and unplug cord from wall outlet. Flame cherry mixture.

Spoon ice cream into individual serving dishes; spoon hot cherry mixture over. Garnish with a dollop of whipped cream.

4 servings.

Whole Wheat Bread and Fruit Pudding

2 cups very warm milk
3 eggs, beaten
2 tablespoons butter or margarine, melted
1/2 cup light brown sugar
1 teaspoon vanilla
1/2 teaspoon ground cinnamon

1/4 teaspoon ground nutmeg
1/4 teaspoon salt
7 slices firm whole wheat bread cut into scant 1/2-inch cubes
1 cup chopped mixed dried fruit
Warm water
Whipped cream

Beat milk, eggs and butter until smooth; mix in sugar, vanilla, cinnamon, nutmeg and salt. Pour mixture over bread cubes and fruit in large bowl; toss to coat evenly. Spoon mixture into 1 1/2-quart greased casserole; place on rack in fry pan. Add 2 inches warm water; heat at 400° until boiling. Reduce heat to simmer, between Warm and 200°; cook, covered, until pudding is set, 1 1/4 to 1 1/2 hours. Remove casserole from fry pan; cool on wire rack. Serve warm with whipped cream.

8 servings.

Creamy Caramels

1 cup granulated sugar
1 cup light brown sugar
2 cups whipping cream or half-and-half

3/4 cup light corn syrup
1/2 cup butter or margarine-butter blend
3/4 cup chopped pecans

Combine sugars, 1 cup cream, corn syrup and butter in fry pan; cook at Warm until butter is melted, stirring occasionally. Stir in remaining 1 cup cream; cook at 300° until boiling. Continue cooking until candy thermometer registers 245° (firm ball), stirring constantly. Turn heat to Off; stir in pecans. Pour candy into aluminum foil lined 8 × 8 inch baking pan. Cool; cut into squares. Store in airtight container.

5 dozen.

Chocolate Clusters

1 pound semi-sweet chocolate, coarsely chopped
2 ounces unsweetened chocolate, coarsely chopped

Warm water
2 cups cocktail peanuts
1 1/2 cups raisins

Place chocolate in metal bowl in fry pan. Add 1 1/2 inches warm water to fry pan. Heat chocolate at Warm until melted, stirring occasionally. Stir in peanuts and raisins; remove bowl from fry pan.

Drop chocolate mixture by rounded tablespoonfuls onto waxed paper lined cookie sheet. Refrigerate until hard, about 15 minutes. Store candies in airtight container.

About 1 3/4 pounds.

Chocolate Almond Bark

Make chocolate mixture as above, substituting 2 1/2 cups toasted blanched whole almonds for the peanuts and raisins. Spread mixture to 1/4-inch thickness on waxed paper lined cookie sheet. Refrigerate until hard, about 15 minutes; break into pieces.

About 2 pounds.

English Toffee

1 cup butter or margarine-butter blend
1 1/3 cups sugar
1/4 cup water
1 tablespoon light corn syrup
1 1/2 cups coarsely chopped almonds, toasted

6 ounces semi-sweet chocolate, coarsely chopped
Warm water

Heat butter in fry pan at Warm until melted. Stir in sugar, 1/4 cup water and corn syrup; cook at 325° until candy thermometer registers 300° (hard-crack), stirring constantly. Turn heat to Off. Stir in 1 cup almonds. Pour toffee mixture into greased 13 × 9 × 2 inch baking pan; cool to room temperature.

Place chocolate in small metal bowl in fry pan. Add 1 inch warm water to fry pan; heat at Warm until chocolate is melted, stirring occasionally. Spread chocolate evenly over toffee; sprinkle with remaining 1/2 cup almonds. Refrigerate until chocolate is hard, about 15 minutes. Break candy into pieces with tip of knife. Store in airtight container.

About 1 1/4 pounds.

Mixed Nut Brittle

1 cup granulated sugar
1 cup light brown sugar
1 cup light corn syrup
1/2 cup water

1/4 cup butter or margarine-butter blend
2 cups mixed nuts, toasted
1 1/2 teaspoons baking soda

Mix sugars, corn syrup and water in fry pan; cook at Warm until sugars dissolve, stirring occasionally. Continue cooking at 300° until mixture boils. Stir in butter until melted; continue cooking until candy thermometer registers 300° (hard-crack). Turn heat to Off. Stir in nuts and soda; pour mixture into greased jelly roll pan, spreading quickly with spatula. Cool to room temperature. Break into pieces. Store in airtight container.

About 2 pounds.

Funnel Cakes

1 1/4 cups all-purpose flour
1 tablespoon granulated sugar
1 teaspoon baking soda
3/4 teaspoon baking powder
1/4 teaspoon salt

3/4 to 1 cup milk
1 egg
Vegetable oil
Powdered sugar
Maple syrup (optional)

Mix flour, sugar, baking soda, baking powder and salt in bowl. Beat together 3/4 cup milk and egg; stir into flour mixture until blended. Stir in additional 1/4 cup milk, if necessary, for batter to flow slowly but evenly through a funnel with 1/2-inch opening.

Heat 2 inches oil in fry pan at 375°. Fill funnel with 1/2 cup batter, holding finger over opening. Remove finger from opening and let batter flow into oil, swirling batter into a spiral pattern; cook until crisp and golden, 1 to 2 minutes on each side. Remove cake from oil with slotted spoon; drain on paper toweling. Repeat with remaining batter. Sprinkle warm cakes with powdered sugar. Serve with syrup.

4 servings.

Fresh Strawberry Tart

Pastry Cream
Sweet Pastry
2 to 3 pints fresh strawberries, hulled

1/3 cup currant jelly
1 to 2 teaspoons water

Make Pastry Cream. Make Sweet Pastry. Place Sweet Pastry on serving dish; spread Pastry Cream evenly over pastry. Arrange berries on Pastry Cream, pointed ends up. Heat currant jelly and water in fry pan at Warm until jelly is melted; brush jelly over strawberries. Cut tart into squares to serve.

6 servings.

TIP: Any desired fresh or drained canned fruit can be substituted for the strawberries. If using a light-colored fruit, such as pineapple, banana or peaches, substitute apple jelly or apricot preserves for the currant jelly.

Pastry Cream

1/2 cup sugar
3 tablespoons all-purpose flour
1/8 teaspoon salt

1 1/2 cups half-and-half or milk
3 egg yolks, beaten
1/2 teaspoon vanilla or almond extract

Mix sugar, flour and salt in fry pan. Stir in half-and-half gradually until blended; cook at 200° until thickened, about 4 minutes, stirring constantly. Stir about 1/2 cup half-and-half mixture into egg yolks. Stir yolk mixture into fry pan; cook until thickened, about 4 minutes, stirring constantly. Stir in vanilla. Pour cream into bowl; cool to room temperature, stirring occasionally. Refrigerate until chilled, about 2 hours.

About 2 cups.

Sweet Pastry

2 cups all-purpose flour
2 tablespoons sugar
1/4 teaspoon salt

1/2 cup cold butter cut into pieces
3 tablespoon vegetable shortening
5 to 6 tablespoons ice water

Mix flour, sugar and salt in bowl; cut in cold butter and shortening until mixture resembles coarse crumbs. Mix in enough ice water to form smooth dough; refrigerate, covered, at least 1 hour.

Heat fry pan at 300°. Roll pastry on lightly floured surface into 10-inch square; trim to 9 inches, rounding corners. Roll pastry onto rolling pin; unroll onto center of piece of aluminum foil 20 inches long. Place foil with pastry in fry pan, allowing edges of foil to extend up sides of fry pan. Pierce pastry with fork; cook, covered, 5 minutes, or until bottom of pastry is golden. Using edges of foil, rotate pastry 1/2 turn in fry pan; cook, covered, 5 minutes. Remove pastry from fry pan; carefully transfer pastry to wire rack. Place rack in fry pan; cook, covered, 15 minutes. Remove from fry pan; cool on wire rack.

One 9-inch pastry.

Chocolate Fudge Cheesecake

3	tablespoons butter or margarine		1	cup granulated sugar
1	cup finely ground pecans		1/4	cup light brown sugar
3/4	cup finely ground walnuts		1/2	cup unsweetened cocoa
3	tablespoons granulated sugar		3	eggs
1/2	teaspoon ground cinnamon		1/4	cup whipping cream or half-and-half
2	8-ounce packages cream cheese, softened		1	teaspoon vanilla

Place butter in bottom of 9-inch spring-form pan. Place pan on rack in fry pan; cook, covered, at 375° until butter is melted. Blend in nuts, 3 tablespoons sugar and cinnamon; reserve 2 tablespoons nut mixture. Pat remaining mixture evenly in bottom and 1/2 inch up side of spring-form pan; cook, covered, at 375° for 15 minutes.

Beat cream cheese in bowl until fluffy. Beat in 1 cup sugar, brown sugar and cocoa until smooth. Beat in eggs, one at a time, beating well after each addition. Mix in cream and vanilla until smooth; pour into crust. Sprinkle with reserved nut mixture; cook, covered, until cheesecake is set, 40 to 45 minutes. Remove spring-form pan from fry pan; cool on wire rack to room temperature.

Refrigerate cheesecake until chilled, 3 to 4 hours. Remove rim of spring-form pan; cut cheesecake into wedges to serve.

8 to 10 servings.

Peach Praline Upside-Down Cake

1 1/4	cups milk		1/3	cup butter or margarine
1	tablespoon lemon juice		2/3	cup pecan halves
1	18.25-ounce package yellow cake mix		3/4	cup light brown sugar
3	eggs		1	teaspoon maple extract
1/3	cup vegetable oil		1	29-ounce can sliced peaches, drained

Mix milk and lemon juice; let stand 15 minutes. Make cake mix according to package directions, using milk mixture, eggs and oil. Reserve batter.

Heat butter in fry pan at Warm until melted. Stir in pecans; cook at 200° until pecans are toasted, 3 to 5 minutes. Stir in brown sugar and maple extract; cook, until sugar is melted, stirring frequently. Arrange peach slices attractively in fry pan. Spoon reserved batter over; cook, with cover 1/2-inch ajar, at 225° until cake springs back when touched in center, 50 to 55 minutes. Invert immediately onto serving plate.

10 to 12 servings.

Fry Pan Cookies

1 1/2	cups chopped mixed dried fruit		2	cups oven-toasted rice cereal
2	eggs, beaten		3/4	cup chopped walnuts or pecans
3/4	cup light brown sugar			

Combine dried fruit, eggs and sugar in fry pan; cook at 200° until sugar is dissolved, 5 to 8 minutes, stirring constantly. Stir in cereal and nuts until blended; turn heat to Off. Drop mixture by heaping teaspoonfuls onto cookie sheet; refrigerate until set, about 15 minutes. Store in airtight container.

3 dozen.

Chocolate Fudge Cheesecake, Fresh
Strawberry Tart, Pears Poached in Port

85

Crepes Suzette

1 cup all-purpose flour
1 tablespoon granulated sugar
2 eggs, beaten
3/4 to 1 cup milk
2 tablespoons orange flavor liqueur (optional)
2 tablespoons butter or margarine, melted

1/2 cup butter or margarine, softened
2 tablespoons orange marmalade
Grated rind of 1 lemon
2 cups powdered sugar
2 tablespoons butter or margarine

Beat flour, sugar, eggs and 3/4 cup milk until smooth. Stir in liqueur and melted butter; let batter stand 15 minutes. Beat softened butter, orange marmalade and lemon rind until fluffy; beat in powdered sugar. Reserve butter mixture.

Stir additional 1/4 cup milk into batter if necessary for proper consistency (batter should be the consistency of whipping cream). Heat fry pan at 350°. Pour 2 tablespoons batter into fry pan; cook crepe until golden on the bottom, about 1 minute. Turn crepe, cook 30 seconds. Remove from fry pan. Repeat with remaining batter.

Spread reserved butter mixture on crepes; fold crepes in half, then in half again. Heat 2 tablespoons butter in fry pan at Warm until melted.

Arrange folded crepes in fry pan; cook at 250° until crepes are browned on the bottom, 3 to 4 minutes. Turn crepes; cook 2 minutes. Serve hot.

6 servings (3 crepes each).

Orange Caramel Flan

3/4 cup sugar
2 cups warm half-and-half
3 eggs, beaten
1/4 cup sugar
2 tablespoons orange flavor liqueur

1 teaspoon vanilla
1/8 teaspoon ground mace
1/8 teaspoon salt
Warm water

Heat fry pan at 300°. Add sugar, cook until sugar is dissolved and golden in color, stirring constantly. Turn heat to Off. Immediately pour sugar syrup into 1 1/2-quart glass casserole. Holding casserole with pot holders, quickly tilt casserole to coat bottom and side with syrup. Let stand while preparing custard. Clean fry pan.

Beat half-and-half and eggs in bowl until well blended; beat in remaining ingredients, except water. Pour custard mixture into casserole; place casserole on rack in fry pan. Add 1 1/2 inches warm water to fry pan; heat, covered at 400° until boiling. Reduce heat to simmer, between Warm and 200°; cook, covered, until custard is set, about 30 minutes. Remove casserole from fry pan; cool on wire rack to room temperature. If moisture has collected on top of custard, carefully blot with paper toweling.

Refrigerate until chilled, 3 to 4 hours. Invert custard onto rimmed serving plate.

4 servings.

Favorite Menus

There are so many things to consider when you're wondering what to serve with what. A balance of protein, carbohydrates, vitamins, and other nutrients is most important, of course. But so is the balance of flavors. Preparation time must be feasible, and so must the cost. Variety is no less essential, nor is attractive appearance. And to complicate matters further, you have to make menu choices almost every day, taking into account yesterday's meals and tomorrow's.

This chapter of complete menus presents ways to resolve all these issues every day of the week. It includes seven breakfasts, lunches, and dinners, as well as a special section of seven menus tailored for just one or two diners. The keys to all of the meals are uncomplicated, simple-to-prepare dishes that enhance one another when served together.

In following these menus, you'll discover comfortable cooking patterns. The recipes indicate which foods can be done ahead and refrigerated and which can be kept warm while you're finishing other dishes. You'll quickly realize how the electric fry pan can be used in tandem with the stove to speed everything along. No doubt you'll soon want to create hundreds of new menus too, by substituting or adding other recipes in this book. But these meal plans are a good place to start, for the recipes are especially easy and the scheduling will fit even the busiest days.

Lumberjack Breakfast

Apricots in Orange Juice
Corned Beef Hash Casserole
Whole Wheat Toast with Apple Butter
Coffee or Tea
Recipes Included

Apricots in Orange Juice

1	11-ounce package dried apricots
2	cups orange juice
1 to 2	tablespoons apricot preserves
2	whole allspice

1	cinnamon stick
1	whole clove
1/8	teaspoon ground mace

Combine all ingredients in fry pan; heat at 400° until boiling. Reduce heat to simmer, between Warm and 200°; cook, covered, until apricots are tender, about 10 minutes. Spoon apricot mixture into serving bowl; let cool.

4 servings.

Corned Beef Hash Casserole

2	15 1/2-ounce cans corned beef hash
1 1/2	tablespoons spicy brown mustard
3	tablespoons finely chopped onion
6	eggs
	Salt

	Pepper
1 1/2	cups shredded Swiss cheese
	Paprika
	Ground nutmeg

Combine hash, mustard and onion; spread mixture evenly in bottom of fry pan. Make 6 evenly spaced depressions, about 2 inches in diameter, in hash mixture. Break 1 egg into each depression; sprinkle lightly with salt and pepper. Sprinkle cheese, paprika and nutmeg over hash mixture and eggs; cook, covered, at 200° until eggs are cooked to desired degree of doneness and cheese is melted, about 25 minutes.

4 to 6 servings.

Sunday Breakfast

Chilled Grapefruit Halves
*Double-Thick French Toast
*Almond Syrup
Sausage Links
Coffee with Cinnamon

*Recipes Included

Double-Thick French Toast

1	loaf unsliced, day old bread		1 1/2	teaspoons ground cinnamon
1 1/2	cups half-and-half or milk		3/4	teaspoon vanilla
3	eggs, beaten		6	tablespoons butter or margarine
2	tablespoons sugar			Almond Syrup

Cut eight 1-inch thick slices from bread, reserving rest of loaf for other use. Beat half-and-half and eggs in shallow bowl until smooth; mix in sugar, cinnamon and vanilla. Heat 3 tablespoons of the butter in fry pan at Warm until melted. Dip 4 slices bread into half-and-half mixture, coating both sides of bread generously with mixture; cook at 275° until golden, 3 to 4 minutes on each side. Remove French toast from fry pan; keep warm. Repeat with remaining butter and bread slices. Serve with Almond Syrup.

4 servings.

Almond Syrup

2	tablespoons butter or margarine		1/3	cup dark corn syrup
3/4	cup slivered almonds		1 to 2	tablespoons lemon juice
2	cups light brown sugar		1	tablespoon grated lemon rind
3/4	cup water			

Heat butter in fry pan at Warm until melted. Add almonds; cook at 200° until almonds are golden. Remove almonds from fry pan. Add sugar, water, corn syrup, lemon juice and lemon rind; cook at 200° until sugar is dissolved and syrup is thickened to desired consistency, about 10 minutes. Stir in almonds. Pour syrup mixture into pitcher or bowl; place in small pan of hot water to keep warm.

About 1 3/4 cups.

Farm Breakfast

Tomato Juice
*Farm-Style Hash Browns and Eggs
*Cinnamon Apple Rings
Buttermilk Biscuits with Strawberry Preserves
Hot Cocoa with Marshmallows

*Recipes Included

Farm-Style Hash Browns and Eggs

1	pound bacon		Salt
1	cup sliced mushrooms		Pepper
1/2	cup chopped green pepper	1	cup shredded cheddar cheese
4	cups unpeeled, diced cooked potatoes		Cinnamon Apple Rings
8	eggs, beaten		

Cook bacon in fry pan at 300° until crisp; remove bacon and crumble. Pour off excess drippings; reserve 2 tablespoons. Add mushrooms and green pepper to drippings in fry pan; cook at 225°, 2 minutes. Stir in potatoes; cook until crisp, about 8 minutes, stirring occasionally. Pour eggs over potato mixture; cook until eggs are set, stirring occasionally. Stir in bacon; season to taste with salt and pepper. Sprinkle cheese over potato mixture; cook, covered, until cheese is melted, about 2 minutes.

Spoon potato mixture on serving platter; cover with aluminum foil to keep warm. Clean fry pan. Make Cinnamon Apple Rings; arrange on platter with potato mixture.

6 servings.

Cinnamon Apple Rings

2	tablespoons butter or margarine	2	medium apples, cored, sliced into 1/4-inch rings
1	tablespoon light brown sugar		
1/8	teaspoon ground cinnamon	1/4	cup golden raisins

Heat butter in fry pan at Warm until melted. Stir in sugar and cinnamon; cook 1 minute. Add apples and raisins; cook, covered, at 200° until apples are tender and glazed, about 2 minutes on each side.

6 servings.

Breakfast on the Run

Chilled Vegetable Juice
*Breakfast Sandwiches
*Honeyed Oranges and Grapefruit
Coffee

*Recipes Included

Breakfast Sandwiches

1/3 cup mayonnaise or salad dressing
  1 teaspoon lemon juice
  1 teaspoon Dijon-style mustard
1/2 teaspoon sugar
  2 English muffins, split
     Butter or margarine, softened

1/2 pound sliced Canadian bacon or ham
  1 tablespoon butter or margarine
  4 eggs
1/2 cup shredded Swiss cheese
     Paprika

Mix mayonnaise, lemon juice, mustard and sugar; reserve sauce. Spread cut sides of muffins lightly with softened butter. Heat fry pan at 275°. Place Canadian bacon and muffins, cut sides down, in fry pan; cook until muffins are golden and Canadian bacon is hot. Remove from fry pan; place Canadian bacon slices on muffins; cover loosely with aluminum foil. Heat 1 tablespoon butter in fry pan at Warm until melted. Fry eggs at 250° to desired degree of doneness. Sprinkle eggs with cheese; cook, covered, until cheese is melted, about 1 minute. Place eggs on Canadian bacon; sprinkle with paprika. Serve with reserved sauce.

4 servings.

Honeyed Oranges and Grapefruit

  1 cup orange juice
  2 tablespoons honey
1/8 teaspoon ground cinnamon
1/8 teaspoon ground nutmeg

1/8 teaspoon ground allspice
  3 medium oranges, peeled, sliced, seeded
  1 large grapefruit, peeled,
     cut into segments

Mix orange juice, honey, cinnamon, nutmeg and allspice in fry pan; cook at 400° until boiling. Stir in oranges and grapefruit; simmer, between Warm and 200°, covered, 5 minutes. Spoon into serving bowl; serve warm or refrigerate, covered, until chilled, serve cold.

4 servings.

Silver Dollar Breakfast

Chilled Melon Wedges
*Whole Wheat Pancakes
*Blueberry Sauce
Scrambled Eggs
Coffee or Tea

*Recipes Included

Whole Wheat Pancakes

1 1/3 cups all-purpose flour	1 teaspoon salt
2/3 cup whole wheat flour	2 cups milk
1/4 cup sugar	1/4 cup vegetable oil
4 teaspoons baking powder	2 eggs, beaten
1 teaspoon ground cinnamon	Vegetable oil
1/4 teaspoon ground nutmeg	Blueberry Sauce

Mix flours, sugar, baking powder, cinnamon, nutmeg and salt in bowl. Beat milk, 1/4 cup oil and eggs; mix into flour mixture until smooth.

Heat fry pan at 350°; brush bottom of fry pan lightly with oil. Pour batter into fry pan, using about 3 tablespoons batter for each pancake; cook until bubbles form on tops of pancakes and bottoms of pancakes are golden. Turn; cook until golden. Serve pancakes with Blueberry Sauce.

4 servings.

Blueberry Sauce

1/2 cup butter or margarine	2 teaspoons grated lemon rind
2 tablespoons light brown sugar	1 16-ounce package frozen blueberries, thawed
1/4 cup seedless red raspberry jam	
2 teaspoons lemon juice	

Heat butter in fry pan at Warm until melted. Stir in sugar; cook 1 minute. Stir in jam, lemon juice and lemon rind; cook 1 minute. Stir in blueberries; cook at 400° until slightly thickened, stirring constantly. Pour blueberry mixture into pitcher or bowl; place in small pan of hot water to keep warm.

About 3 cups.

Orange Omelet Souffle, Grilled Canadian Bacon

Special Occasion Brunch

Fresh Strawberries and Cream
*Orange Omelet Souffle
*Grilled Canadian Bacon
Warm Croissants with Whipped Honey
Chilled Champagne or Coffee
*Recipes Included

Orange Omelet Souffle

Butter or margarine, softened
6 egg whites
1/8 teaspoon cream of tartar
6 egg yolks
1 tablespoon orange flavor liqueur or orange juice
1/8 teaspoon ground mace

1/4 teaspoon salt
1/8 teaspoon white pepper
1/4 cup orange marmalade
Orange twists
Mint or parsley sprigs
Grilled Canadian Bacon

Cut double thickness of aluminum foil 20 inches long; place in fry pan, allowing edges of foil to extend up sides of fry pan. Butter bottom of foil generously.

Beat egg whites and cream of tartar in large bowl until stiff, but not dry, peaks form. Beat egg yolks, liqueur, mace, salt and pepper in large bowl until thick and lemon colored, about 5 minutes. Stir about a fourth of the egg whites into yolk mixture; fold yolk mixture into remaining whites.

Heat fry pan at 250°. Pour egg mixture into fry pan; cook, covered, 30 minutes (omelet will appear moist on top but will feel firm when touched). Loosen edges of omelet with plastic or wooden spatula; lift from fry pan, using foil; invert on serving platter. Spread top of omelet with marmalade; garnish with orange twists and mint. Cover loosely with aluminum foil to keep warm.

Make Grilled Canadian Bacon; arrange on platter with omelet.

4 servings.

Grilled Canadian Bacon

3 tablespoons butter or margarine
2 teaspoons dried chives

1/4 teaspoon prepared horseradish
8 ounces sliced Canadian Bacon

Heat butter in fry pan at Warm until melted. Stir in chives, horseradish and Canadian bacon; cook, covered, at 275°, 2 minutes.

4 servings.

Steak 'N' Egger

Chilled Orange Juice
*Steak 'n' Cheese Scrambled Eggs
*Grilled Herb Toast
Cottage Fried Potatoes
Coffee
*Recipes Included

Steak 'N' Cheese Scrambled Eggs

4	3-ounce beef sandwich steaks		8	eggs
1/4	cup Worcestershire sauce		1/4	cup chopped green onions and tops
3	tablespoons spicy brown mustard			Salt
2	tablespoons butter or margarine			White pepper
1	3-ounce package cream cheese, cubed			

Brush steaks generously on both sides with mixture of Worcestershire sauce and mustard; let stand 5 minutes. Heat 1 tablespoon butter in fry pan at Warm until melted. Add steaks; cook, covered, at 300° until browned, about 2 minutes on each side. Remove steaks; keep warm.

Add remaining 1 tablespoon butter and cream cheese to fry pan; cook at 200° until cheese is melted. Beat eggs until foamy; stir in onions. Add egg mixture to fry pan; cook until eggs are set, 1 to 2 minutes, stirring occasionally. Season to taste with salt and pepper. Arrange steaks and eggs on serving platter.

4 servings.

Grilled Herb Toast

4	hoagie or small French rolls, cut in half		1/2	teaspoon garlic powder
	Butter or margarine		1/4	teaspoon dried thyme leaves

Spread cut sides of rolls lightly with butter. Mix garlic powder and thyme; sprinkle evenly over butter. Heat fry pan at 275°. Place rolls, cut sides down, in fry pan; cook until golden, about 2 minutes.

4 servings.

El Luncho

Peruvian Beef
Sliced Avocados with Cherry Tomato Halves
Lemon Vinaigrette Dressing
Glazed Carrot Walnut Cake

*Recipes Included

Peruvian Beef

6   tablespoons vegetable oil
1   10-ounce package frozen shoestring potatoes
1   pound beef top round or sirloin steak, cut into thin strips
1   cup chopped onions
1   cup chopped green pepper
1   clove garlic, minced

1   16-ounce can tomatoes, drained, coarsely chopped
1 1/2   tablespoons red wine vinegar
1   teaspoon Worcestershire sauce
    Salt
    Pepper
    Hot cooked rice (optional)

Heat fry pan at 375°. Add 4 tablespoons oil and potatoes; cook until golden and crisp; about 10 minutes. Remove potatoes from fry pan; drain on paper toweling. Clean fry pan.

Heat fry pan at 325°. Add remaining 3 tablespoons oil and beef; cook until brown, 2 to 3 minutes, stirring frequently. Stir in onion, green pepper and garlic; cook 4 minutes. Stir in tomatoes, vinegar and Worcestershire sauce; cook until liquid is absorbed, 6 to 7 minutes. Season to taste with salt and pepper. Stir in potatoes; cook until heated through, about 1 minute. Serve with hot cooked rice.

4 servings.

Glazed Carrot Walnut Cake

1   9-ounce package yellow cake mix
1   egg
1/3   cup water
1/2   cup shredded carrots
1/4   cup chopped walnuts

3/4   teaspoon ground cinnamon
1/4   teaspoon ground nutmeg
1/4   teaspoon ground ginger
    Browned Butter Glaze
    Walnut halves

Make cake mix according to package directions, using egg and water; stir in carrots, walnuts, cinnamon, nutmeg and ginger. Heat fry pan at 350°. Pour batter into greased and floured 8-inch round cake pan. Place cake pan on rack in fry pan; cook, with cover 1/2-inch ajar, until toothpick inserted near center of cake comes out clean, 40 to 45 minutes. Remove cake pan from fry pan; cool on wire rack 10 minutes. Remove cake to serving plate.

Make Browned Butter Glaze; spoon glaze over cake. Garnish edge of cake with walnut halves.

6 to 8 servings.

Browned Butter Glaze

1/4   cup butter or margarine-butter blend
1   tablespoon dark corn syrup
1   cup powdered sugar

1 1/2 to 2   tablespoons milk
1/4   teaspoon vanilla
    Dash salt

Heat butter in fry pan at Warm until melted; cook until butter is browned, about 1 minute, stirring constantly. Turn heat to Off; add corn syrup. Stir in powdered sugar and milk alternately, using enough milk to obtain thin glaze consistency. Stir in vanilla and salt.

About 2/3 cup.

Soup 'N' Sandwich Special

Cream of Tomato Soup with Dill
*Cube Steak Sandwiches with Blue Cheese
*Green Beans and Onions
*Sweet Strip Lemon Pie
Recipes Included

Cube Steak Sandwiches with Blue Cheese

4	slices Italian bread, 3/4 inch thick	1	teaspoon dried chives
	Butter or margarine, softened	1/2	teaspoon Bavarian-style mustard
3	tablespoons butter or margarine	1/4	teaspoon prepared horseradish
4	beef cube steaks	2	tablespoons crumbled blue cheese

Spread bread slices lightly with softened butter. Heat fry pan at 275°. Place bread, buttered sides down in fry pan; cook until toasted. Remove toasted bread from fry pan. Add 3 tablespoons butter and steaks to fry pan; cook at 300° to desired degree of doneness. Place toasted bread on serving plates; top with steaks. Stir in chives, mustard and horseradish; cook 2 minutes. Stir in blue cheese until beginning to melt; spoon sauce over steaks. Keep warm while making Green Beans and Onions.

4 servings.

Green Beans and Onions

3 to 4	tablespoons butter or margarine	1 to 1 1/2	tablespoons lemon juice
1	10-ounce package frozen cut green beans		Salt
2	green onions and tops, thinly sliced		Pepper

Heat butter in fry pan at Warm until melted. Stir in beans and onions; cook, covered, at 225° until vegetables are crisp-tender, about 5 minutes. Stir in lemon juice; season to taste with salt and pepper.

4 servings.

Sweet Strip Lemon Pie

	Pastry for double-crust pie	1	cup light corn syrup
1/2	cup granulated sugar	1	cup water
1/3	cup light brown sugar	2	tablespoons lemon juice
3	tablespoons all-purpose flour	2	tablespoons butter or margarine, softened
1	teaspoon grated lemon rind		
2	dashes salt	2	eggs, beaten

Roll scant two-thirds pastry on lightly floured surface into circle 1 inch larger than inverted 9-inch pie pan. Ease pastry into pan. Refrigerate pastry in pan; wrap and refrigerate remaining unrolled pastry.

Mix sugars, flour, lemon rind and salt in fry pan. Stir in corn syrup, water, lemon juice and butter until blended; cook at Warm until mixture is quite warm, about 5 minutes, stirring constantly. Stir about 1/2 cup lemon mixture into eggs. Stir egg mixture into lemon mixture in fry pan; cook at 200° until thickened, 5 to 7 minutes, stirring constantly. Turn heat to Off; let stand 5 minutes.

Roll remaining pastry on lightly floured surface to 1/8 inch thickness; cut into 3/4-inch strips. Pour lemon mixture into pastry lined pie pan; make lattice top with pastry strips. Trim and flute edge of pastry.

Bake pie in conventional oven at 350° until filling is set, about 35 minutes. Cool on wire rack; serve warm or at room temperature.

8 to 10 servings.

Deli Delights

Pastrami Reubens

1/4 cup mayonnaise or salad dressing
  1 teaspoon spicy brown mustard
1/4 teaspoon caraway seed
  8 slices rye bread
 12 ounces sliced pastrami

  1 16-ounce can sauerkraut, drained
  4 1-ounce slices Monterey Jack cheese
  1 tablespoon butter or margarine
  1 tablespoon vegetable oil

Mix mayonnaise, mustard and caraway seed; spread on 4 slices of bread. Top with pastrami, sauerkraut, cheese and remaining bread slices. Heat butter and oil in fry pan at Warm until butter is melted. Add sandwiches; cook, covered, at 275° until golden, about 3 minutes on each side. Remove sandwiches from fry pan; keep warm while making Dilled Potato Nuggets.

4 servings.

Dilled Potato Nuggets

  2 tablespoons vegetable oil
  1 tablespoon butter or margarine
  4 cups frozen potato nuggets

1/2 teaspoon dried dillweed
1/4 teaspoon onion powder
1/4 teaspoon paprika

Heat oil and butter in fry pan at Warm until butter is melted. Stir in potato nuggets; cook, covered, at 275° until browned and crisp, 5 to 6 minutes, stirring occasionally. Sprinkle potatoes with dillweed, onion powder and paprika; cook 1 minute.

4 servings.

For the Lunch Bunch

Garden Vegetable Soup
*Sausage Mac 'n' Cheese
*Grilled Tomato Slices
Cherry Gelatin with Fruit Cocktail

*Recipes Included

Sausage Mac 'N' Cheese

1	14-ounce package macaroni and cheese deluxe dinner		1/4	cup thinly sliced celery
2	quarts water		1	cup sour cream or sour half-and-half
1	teaspoon salt		1	tablespoon mayonnaise or salad dressing
12	ounces bulk pork sausage, crumbled		1/8	teaspoon dried sage leaves
1/2	cup chopped green onions		1/8	teaspoon dried marjoram leaves

Cook macaroni in fry pan according to package directions, using water and salt. Drain macaroni and reserve. Cook sausage, onion and celery in fry pan at 300° until sausage is brown, about 5 minutes; drain excess fat. Stir in reserved macaroni, cheese sauce, sour cream, mayonnaise, sage and marjoram; cook, covered, at 200° until heated, about 5 minutes, stirring occasionally. Spoon macaroni into serving bowl; keep warm while making Grilled Tomato Slices.

6 servings.

Grilled Tomato Slices

1/4	cup butter or margarine		1/16	teaspoon dried sage leaves
1/2	cup dry bread crumbs		2	dashes salt
1/8	teaspoon dried tarragon leaves		3	medium tomatoes, cut into 1/2-inch slices

Heat butter in fry pan at Warm until melted. Stir in bread crumbs, tarragon, sage and salt; cook at 200° until crumbs are browned, about 2 minutes. Add tomato slices, spoon crumb mixture over slices; cook, covered, until tomatoes are heated, about 2 minutes.

6 servings.

Hearty Home Cooking

Hot Ham Salad Patties
Brown Sugar Pineapple Rings
Grated Carrot and Raisin Salad
Pear Halves with Gingersnap Crumbs

*Recipes Included

Hot Ham Salad Patties

1/2	pound lean ground beef
1/2	pound finely chopped or ground baked ham
1	cup fresh bread crumbs
3	tablespoons chopped pecans
2	tablespoon chopped onion
1/3	cup mayonnaise or salad dressing

1/3	cup sour cream or sour half-and-half
2	eggs
1	teaspoon Dijon-style mustard
1/4	teaspoon celery seed
2	tablespoons butter or margarine

Combine all ingredients, except butter, until thoroughly blended; form into 4 patties. Heat butter in fry pan at Warm until melted. Add patties; cook at 275° until patties are browned and cooked through, 3 to 4 minutes on each side. Arrange patties on serving platter; keep warm while making Brown Sugar Pineapple Rings.

4 servings.

Brown Sugar Pineapple Rings

1/4	cup butter or margarine
1/3	cup light brown sugar
1	teaspoon vanilla

1/4	teaspoon ground cinnamon
1	20-ounce can pineapple slices, drained

Heat butter and sugar in fry pan at Warm until butter is melted. Stir in vanilla and cinnamon. Add pineapple slices; cook at 225° until heated, about 2 minutes, spooning sauce over pineapple. Arrange on platter with ham patties.

4 servings.

South of the Border

Iced Gazpacho
Eggs Scrambled with Tortillas
Zucchini Wedges
Lime Sherbet and Butter Cookies

*Recipes Included

Eggs Scrambled with Tortillas

1/4 cup butter or margarine

4 corn tortillas, cut into 1/2-inch strips

1/4 cup chopped green onions and tops

6 eggs, beaten

3 tablespoons milk

1/2 cup shredded Monterey Jack cheese

1 4-ounce can chopped mild or hot green chilies, drained

Salt

Pepper

Heat butter in fry pan at Warm until melted. Add tortillas; cook at 300° until crisp, about 30 seconds. Remove tortillas and drain on paper toweling. Add onions; cook at 225°, 1 minute. Stir in eggs, milk, cheese, chilies and tortillas; cook until eggs are set, stirring occasionally. Season eggs to taste with salt and pepper. Spoon onto serving platter; keep warm while making Zucchini Wedges.

4 servings.

Zucchini Wedges

2 small zucchini

2 tablespoons butter or margarine

1 small clove garlic, minced

1/4 cup water

1/4 teaspoon chicken flavor instant bouillon

1/4 teaspoon ground cumin

Cut zucchini into 1-inch pieces, cut pieces into fourths. Heat butter in fry pan at Warm until melted. Add zucchini and garlic; cook at 225°, 2 minutes. Add water, bouillon and cumin; cook, covered, until zucchini is tender, about 2 minutes.

4 servings.

School Fuel

Sloppy Moes
Cheddar Hamburger Buns
Shoestring Potatoes
Bread and Butter Pickle Slices
Chocolate Ice Cream Sundaes
*Recipes Included

Sloppy Moes

Cheddar Hamburger Buns
1 pound lean ground beef
2 hot dogs, cut into 1/4-inch slices
1/2 cup chopped onions
1/4 cup chopped green pepper

1/2 cup chili sauce
1/2 cup catsup
2 to 4 tablespoons grape or currant jelly
1/2 teaspoon Worcestershire sauce
1/8 teaspoon pepper

Make Cheddar Hamburger Buns, set aside. Heat fry pan at 275°. Add ground beef, hot dogs, onion and green pepper; cook until beef is brown, about 5 minutes, stirring frequently. Drain excess fat. Stir in remaining ingredients, except buns; cook at 200° until heated through. Spoon into Cheddar Hamburger Buns.

6 servings.

Cheddar Hamburger Buns

1 13 3/4-ounce package hot roll mix
3/4 cup warm water (110°)
1 egg
1/2 cup shredded cheddar cheese

Vegetable oil
1 egg yolk, beaten
1 tablespoon water
Sesame seed

Make hot roll mix according to package directions, using warm water and egg; stir in cheese after adding half the flour mixture. Knead dough on lightly floured surface until smooth and elastic, about 5 minutes. Divide dough into 6 equal pieces; roll into balls and flatten into bun shapes, about 3 1/2 inches in diameter.

Place rack in fry pan; cover rack with aluminum foil and oil lightly. Place dough pieces on foil; heat, covered at warm, 1 minute. Turn heat to Off; let stand, covered, until dough has doubled in size, about 30 minutes. Mix egg yolk and 1 tablespoon water; brush on dough. Sprinkle with sesame seed. Heat fry pan at 375°. Place buns on rack in fry pan; cook until buns are deep golden on the bottom, about 40 minutes. Remove from fry pan; cool on wire rack. Cut into halves.

6 buns.

Tradition at the Table

Savory Chuck Roast
Steamed Vegetable Medley
Iceberg Lettuce Wedges with Thousand Island Dressing
Poppy Seed Pan Rolls
Mincemeat Baked Apples

Recipes Included

Savory Chuck Roast

2 tablespoons vegetable oil	1/4 cup sweet vermouth (optional)
4 pound beef blade or round bone chuck roast	1 bay leaf
1/4 cup chopped onion	1 whole clove
1 clove garlic, minced	3 peppercorns
1/4 cup all-purpose flour	2 tablespoons chopped red pepper
2 cups warm water	Salt
1 teaspoon beef flavor instant bouillon	Pepper

Heat fry pan at 325°. Add oil and beef; cook until browned, about 5 minutes on each side. Remove meat. Add onion and garlic; cook at 225° until onion is tender, about 2 minutes. Stir in flour; cook 1 minute. Stir in water, bouillon, vermouth, bay leaf, clove and peppercorns; cook at 400° until boiling, scraping drippings from bottom of fry pan with plastic or wooden utensil. Reduce heat to simmer, between Warm and 200°. Add meat; cook, covered, until meat is tender, about 2 hours, turning meat over twice during cooking. Remove meat to serving platter.

Stir red pepper into sauce; season to taste with salt and pepper. Spoon sauce over meat; keep warm while making Steamed Vegetable Medley.

6 to 8 servings.

Steamed Vegetable Medley

1 pound small carrots, cut in half lengthwise	1/4 cup melted butter or margarine
1/2 pound fresh or thawed frozen green beans, cut diagonally into halves	Salt
1 16-ounce jar boiled whole onions	Pepper
Water	Minced parsley

Arrange vegetables in steaming rack in fry pan. Add 1 inch water; heat at 400° until boiling. Reduce heat to simmer, between Warm and 200°; cook, covered, until vegetables are crisp-tender, 10 to 12 minutes. Arrange vegetables around meat on platter; drizzle vegetables with butter and sprinkle lightly with salt, pepper and parsley.

6 to 8 servings.

Poppy Seed Pan Rolls

1	1/4-ounce package active dry yeast	2	eggs
1/4	cup warm milk (110°)	2 1/2	cups all-purpose flour
1/4	cup warm water (110°)	3/4	teaspoon salt
1/4	cup butter or margarine, softened		Melted butter or margarine
2	tablespoons sugar		Poppy seed

Stir yeast into warm milk and water in small bowl; let stand 5 minutes. Beat softened butter and sugar in bowl until fluffy; beat in eggs, 1 at a time. Mix in 1 cup flour and salt. Mix in remaining 1 1/2 cups flour alternately with yeast mixture, beating well after each addition (dough will be very soft and sticky). Spoon dough into 2 greased 6-cup muffin pans, filling each about half full. Brush tops of dough with melted butter; sprinkle lightly with poppy seed. Refrigerate 1 muffin pan, loosely covered with waxed paper.

Place remaining muffin pan on rack in fry pan. Heat, covered, at Warm for 1 minute. Turn heat to Off; let stand, covered, until dough has doubled in size, 30 to 35 minutes. Heat fry pan at 375°. Place muffin pan on rack; cook, covered, until deep golden on bottom, 22 to 25 minutes. Remove rolls from muffin pan; cool on wire rack. Turn heat to Off.

Remove the other muffin pan from refrigerator when beginning to cook first pan; let stand at room temperature. When first pan of rolls is done, place other pan on rack in fry pan. If fry pan has cooled, heat, covered, at Warm for 1 minute. Turn heat to Off, let stand, covered, until dough has doubled in size, 45 to 55 minutes. Cook, covered, as above.

1 dozen.

Mincemeat Baked Apples

4	large baking apples	1 to 2	teaspoons brandy (optional)
1/2	cup mincemeat		Warm water
1/4	cup chopped walnuts		Whipped cream

Core apples; peel 1-inch strip from tops of apples. Combine mincemeat, walnuts and brandy; spoon mixture into apples. Place apples in baking pan; place pan on rack in fry pan. Add 1 inch warm water to fry pan; heat at 400° until boiling. Reduce heat to simmer, between Warm and 200°; cook, covered, until apples are tender, 15 to 20 minutes. Serve apples warm with whipped cream.

4 servings.

Saucy Swiss Steaks, Mushrooms Braised in Wine,
Savory Chuck Roast with Steamed Vegetable Medley, Orange Chicken with Raisins and Almonds

Entertaining Your In-Laws

Saucy Swiss Steaks
Mushrooms Braised in Wine
Whipped Potatoes
Tossed Green Salad with Creamy Garlic Dressing
Individual Dinner Rolls
Brandied Fruit Compote
*Recipes Included

Saucy Swiss Steaks

1 3/4   pounds round steak, cut into serving-size pieces
1/2   cup all-purpose flour
1/2   teaspoon salt
1/4   teaspoon pepper
  2   tablespoons vegetable oil
1/2   cup chopped onions
  1   clove garlic, minced
  1   cup chopped green pepper

1/2   cup chopped celery
  1   15-ounce can tomato sauce
1/2   cup hot water
1/4   teaspoon beef flavor instant bouillon
  1   bay leaf
1/2   teaspoon dried basil leaves
    Salt
    Pepper

Coat beef with mixture of flour, 1/2 teaspoon salt and 1/4 teaspoon pepper. Heat fry pan at 325°. Add oil and meat; cook until well browned, about 5 minutes on each side. Remove meat. Add onion and garlic; cook at 225°, 2 minutes. Stir in green pepper and celery; cook for 2 minutes. Stir in remaining ingredients, except salt and pepper; cook at 400° until boiling. Reduce heat to simmer, between Warm and 200°. Season sauce to taste with salt and pepper. Return meat to fry pan; cook, covered, until tender, 1 1/2 to 1 3/4 hours. Remove to serving platter; keep warm while making Mushrooms Braised in Wine.

4 to 6 servings.

Mushrooms Braised in Wine

1   tablespoon butter or margarine
1   tablespoon vegetable oil
8   ounces mushrooms, cut into halves
2   green onions and tops, sliced diagonally into 1/4-inch slices

1/4   cup dry white wine
1/4   teaspoon dried tarragon leaves
    Salt
    Pepper

Heat butter and oil in fry pan at Warm until butter is melted. Add mushrooms and onions; cook at 225°, 1 minute. Stir in wine and tarragon; cook, covered, until vegetables are tender, about 2 minutes. Season to taste with salt and pepper.

4 to 6 servings.

Brandied Fruit Compote

2   11-ounce boxes mixed dried fruit
1   cup golden raisins
3   cups water
1   cup light brown sugar
1   small lemon, sliced

1   tablespoon lemon juice
1   cinnamon stick
4   whole cloves
1/4 to 1/2   cup brandy

Pit prunes; combine dried fruit and raisins in fry pan. Stir in remaining ingredients, except brandy; cook, covered, at 400° until boiling. Reduce heat to simmer, between Warm and 200°; cook, covered, 20 minutes or until fruit is soft and plumped. Stir in brandy; spoon mixture into bowl and cool to room temperature. Refrigerate, covered, several hours for flavors to blend. Serve warm or at room temperature.

8 servings.

The Italian Alternative

Shrimp with Spinach-Pesto Sauce
Sautéed Cherry Tomatoes
Boston Lettuce with Marinated Artichoke Hearts
Sesame Seed Breadsticks
Italian Lemon Ices or Sherbet
with Dark Sweet Cherries
Recipes Included

Shrimp with Spinach-Pesto Sauce

Spinach-Pesto Sauce
1 tablespoon butter or margarine
1 tablespoon olive oil
1 pound peeled, deveined uncooked shrimp
1/2 cup dry white wine

2 tablespoons lemon juice
1/4 teaspoon salt
1/4 teaspoon white pepper
6 cups hot cooked rice or spaghetti
2 tablespoons grated Parmesan cheese

Make Spinach-Pesto Sauce; reserve. Heat butter and oil in fry pan at Warm until butter is melted. Add shrimp; cook at 325° until shrimp are pink and done, 2 to 3 minutes. Stir in wine and lemon juice; cook at 400° until liquid is nearly evaporated, about 2 minutes. Reduce heat to 200°. Stir in salt, pepper and reserved Spinach-Pesto Sauce; cook, covered, until heated, about 2 minutes. Serve over rice or spaghetti; sprinkle with Parmesan cheese.

4 servings.

Spinach-Pesto Sauce

1/4 10-ounce package frozen chopped spinach, thawed
1/4 cup olive or vegetable oil
1/4 cup butter or margarine, softened
1/4 cup walnuts

1 tablespoon dried basil leaves
1 clove garlic, minced
1/8 teaspoon salt
1/8 teaspoon pepper

Squeeze moisture from spinach. Process all ingredients in food processor or blender until smooth.

About 3/4 cup.

Sautéed Cherry Tomatoes

1 tablespoon butter or margarine
1 tablespoon olive or vegetable oil
1 pint cherry tomatoes
1/4 teaspoon dried tarragon leaves

1 teaspoon lemon juice
Salt
Pepper

Heat butter and oil in fry pan at Warm until butter is melted. Add tomatoes; cook, covered, at 225°, 2 to 3 minutes. Sprinkle with tarragon and lemon juice; season to taste with salt and pepper.

4 servings.

The Orient Express

Won Tons with Sweet-Sour Sauce
*Beef Chow Mein
*Fried Chinese Noodles
Orange Sherbet
*Fortune Cookies
*Recipes Included

Fried Won Tons with Sweet-Sour Sauce

8 egg roll wrappers
   Vegetable oil

Sweet-Sour Sauce

Cut egg roll wrappers in 1-inch strips. Heat 1 1/2 inches oil in fry pan at 350°. Twist strips into spiral shapes; cook in oil until golden and crisp, about 1 minute. Drain on paper toweling.

Make Sweet-Sour Sauce; spoon into small bowl. Serve fried strips with sauce for dipping.

8 servings.

Sweet-Sour Sauce

1/2 cup apricot preserves
  1 tablespoon cider vinegar

1   teaspoon soy sauce
1/2 teaspoon prepared mustard

Mix all ingredients.

About 2/3 cup.

Beef Chow Mein

  2 tablespoons vegetable oil
  1 cup sliced mushrooms
3/4 cup chopped onions
  1 cup chopped red or green pepper
  2 cloves garlic, minced
  3 cups diced cooked beef
  3 cups water
  3 teaspoons beef flavor instant bouillon

  3 tablespoons soy sauce
1/4 teaspoon Chinese 5-spice powder (optional)
  3 tablespoons cornstarch
1/3 cup cold water
  2 cups fresh or drained canned bean sprouts
  1 cup sliced water chestnuts

Heat fry pan at 225°. Add oil, mushrooms, onion, pepper and garlic; cook until vegetables are tender, about 5 minutes. Stir in beef; cook until hot, 3 to 4 minutes, stirring occasionally. Add 3 cups water, bouillon, soy sauce and 5-spice powder; cook at 400° until boiling. Reduce heat to simmer, between Warm and 200°. Stir in cornstarch and cold water; cook until thickened, stirring constantly. Stir in bean sprouts and water chestnuts; cook until heated, 3 to 4 minutes. Spoon chow mein into serving bowl; keep warm while making Fried Chinese Noodles.

4 servings.

TIP: Chinese 5-spice powder may be purchased in Oriental groceries or specialty food stores.

Fried Chinese Noodles

1 pound presteamed Cantonese noodles	3 tablespoons vegetable oil
Warm water	1 teaspoon sesame oil (optional)
Cold water	

Rinse noodles in warm water, then in cold water; drain well. Heat fry pan at 225°. Add oils and noodles; fry until crisp, about 3 minutes, stirring occasionally.

4 servings.

TIP: Presteamed Cantonese noodles are available in Oriental groceries and specialty food stores; there is no substitute.

TIP: Chow mein can be served on rice. Cook regular or quick-cooking rice in fry pan according to package directions.

Fortune Cookies

1/2 cup all-purpose flour	2/3 cup water
1/3 cup sugar	1/3 cup vegetable oil
1 tablespoon cornstarch	1 egg white
1/8 teaspoon salt	1 teaspoon vegetable oil

Mix flour, sugar, cornstarch, and salt in small bowl. Mix water, 1/3 cup oil and egg white in small bowl until blended. Whisk water mixture into flour mixture to make thin batter.

Heat fry pan at 300°; brush fry pan with 1 teaspoon oil. Pour scant tablespoon batter into fry pan, spreading with back of spoon to make 2-inch circle; cook until golden on the bottom, about 2 minutes. Turn; cook until golden, 2 minutes. Remove from fry pan; fold warm cookie in half; form into shape of fortune cookie by bringing 2 ends together and creasing center (cookies can be folded against the edge of a table). Cool on wire rack. Repeat with remaining batter, making cookies 1 at a time.

2 dozen.

TIP: If desired, fortunes can be added to the cookies. Write or type fortunes on strips of paper 1 1/2 inches long. Lay paper on cookie before folding in half.

An Elegant Evening at Home

Orange Chicken with Raisins and Almonds
Tumeric Rice
Bibb Lettuce with Chilled Steamed Asparagus
Mustard Vinaigrette Dressing
Crusty French Bread
Fudge Brownie Ice Cream Pie

*Recipes Included

Orange Chicken with Raisins and Almonds

3 to 3 1/2	pounds chicken pieces		1/4	teaspoon ground cinnamon
1/2	cup all-purpose flour		1/16	teaspoon ground mace
1/2	teaspoon ground cinnamon		1	tablespoon almond or orange flavor liqueur (optional)
1	teaspoon salt		2	tablespoons cornstarch
1/16	teaspoon white pepper		1/4	cup cold water
3	tablespoons vegetable oil			Salt
3	cups water			White pepper
1 1/2	teaspoon chicken flavor instant bouillon		1/2	cup golden raisins
	Water		1/4	cup slivered almonds, toasted
2/3	cup undiluted frozen orange juice concentrate			Tumeric Rice

Coat chicken pieces with mixture of flour, 1/2 teaspoon cinnamon, 1 teaspoon salt and 1/16 teaspoon pepper. Heat fry pan at 325°. Add oil and chicken; cook, covered, until browned on all sides, 10 to 15 minutes. Remove chicken; drain fry pan. Add 3 cups water and bouillon; cook at 400° until boiling, scraping drippings from bottom of fry pan with plastic or wooden utensil. Return chicken to fry pan; reduce heat to simmer, between Warm and 200°; cook, covered, until chicken is tender and juices are clear when thickest parts are pierced with a fork, 40 to 50 minutes. Remove chicken to serving platter; keep warm. Strain cooking liquid; discard fat. Clean fry pan.

Add enough water to cooking liquid to make 2 1/2 cups; pour into fry pan. Stir in orange juice concentrate, 1/4 teaspoon cinnamon and mace; heat at 400° until boiling. Reduce heat to simmer, between Warm and 200°. Stir in liqueur. Mix cornstarch and cold water; whisk into fry pan, stirring constantly until thickened. Season sauce to taste with salt and pepper. Stir in raisins and almonds; cook until heated, about 1 minute. Spoon sauce over chicken and keep warm while making Tumeric Rice. Serve chicken with rice.

4 to 6 servings.

Tumeric Rice

2 1/4 cups enriched precooked rice
2 1/4 cups water
3/4 teaspoon salt
1 tablespoon butter

1 teaspoon grated orange rind
1/4 teaspoon ground tumeric
Minced parsley

Cook rice in fry pan according to package directions, using water, salt and butter. Stir orange rind and tumeric into rice. Spoon rice into bowl; sprinkle with parsley.

4 to 6 servings.

Fudge Brownie Ice Cream Pie

1/4 cup butter or margarine
1 ounce unsweetened chocolate, coarsely chopped
Warm water
1/2 cup sugar
1 egg
1/4 teaspoon almond extract

1/4 cup all purpose flour
1/4 teaspoon baking powder
1/4 teaspoon salt
1 quart chocolate chip or vanilla ice cream, slightly softened
2 tablespoons sliced almonds, toasted
Fudge ice cream sauce

Place butter and chocolate in small metal bowl in fry pan. Add 1 inch warm water to fry pan; heat at Warm until butter and chocolate are melted, stirring occasionally. Remove bowl from fry pan; discard water in fry pan. Stir sugar, egg, almond extract, flour, baking powder and salt into butter mixture; spread batter evenly in greased 8-inch pie pan. Heat fry pan at 350°. Place pie pan on rack in fry pan; cook, covered, until cake is firm to touch, about 30 minutes. Remove pie pan; cool on wire rack.

Spoon ice cream over cake in pie pan; sprinkle with almonds. Freeze until hard, 8 hours or overnight. Cut into wedges to serve; spoon fudge sauce over.

8 servings.

Pasta Pleaser

Minestrone Soup
*Sausage and Cheese Manicotti
*Antipasto Vegetable Salad
Garlic Bread
*Bow Tie Cookies

*Recipes Included

Sausage and Cheese Manicotti

Parmesan White Sauce

1/2 pound mild or hot Italian sausage, casing removed, crumbled

1/2 cup finely chopped onions

1 clove garlic, minced

2 cups ricotta cheese

2 eggs, beaten

1/2 10-ounce package frozen spinach, cooked

2 tablespoons grated Parmesan cheese

1/8 teaspoon ground cinnamon

1/2 teaspoon salt

1/8 teaspoon white pepper

8 manicotti shells, cooked

1 15 1/2-ounce jar spaghetti sauce

1 cup shredded mozzarella cheese

Make Parmesan White Sauce in fry pan; reserve. Clean fry pan. Cook sausage in fry pan at 325° until brown. Add onion and garlic; cook at 225° for 5 minutes. Remove sausage from fry pan and drain. Mix ricotta cheese and eggs in bowl. Drain spinach well between paper toweling; stir into ricotta cheese mixture. Stir in sausage, Parmesan cheese, cinnamon, salt and pepper; stuff mixture into manicotti shells.

Spread spaghetti sauce in bottom of fry pan; arrange stuffed manicotti over sauce. Spoon reserved Parmesan White Sauce over manicotti. Sprinkle with mozzarella cheese; cook, covered, at 200° until manicotti are heated through, about 30 minutes.

4 servings.

Parmesan White Sauce

1/4 cup butter or margarine

1/4 cup all-purpose flour

2 cups milk

1 cup half-and-half

1/4 cup grated Parmesan cheese

1/2 teaspoon grated lemon rind

1/8 teaspoon ground nutmeg

1/2 teaspoon salt

1/8 teaspoon white pepper

Heat butter in fry pan at Warm until melted. Stir in flour, cook 1 minute. Stir in milk and half-and-half; cook at 400° until boiling. Reduce heat to simmer, between Warm and 200°; cook until sauce is thickened, stirring constantly. Turn heat to Off; stir in remaining ingredients.

About 3 cups.

Antipasto Vegetable Salad

1/2 pound fresh asparagus, cut diagonally
    into 1-inch pieces

  1 small zucchini, scored, sliced
    1/4 inch thick

  2 medium carrots, cut into julienne strips

  1 rib celery, slice 1/4 inch thick

Water

Tarragon Dressing

  2 ounces brick cheese, cut into
    julienne strips

Lettuce leaves

Place vegetables in vegetable steamer; place steamer in fry pan. Add 1/2 inch water to fry pan; cook, covered, at 400° until boiling. Reduce heat to simmer, between Warm and 200°; cook, covered, until vegetables are just crisp-tender, 3 to 5 minutes. Remove vegetables and keep warm; discard water.

Pour Tarragon Dressing over vegetables and toss. Serve warm or refrigerate until chilled. Add cheese; toss before serving. Serve on lettuce leaves.

4 servings.

TIP: Thawed frozen asparagus may be substituted for the fresh asparagus. Prepare and cook as above.

Tarragon Dressing

1/4 cup olive oil

1/4 cup vegetable oil

  1 clove garlic, crushed

1/4 cup white wine vinegar

  1 tablespoon finely chopped onion

1/2 teaspoon Dijon-style mustard

1/2 teaspoon dried tarragon leaves

1/2 to 3/4 teaspoon salt

1/8 teaspoon pepper

Heat fry pan at 225°. Add oils and garlic; cook 1 minute, stirring constantly. Discard garlic. Stir in remaining ingredients; cook at 200° until simmering.

About 3/4 cup.

Bow Tie Cookies

2 1/4 cups all-purpose flour

1/2 teaspoon salt

  2 tablespoons finely ground almonds

  2 tablespoons cold butter,
    cut into pieces

  3 eggs, beaten

  2 tablespoons almond flavor liqueur

Vegetable oil

Powdered sugar

Mix flour, salt and almonds in small bowl; cut in butter until mixture resembles coarse crumbs. Stir in eggs and liqueur to form dough; knead on lightly floured surface 5 times. Roll a fourth of the dough on lightly floured surface into rectangle 12 × 6 inches; cut into strips, 6 × 1 inches. Tie each strip into loose knot.

Heat 1 inch oil in fry pan at 350°. Add cookies; cook, several at a time, until golden, about 1 minute on each side. Remove from oil with slotted spoon; drain on paper toweling. Sprinkle warm cookies with powdered sugar. Repeat with remaining dough. Store cookies in airtight container.

About 4 dozen.

Catch of the Day

Manhattan Clam Chowder
*Fish 'n' Chips
Creamy Coleslaw
Grilled Buttered French Bread
*English Trifle

*Recipes Included

Fish 'N' Chips

Powdered Salt (see recipe, page 26)
1 cup all-purpose flour
2/3 cup water
1 teaspoon salt
1 teaspoon baking powder

Vegetable oil
1 pound frozen french fries
2 pounds fresh or thawed frozen cod, cut into 2-inch pieces
Malt or cider vinegar

Make Powdered Salt; reserve. Mix flour, water and 1 teaspoon salt in shallow bowl until smooth; let batter stand 20 minutes. Stir in baking powder.

Heat 2 inches oil in fry pan at 350°. Add frozen potatoes; cook until golden, about 5 minutes. Drain on paper toweling; sprinkle lightly with reserved Powdered Salt. Keep warm.

Dip fish into batter, allowing excess batter to drain. Cook fish in oil in fry pan at 375° until golden, about 3 minutes. Drain on paper toweling. Sprinkle fish lightly with reserved Powdered Salt.

Arrange potatoes and fish on serving platter; sprinkle lightly with vinegar.

4 servings.

English Trifle

Pastry Cream (see recipe, page 84)
2 cups half-and-half or milk
1 10 3/4-ounce frozen pound cake, thawed
1/2 cup almond flavor liqueur
2/3 cup raspberry preserves

3/4 cup sliced almonds, toasted
1 cup whipping cream
1/4 cup powdered sugar
1/4 teaspoon vanilla

Make Pastry Cream in fry pan, using 2 cups half-and-half instead of 1 1/2 cups half-and-half. Refrigerate, covered, until chilled.

Cut pound cake lengthwise into halves; cut into 1/2-inch slices. Arrange half the cake slices on bottom of straight-sided glass bowl or soufflé dish, cutting pieces, if necessary, to fill spaces. Sprinkle cake with 1/4 cup of the liqueur; spread with 1/3 cup of the preserves and 1 cup of the Pastry Cream. Sprinkle with 1/4 cup of the almonds. Repeat layers, reserving remaining 1/4 cup almonds. Refrigerate, covered, 4 hours or overnight.

Whip cream until stiff peaks form, gradually adding powdered sugar and vanilla. Spread cream mixture over trifle; sprinkle with reserved 1/4 cup almonds.

6 to 8 servings.

Dinner By Candlelight

Cornish Hens with Orange-Curry Sauce
†*Fruit and Nut Rice*
French-cut Green Beans with Lemon Butter
Mixed Green Salad
Sesame Seed Dinner Rolls
Chocolate Pudding Cake

*Recipes Included
†Recipe on page 62

Cornish Hens with Orange-Curry Sauce

2 1-pound Cornish hens	1/4 teaspoon ground cinnamon
Garlic powder	1 cup orange juice
Salt	1 tablespoon light rum (optional)
Pepper	1 teaspoon light brown sugar
2 tablespoons vegetable oil	1 tablespoon butter
1/2 cup finely chopped onions	Salt
1 clove garlic, minced	Pepper
1 teaspoon curry powder	

Sprinkle cavities of hens lightly with garlic powder, salt and pepper. Heat fry pan at 325°. Add oil and hens; cook, covered, until golden, about 4 minutes on each side. Remove hens from fry pan; drain all but 1 tablespoon fat.

Add onion, garlic, curry powder and cinnamon; cook at 225° for 2 minutes. Stir in orange juice and rum; cook at 400° until boiling. Add hens to fry pan. Reduce heat to simmer, between Warm and 200°; cook, covered, until hens are tender and juices are clear when thickest parts are pierced with a fork, about 45 minutes. Arrange hens on serving platter; keep warm.

Stir sugar and butter into fry pan. Season sauce to taste with salt and pepper. Serve sauce with hens.

2 servings.

Chocolate Pudding Cake

1/4 cup water	1/4 cup cornstarch
6 ounces semi-sweet chocolate, coarsely chopped	1/4 cup all-purpose flour
	Dash salt
2 teaspoons instant coffee crystals	1 1/4 cups raspberry flavor liqueur (or orange juice)
3/4 cup butter, cut into small pieces	
5 egg yolks	5 egg whites
3/4 cup sugar	Water

Heat 1/4 cup water in fry pan at Warm. Add chocolate and coffee, stirring until chocolate is melted. Stir in butter, several pieces at a time, until melted; turn heat to Off. Beat egg yolks and sugar until smooth; stir gradually into chocolate mixture. Stir in combined cornstarch, flour and salt. Stir in liqueur.

Beat egg whites in large bowl until stiff, but not dry, peaks form. Stir about a fourth of the egg whites into chocolate mixture. Fold chocolate mixture into egg whites. Clean fry pan. Pour chocolate mixture into greased and sugared 2-quart soufflé dish.

Place 2 or 3 metal skewers in fry pan; place soufflé dish on skewers. Add 1 1/2 inches water; heat at 400° until boiling. Reduce heat to simmer, between Warm and 200°; cook, covered, until pudding is set, about 50 minutes. Serve warm or refrigerate until chilled and serve cold.

About 8 servings.

Monday Night Football Fixings

Gyros Burgers
Minted Peas
Deep-fried Potato Wedges
Coconut Cream Pie

*Recipes Included

Gyros Burgers

1/4 pound lean ground beef	1 small cucumber, seeded, chopped
1/4 pound lean ground lamb or beef	1 small tomato, chopped
1 tablespoon chopped onion	1 green onion, sliced
1 clove garlic, minced	1/3 cup plain yogurt
1/4 teaspoon dried oregano leaves	1/4 teaspoon dried mint leaves
1/2 teaspoon salt	1/4 teaspoon dried oregano leaves
2 pita breads	

Combine ground beef, ground lamb, onion, garlic, 1/4 teaspoon oregano and salt until blended; shape into 2 patties. Heat fry pan at 250°. Add meat patties; cook to desired degree of doneness, about 5 minutes on each side for medium. Remove patties. Clean fry pan.

Cut tops of pita breads to form pockets. Place meat patties in breads; add cucumber, tomato and onion. Mix yogurt, mint and 1/4 teaspoon oregano; spoon into sandwiches.

2 servings.

Minted Peas

2 tablespoons butter or margarine	1/4 teaspoon dried mint leaves
1 1/2 cup frozen peas, thawed	Salt
1/2 teaspoon grated lemon rind	Pepper

Heat butter in fry pan at Warm until melted. Add peas; cook at 225°, 2 minutes. Stir in lemon rind and mint; cook until peas are tender, about 2 minutes, stirring occasionally. Season to taste with salt and pepper.

2 servings.

Harvest Repast

*Pineapple-Orange Ham Kabobs
†Sweet Potatoes with Nut Butter
Sautéed Spinach with Raisins
Caesar Salad
Whole Wheat Muffins
*Pears Poached in Port Wine

*Recipes Included
†Recipe on page 27

Pineapple-Orange Ham Kabobs

1/2 pound baked ham, cut into
    1-inch cubes
1 medium orange, cut into 8 wedges
8 medium mushrooms
    Vegetable oil

1/4 cup pineapple preserves
1 tablespoon soy sauce
1 teaspoon Dijon-style mustard
1/8 teaspoon ground ginger

Arrange ham, orange wedges and mushrooms alternately on 4 metal skewers. Heat fry pan at 225°. Brush bottom of fry pan lightly with oil. Arrange skewers in fry pan; cook until light brown, about 2 minutes on each side.

Mix pineapple preserves, soy sauce, mustard and ginger. Brush generously on kabobs; cook at 250° for 3 to 4 minutes, brushing several times with pineapple mixture. Arrange kabobs on serving platter.

2 servings.

Pears Poached in Port Wine

4 medium pears
2 cups port wine
1 cup water
1 tablespoon orange flavor liqueur or
    undiluted frozen orange juice
    concentrate
1/4 cup sugar
1 cinnamon stick

Dash ground cloves
1 small orange, cut into 1/4-inch slices
3 tablespoons cornstarch
1/3 cup cold water
    Whipped cream (optional)
    Ground nutmeg

Peel pears; cut lengthwise into halves. Core pear halves, leaving stems intact. Combine wine, 1 cup water, liqueur, sugar, cinnamon and cloves in fry pan; heat at 400° until boiling. Reduce heat to simmer, between Warm and 200°. Add pear halves, cut sides down, and orange slices; cook, covered, until pears are tender when pierced with a sharp knife, 10 to 15 minutes. Remove pears; cool to room temperature and refrigerate, covered. Strain cooking liquid; discard spices and orange slices.

Return cooking liquid to fry pan; heat at 400° until boiling. Reduce heat to simmer, between Warm and 200°. Mix cornstarch and cold water, whisk into simmering liquid. Cook until thickened, whisking constantly. Arrange pear halves in serving dishes; spoon hot sauce over. Garnish with whipped cream. Sprinkle lightly with nutmeg.

8 servings.

Oktoberfeast

Marinated Herring and Onions
*Wiener Schnitzel
†Poppy Seed Noodles
Braised Celery
Caraway Rye Bread
*Apple Steamed Pudding

*Recipes Included
†Recipe on page 62

Wiener Schnitzel

2	veal cutlets		Salt
	Flour		Pepper
1	egg, beaten	1	ounce thinly sliced baked ham
	Dry bread crumbs	1/4	cup shredded Muenster cheese
2	tablespoons olive or vegetable oil		

Pound veal with flat side of mallet until 1/4 inch thick; cut into serving-size pieces. Coat veal lightly with flour; dip into egg and coat with bread crumbs. Heat fry pan at 325°. Add oil and veal; cook until golden, about 1 1/2 minutes on each side. Sprinkle lightly with salt and pepper. Arrange ham on veal. Sprinkle with cheese; cook, covered, until cheese is melted, about 2 minutes. Arrange on serving plate; keep warm.

2 servings.

Apple Steamed Pudding

3/4	cup applesauce	1/2	teaspoon salt
1/2	cup ground beef suet	1	cup all-purpose flour
1/4	cup granulated sugar	1/2	teaspoon baking powder
1/4	cup light brown sugar	1/4	teaspoon baking soda
1	egg	1	cup golden raisins
1/2	teaspoon ground cinnamon	1/3	cup chopped walnuts
1/4	teaspoon ground allspice		Water
1/4	teaspoon ground nutmeg		Whipped Cream

Mix applesauce, suet, sugars, egg, cinnamon, allspice, nutmeg and salt in bowl until smooth; mix in combined flour, baking powder and soda. Mix in raisins and walnuts. Spoon batter into greased 1-quart mold or soufflé dish; firmly cover with aluminum foil.

Place mold on rack in fry pan; add 2 inches water to fry pan. Heat at 400° until boiling. Reduce heat to simmer, between Warm and 200°; cook, covered, until toothpick inserted in center of pudding comes out clean, about 1 1/2 hours.

Unmold onto serving platter; serve warm with whipped cream.

8 servings.

His Turn to Cook

†Braised Turkey Legs
*Mustard-glazed Carrots
Brown Rice with Onions and Red Peppers
Cucumber Salad
Crusty Dinner Rolls
*Chocolate Apricot Date Bars

*Recipes Included
†Recipe on page 50

Mustard-Glazed Carrots

1	10-ounce package frozen carrots	2	teaspoons lemon juice
2	cups water	1/2	teaspoon salt
2	tablespoons butter or margarine	1/16	teaspoon white pepper
1	tablespoon honey	1	teaspoon minced parsley
2	teaspoons Dijon-style mustard		

Place carrots in small bowl; place on rack in fry pan. Add water, cook, covered, 8 to 10 minutes. Remove from fry pan and drain.

Add butter to fry pan; heat at Warm until melted. Stir in honey, mustard, lemon juice; cook 1 minute. Stir in carrots; cook, covered, at 200° until heated through, about 1 minute. Season to taste with salt and pepper; sprinkle with parsley.

2 servings.

Chocolate-Apricot Date Bars

6	ounces dried apricots, finely chopped	1/2	cup butter or margarine
6	ounces pitted dates, finely chopped	1	18.25-ounce package yellow cake mix
1	cup water	1	cup quick-cooking oats
1/3	cup sugar	1	cup chopped pecans
4	ounces unsweetened chocolate, coarsely chopped	1	egg
1	teaspoon vanilla		Water

Combine apricots, dates, 1 cup water and sugar in fry pan; heat at 400° until boiling. Reduce heat to Warm. Stir in chocolate until melted; cook until thickened, about 8 minutes, stirring occasionally. Stir in vanilla. Remove fruit mixture and reserve. Clean fry pan.

Heat butter in fry pan at Warm until melted. Stir in cake mix, oats and 1/2 cup of the pecans. Break egg into measuring cup; add enough water to make 1/2 cup. Stir egg mixture into fry pan until well blended. Smooth batter into even layer; cook at 200°, with cover 1/2-inch ajar, until cake appears dry on the surface, 15 to 18 minutes. Spread reserved fruit mixture over cake. Sprinkle with remaining 1/2 cup pecans; cook with cover 1/2-inch ajar, 35 minutes. Cool in fry pan; cut into squares.

2 dozen.

Subzero Supper

Split Pea Soup
*Pork Cutlets with Onion and Fennel
*Cabbage in Cream Sauce
Waldorf Salad on Leaf Lettuce
Salt Sticks
*Rice Pudding with Raspberry Sauce
*Recipes Included

Pork Cutlets with Onion and Fennel

1 tablespoon vegetable oil	1/2 teaspoon chicken flavor instant bouillon
2 pork cutlets or chops, 3/4 inch thick	
1/4 cup chopped onion	1/8 teaspoon fennel seed, crushed
1 cup water	1/16 teaspoon white pepper

Heat fry pan at 325°. Add oil and pork cutlets; cook, covered, until brown, about 2 minutes on each side. Remove pork cutlets. Add onion; cook at 225° for 2 minutes. Stir in remaining ingredients; cook at 400° until boiling. Reduce heat to simmer, between Warm and 200°. Add pork cutlets; cook, covered, until cutlets are tender, about 45 minutes. Remove cutlets to serving platter. Reserve onion mixture in fry pan for Cabbage in Cream sauce.

2 servings.

Cabbage in Cream Sauce

Reserved onion mixture (from Pork Cutlets with Onion and Fennel)	1 tablespoon all-purpose flour
	Ground nutmeg
2 cups thinly sliced cabbage	
1/2 cup half-and-half	

Heat reserved onion mixture in fry pan at 200°. Stir in cabbage; cook, covered, 5 minutes. Stir half-and-half and flour into cabbage mixture; cook, covered, until cabbage is tender, about 4 minutes; sprinkle lightly with nutmeg.

2 servings.

Rice Pudding
with Raspberry Sauce

3 cups milk
2 cups water
1/2 cup sugar
1/8 teaspoon ground mace
1/4 teaspoon salt
2 cups white long grain rice

1/4 cup butter or margarine, softened
1/3 cup almond flavor liqueur
2 cups whipping cream
2 tablespoons sugar
1 cup slivered almonds, toasted
Raspberry Sauce

Mix milk, water, 1/2 cup sugar, mace and salt in fry pan; heat at 400° until boiling. Stir in rice. Reduce heat to simmer, between Warm and 200°; cook, covered, until rice is tender and liquid is absorbed, about 30 minutes, stirring occasionally. Stir in butter and liqueur. Remove to large bowl; cool to room temperature.

Whip cream and 2 tablespoons sugar in bowl until stiff peaks form. Fold whipped cream into rice mixture. Fold in almonds. Refrigerate, covered, until chilled, 2 to 3 hours.

Make Raspberry Sauce. Spoon rice pudding into individual serving bowls; serve with sauce.

12 servings.

Raspberry Sauce

1 10-ounce package frozen raspberries, thawed

1 tablespoon almond flavor liqueur

Process raspberries and liqueur in food processor or blender until smooth. Refrigerate, covered, until serving time.

1 cup.

Patio Dinner Alfresco

Sliced Tomatoes, Black Olives and Mozzarella Cubes
*Spaghetti Carbonara
*Italian-style Broccoli
Bibb and Boston Salad with Italian Dressing
Basil-Garlic Bread
Spumoni Ice Cream

*Recipes Included

Spaghetti Carbonara

1	tablespoon vegetable oil		2	eggs, beaten
1/2	tablespoon olive or vegetable oil		1/4	cup grated Parmesan cheese
1/2	cup coarsely chopped baked ham		1/4	teaspoon salt
1	clove garlic, minced		1/16	teaspoon cayenne pepper
1/4	cup frozen peas, thawed			White pepper
8	ounces spaghetti, cooked			

Heat fry pan at 225°. Add oil, ham and garlic; cook for 2 minutes. Stir in peas and spaghetti; cook until heated through, 3 to 4 minutes, stirring occasionally. Mix eggs, cheese, salt and cayenne pepper; pour egg mixture over spaghetti. Turn heat to Off; toss spaghetti until egg mixture is set, 2 to 3 minutes. Season to taste with white pepper. Spoon into serving bowl.

2 servings.

Italian-Style Broccoli

2	tablespoons olive or vegetable oil		Salt
2	cups frozen sliced broccoli, thawed		Pepper
1	clove garlic, minced		
2	tablespoons pine nuts or slivered almonds, toasted		

Heat fry pan at 225°. Add oil, broccoli and garlic; cook until broccoli is crisp-tender and beginning to brown, about 4 mintues, stirring occasionally. Stir in pine nuts; season to taste with salt and pepper.

2 servings.

Meals in a Fry Pan

With their robust flavors and rich aromas, one-pan meals can be the most comforting kind of fare—both for diners and for the cook. A generous stew or casserole, a steaming bowl of chowder or chili, a homemade pizza or pan of enchiladas—these favorites never fail to kindle mealtime excitement. Yet they are also the cook's best standbys for busy days. The recipes need minimal accompaniment—a simple salad and fresh fruit at most. There's only one pan to clean up afterwards. And almost every dish can be reheated, even a day or two later, with excellent results.

When everyone's asking "What's for dinner?" you can lift the fry pan lid to reveal answers ranging from Chicken and Pork Fried Rice to Veal Paprikash with Buttered Noodles. Even a stew can surprise—if it's as irresistible as Three-Meat Stew, Irish Lamb Stew, or Beef Vegetable Stew with Dill Dumplings. The spicy fragrance of apple juice-simmered sauerkraut and sausages brings a new dimension to Pork and Kraut Casserole. The lightest egg batter turns stuffed peppers into delectable Mexican-style Peppers Rellenos. A mating of two delicate-tasting ingredients produces the refinement of Chicken and Artichoke Casserole. But the most popular answers in your home may well be crusty, cheesy Deep Pan Pizza or extra-meaty, extra-spicy Fire Fighter's Chili.

Irish Lamb Stew

2	tablespoons vegetable oil
1 1/2	pounds lamb cubes
2	medium onions, sliced
3	tablespoons all-purpose flour
2	cups water
1 1/2	teaspoons chicken flavor instant bouillon
1 1/2	teaspoons Worcestershire sauce

1	teaspoon minced parsley
1/4	teaspoon dried thyme leaves
1	bay leaf
4	small potatoes, peeled, cut into fourths
4	medium carrots, cut into 1/2-inch slices
	Salt
	Pepper

Heat fry pan at 300°. Add oil and lamb; cook until brown. Remove lamb. Add onions; cook at 225° until tender. Stir in flour; cook 2 minutes. Add lamb, water, bouillon, Worcestershire sauce, parsley, thyme and bay leaf; cook at 400° until boiling. Reduce heat to simmer, between Warm and 200°; cook, covered, until lamb is tender, 1 1/4 to 1 1/2 hours. Add potatoes and carrots during last 30 minutes of cooking time. Season to taste with salt and pepper.

4 servings.

Chicken and Pork Fried Rice

4	dried Chinese mushrooms
1/4	cup hot water
2	tablespoons vegetable oil
4	cups cooked rice
1	cup coarsely chopped cooked chicken (light and dark meat)
3/4	cup coarsely chopped cooked pork

1/2	cup thinly sliced green onions and tops
1/4	cup chopped celery
3	eggs, beaten
3	tablespoons soy sauce
1	teaspoon sugar
1/4	teaspoon ground ginger

Combine Chinese mushrooms and hot water in small bowl; let stand until mushrooms are soft, about 15 minutes. Drain mushrooms; reserving liquid. Chop mushrooms coarsely, discarding tough centers.

Heat fry pan at 200°. Add oil and rice; cook until heated through, 6 to 8 minutes, stirring occasionally. Stir in chicken, pork, 1/3 cup onions, celery, mushrooms and reserved liquid; cook until heated through, 3 to 5 minutes. Mix eggs, soy sauce, sugar and ginger. Add to rice mixture; cook until eggs are set, stirring occasionally. Spoon rice mixture into serving bowl; sprinkle with remaining onions.

4 servings.

Chicken Enchilada Casserole

1 15-ounce can tomato sauce
1/2 cup water
2 tablespoons distilled white vinegar
1 tablespoon sugar
2 teaspoons chili powder
1 teaspoon paprika
1/2 teaspoon dried oregano leaves
1/4 teaspoon ground cumin
1/4 teaspoon cayenne pepper
1 teaspoon salt
2 cups shredded cooked chicken

1/2 cup chopped onion
1 clove garlic, minced
1 4-ounce can chopped mild or hot chilies
12 corn tortillas
2 cups shredded cheddar or Monterey Jack cheese
Sliced black olives
Chopped avocado
Sour cream

Mix tomato sauce, water, vinegar, sugar, chili powder, paprika, oregano, cumin, cayenne pepper and salt in fry pan; cook at 400° until boiling. Turn heat to Off.

Combine chicken, onion, garlic, and chilies; stir in 1 cup of the sauce from fry pan. Dip 1 tortilla in sauce in fry pan to soften. Spoon about 2 tablespoons of the chicken mixture and 2 tablespoons cheese on tortilla; roll up. Repeat with remaining tortillas.

Arrange tortillas, seam sides down, in sauce in fry pan; heat at 400° until boiling. Reduce heat to Warm. Sprinkle remaining cheese over tortillas; cook, covered, at Warm until tortillas are heated, about 15 minutes. Sprinkle with olives and avocado; serve with sour cream on the side.

6 servings.

Hearty Meatball Stew

1 1/4 pounds ground beef
1/4 cup finely chopped onion
1 egg
1/2 cup dry bread crumbs
1 clove garlic, crushed
2 teaspoons beef flavor instant bouillon
3/4 teaspoon salt
1/4 teaspoon pepper
2 tablespoons vegetable oil
1 cup water
1 16-ounce can tomatoes, undrained, coarsely chopped

1/2 cup tomato juice
1/2 teaspoon dried basil leaves
1/4 teaspoon dried rosemary leaves
2 medium zucchini, sliced
2 medium carrots, sliced
1/2 medium green pepper, cubed
4 ounces mushrooms, cut into halves
2 tablespoons cornstarch
1/4 cup cold water
Salt
Pepper

Combine ground beef, onion, egg, bread crumbs, garlic, 1 teaspoon bouillon, 3/4 teaspoon salt and 1/4 teaspoon pepper; shape into 16 meatballs. Heat fry pan at 300°. Add oil and meatballs; cook until browned on all sides, about 8 minutes. Add 1 cup water, tomatoes with liquid, tomato juice, remaining 1 teaspoon bouillon, basil and rosemary; cook at 400° until boiling. Reduce heat to simmer, between Warm and 200°; cook, covered, 15 minutes. Add vegetables; cook, covered, until meatballs are no longer pink in the center and vegetables are tender, 10 to 15 minutes. Mix cornstarch and cold water; stir into stew. Cook until thickened. Season to taste with salt and pepper.

4 servings.

Veal Paprikás With Buttered Noodles

2	tablespoons vegetable oil		3/4	teaspoon beef flavor instant bouillon
2	pounds veal cubes		1/2	cup dry white wine
2	cups chopped onions		1/2	cup tomato sauce
1	clove garlic, minced		1	tablespoon tomato paste
1/2	pound sliced mushrooms		1/2	cup sour cream or sour half-and-half
1/4	cup flour		1	tablespoon all-purpose flour
2 1/2	tablespoons paprika			Salt
1/16	teaspoon cayenne pepper			Black pepper
1 1/2	cups water			Hot buttered noodles
3/4	teaspoon chicken flavor instant bouillon			

Heat fry pan at 325°. Add oil and veal; cook until brown, 8 to 10 minutes. Remove meat from fry pan. Add onion and garlic; cook at 225°, 3 minutes. Stir in mushrooms; cook 2 minutes. Stir in 1/4 cup flour, paprika and cayenne pepper; cook 2 minutes. Return meat to fry pan. Stir in water, chicken bouillon, beef bouillon, wine, tomato sauce and tomato paste; cook at 400° until boiling. Reduce heat to simmer, between Warm and 200°; cook, covered, until meat is tender and sauce is quite thick, 1 3/4 to 2 hours, stirring occasionally. Reduce heat to Warm. Mix sour cream and 1 tablespoon flour; stir into meat mixture. Season to taste with salt and black pepper. Serve over hot buttered noodles.

6 servings.

Down East Fish Chowder

4	slices bacon		1/4	cup all-purpose flour
1/2	cup chopped onions		2	cups milk
1	clove garlic, minced		1	cup clam juice
2	medium potatoes, peeled, cut into scant 1/2-inch cubes		12	ounces fresh or thawed frozen sole, cod or other white fish fillets, cut into 1 1/2-inch pieces.
1/2	cup chopped celery			
1/2	cup chopped carrot		4	ounces peeled, deveined, uncooked shrimp
1/2	cup chopped red or green pepper		1/2	cup whipping cream or half-and-half
1/2	teaspoon dried dillweed		1	tablespoon dry sherry (optional)
1/2	teaspoon dried marjoram leaves			Salt
1/4	teaspoon ground allspice			White pepper
2	dashes cayenne pepper			

Cook bacon in fry pan at 300° until crisp; remove bacon and crumble. Reserve 1 tablespoon drippings. Add onion and garlic to drippings in fry pan; cook 2 minutes. Stir in potatoes, celery, carrot and red pepper; cook 2 minutes. Stir in dillweed, marjoram, allspice and cayenne pepper; cook 1 minute. Stir in flour; cook 1 minute. Add milk and clam juice; cook at 400° until boiling. Reduce heat to simmer, between Warm and 200°; cook, covered, until vegetables are tender, about 30 minutes. Stir in fish and shrimp; cook, covered, until fish is tender and flakes with a fork, about 5 minutes. Stir in cream and sherry; season to taste with salt and white pepper.

4 servings.

Deep-Pan Pizza

Deep-Pan Pizza

1	13 3/4-ounce package hot roll mix		1	cup sliced mushrooms
3/4	cup warm water (110°)		1/2	cup chopped green pepper
1	egg		1/2	cup chopped onions
1	cup tomato sauce			Vegetable oil
1	teaspoon dried basil leaves			Cornmeal
1/4	teaspoon dried oregano leaves		1 to 2	ounces sliced pepperoni
1	tablespoon vegetable oil		2	cups shredded mozzarella cheese

Make hot roll mix according to package directions, using 3/4 cup warm water and the egg. Let stand, covered, 15 to 30 minutes.

Mix tomato sauce, basil and oregano; reserve. Heat fry pan at 225°. Add 1 tablespoon oil, mushrooms, green pepper and onion; cook until onion is tender. Remove vegetable mixture from fry pan; reserve. Clean fry pan.

Grease bottom of fry pan lightly with oil; sprinkle lightly with cornmeal. Pat dough out evenly in bottom of fry pan; cook, covered, at Warm 20 minutes. Lightly brush top of dough with oil and sprinkle lightly with cornmeal. Carefully turn dough over in fry pan; cook, covered, 5 minutes.

Spoon reserved sauce mixture evenly on crust. Top with reserved vegetable mixture. Arrange pepperoni on vegetable mixture. Sprinkle cheese over all; cook, covered, at 250° until cooked through, 40 to 45 minutes. Cut into squares with plastic or wooden utensil.

4 servings.

Beef-Vegetable Stew with Dill Dumplings

3	tablespoons vegetable oil		1	bay leaf
1 1/2	pounds beef cubes		1/2	teaspoon curry powder
1	cup chopped onions		3	large carrots, cut diagonally into 1 1/2-inch pieces
1	clove garlic, minced			
3	tablespoons all-purpose flour		4	ounces mushrooms, cut into fourths
3	cups water		1	cup frozen peas
1 1/2	teaspoons beef flavor instant bouillon			Dill Dumplings
2/3	cup tomato sauce			

Heat fry pan at 325°. Add oil and beef; cook until brown, about 8 minutes. Remove beef; reserve 1 tablespoon oil in fry pan. Add onions and garlic; cook at 225° until onions are tender. Stir in flour; cook 2 minutes. Stir in water, bouillon, tomato sauce, bay leaf and curry powder; heat at 400° until boiling. Reduce heat to simmer, between Warm and 200°; cook, covered, until meat is tender, about 1 1/2 hours. Add carrots during last 30 minutes of cooking time. Stir in mushrooms and peas.

Make Dill Dumplings. Drop dough by tablespoons onto stew; cook, uncovered, 10 minutes. Cook, covered, until dumplings are puffed and cooked through, 10 to 15 minutes.

6 servings.

Dill Dumplings

1 1/2	cups buttermilk baking mix		1 1/2	teaspoons dried dillweed
1/2	cup milk			

Mix all ingredients to form dough.

6 servings.

Pork and Kraut Casserole

1 tablespoon vegetable oil
4 pork chops, 3/4 inch thick
4 fully cooked Polish sausages (about 8 ounces)
1 large onion, sliced
2 16-ounce cans sauerkraut, drained
4 potatoes, peeled, cut into halves
1 1/2 cups apple juice

2 tablespoons cider vinegar
1 tablespoon light brown sugar
4 whole cloves
1/4 teaspoon ground nutmeg
Salt
Pepper

Heat fry pan at 300°. Add oil, pork chops and sausages; cook until well browned, about 3 minutes on each side. Remove meats. Add onion; cook at 225°, 2 minutes. Add pork chops, sauerkraut, potatoes, apple juice, vinegar, sugar, cloves and nutmeg; cook at 400° until boiling. Reduce heat to simmer, between Warm and 200°; cook, covered, until pork chops are tender, 1 to 1 1/2 hours. Add sausages to fry pan during last 15 minutes of cooking time. Season to taste with salt and pepper. Arrange meats and sauerkraut on serving platter.

4 servings.

Chicken and Artichoke Casserole

6 chicken breast halves (about 2½ pounds)
All-purpose flour
2 tablespoons vegetable oil
Salt
Pepper
1 cup water
1/2 teaspoon chicken flavor instant bouillon
1/4 cup dry sherry
1/4 teaspoon dried rosemary leaves

1/4 teaspoon dried tarragon leaves
1/8 teaspoon dried marjoram leaves
1 9-ounce package frozen artichoke hearts
2 tomatoes, cut into wedges
1 medium onion, sliced
1 medium green pepper, sliced
1 cup mushrooms, cut into halves
Hot cooked rice

Coat chicken lightly with flour. Heat fry pan at 300°. Add oil and chicken; cook, covered, until golden, about 5 minutes on each side. Sprinkle chicken lightly with salt and pepper. Add water, bouillon, sherry, rosemary, tarragon and marjoram; heat at 400° until boiling. Reduce heat to simmer, between Warm and 200°; cook, covered, 30 minutes. Add artichoke hearts, tomatoes, onion and green pepper; cook, covered, until artichokes are tender, about 10 minutes. Stir in mushrooms; cook, covered, 5 minutes. Serve with hot cooked rice.

4 to 6 servings.

Fire Fighter's Chili

1/2 pound mild or hot Italian sausage, casing removed, crumbled
1/2 pound lean ground beef
1/3 cup chopped onion
2 cloves garlic, minced
2 16-ounce cans tomatoes, undrained, coarsely chopped
1 16-ounce can kidney or pinto beans, drained, rinsed
1/2 cup dry red wine
1/2 cup water

1/2 teaspoon beef flavor instant bouillon
1/3 cup Worcestershire sauce
2 to 3 tablespoons chili powder
1 tablespoon honey
1/4 teaspoon dried red pepper
1/4 teaspoon celery seed
1/4 teaspoon red pepper sauce
Salt
Pepper

Cook sausage and ground beef in fry pan at 300° until brown. Remove from fry pan and drain, reserving 1 tablespoon drippings in fry pan. Add onion and garlic; cook 3 minutes. Stir in meats and remaining ingredients, except salt and pepper; heat at 400° until boiling. Reduce heat to simmer, between Warm and 200°; cook, covered, 30 minutes, stirring occasionally. Season to taste with salt and pepper.

4 servings.

Stuffed Pork Chops with Spiced Peaches

2 tablespoons butter or margarine	6 pork chops, 1 inch thick
2 tablespoons vegetable oil	Salt
1/2 cup chopped green pepper	Pepper
1/4 cup chopped onion	3/4 cup water
1/2 cup whole kernel corn	1/2 teaspoon chicken flavor instant bouillon
1 6-ounce package stuffing mix for pork	Spiced peaches
1 2/3 cups water	
1/4 cup butter or margarine	

Heat 1 tablespoon butter and 1 tablespoon oil in fry pan at 225° until butter is melted. Add green pepper and onion; cook until tender, about 5 minutes. Stir in corn; remove vegetable mixture from fry pan. Clean fry pan.

Make stuffing mix in fry pan according to package directions, using 1 2/3 cups water and 1/4 cup butter; cook at 200°, 4 minutes. Stir in vegetable mixture. Cut pockets in pork chops; spoon stuffing into each chop. Wrap remaining stuffing in aluminum foil and reserve. Clean fry pan.

Add remaining oil and butter to fry pan. Heat fry pan at 325°. Add pork chops; cook until browned, about 4 minutes on each side. Drain excess fat. Sprinkle chops lightly with salt and pepper. Add 3/4 cup water and bouillon; heat at 400° until boiling. Reduce heat to simmer, between Warm and 200°; cook, covered, until pork chops are tender, 45 minutes to 1 hour, turning after 20 minutes. Add more water, if necessary. Add reserved foil package of stuffing to fry pan during last 20 minutes of cooking time. Arrange chops and stuffing on serving platter; garnish with spiced peaches.   4 to 6 servings.

Hash-Stuffed Pepper Rellenos

Hearty Roast Beef Hash (see recipe, page 34)	Water
1 cup shredded Swiss cheese	3 egg whites
2/3 cup sour cream or sour half-and-half	3 egg yolks, beaten
1 teaspoon dried tarragon leaves	1/4 teaspoon paprika
1/2 teaspoon paprika	1/4 teaspoon salt
1/2 teaspoon salt	1/8 teaspoon white pepper
1/4 teaspoon black pepper	Flour
6 large green peppers	Vegetable oil

Make Hearty Roast Beef Hash in fry pan. Stir in cheese, sour cream, tarragon, 1/2 teaspoon paprika 1/2 teaspoon salt, and 1/4 teaspoon black pepper. Remove hash mixture from fry pan and reserve. Clean fry pan.

Cut tops off peppers; remove cores and seeds. Place peppers upside down on rack in fry pan. Add 1/2 inch water; heat at 400° until boiling. Reduce heat to simmer, between Warm and 200°; cook, covered, 10 minutes. Remove peppers from fry pan and cool; discard water. Cut peppers lengthwise into halves and fill with reserved hash mixture.

Beat egg whites until soft peaks form. Mix egg yolks, 1/4 teaspoon paprika, 1/4 teaspoon salt and white pepper. Mix about a fourth of the egg whites into yolk mixture; fold yolk mixture into whites. Coat stuffed side of peppers lightly with flour, dip into egg mixture. Coat again with flour and dip into egg mixture.

Heat 1 inch oil in fry pan at 250°. Place peppers, filled sides down, in fry pan; cook until peppers are golden and hash filling is heated through, 3 to 4 minutes on each side. Serve immediately.

6 servings.

Three-Meat Stew

3 tablespoons vegetable oil
1 pound beef cubes
1 pound veal cubes
1 pound pork cubes
2 cups chopped onions
1 cup chopped green pepper
1 clove garlic, minced
2 cups sliced mushrooms
1/4 cup all-purpose flour
2 tablespoons paprika

1 1/2 cups water
3/4 teaspoon beef flavor instant bouillon
1 16-ounce can tomatoes, undrained, coarsely chopped
2/3 cup tomato sauce
1/4 teaspoon caraway seed, crushed
1 bay leaf
Salt
Pepper

Heat fry pan at 300°. Add oil and beef; cook until brown. Remove beef. Repeat with veal and pork. Add onion, green pepper and garlic; cook at 225°, 5 minutes. Stir in mushrooms; cook 2 minutes. Stir in flour and paprika; cook 1 minute. Stir in meats, water, bouillon, tomatoes with liquid, tomato sauce, caraway seed and bay leaf; heat at 400° until boiling. Reduce heat to simmer, between Warm and 200°; cook, covered, until meats are tender, 1 3/4 to 2 hours. Season to taste with salt and pepper.

6 servings.

Shrimp and Vegetables Tempura

Powdered Salt (see recipe, page 26)
3 egg whites
1 1/2 cups all-purpose flour
1 tablespoon cornstarch
1 teaspoon baking powder
1 1/2 teaspoons salt
3 egg yolks, beaten
1 10-ounce bottle club soda
Vegetable oil
3/4 to 1 pound peeled, deveined, uncooked shrimp

1 small eggplant, peeled, sliced (optional)
1 large green pepper, cut into strips
1 medium sweet potato, peeled, sliced
1 medium onion, sliced
4 ounces green beans, cut into 2-inch pieces
2 large carrots, cut into sticks

Make Powdered Salt; reserve. Beat egg whites until soft peaks form. Mix flour, cornstarch, baking powder and salt into egg yolks alternately with club soda. Mix about a fourth of the egg whites into yolk mixture; fold yolk mixture into whites.

Heat 1 inch oil in fry pan at 375°. Dip shrimp and vegetables into batter; cook in oil until golden, 2 to 4 minutes. Remove from oil with slotted spoon; drain on paper toweling. Sprinkle lightly with reserved Powdered Salt.

4 servings.

Menus for Entertaining

Often, the most challenging aspect of entertaining is planning the cooking so that everything is ready to serve without a lot of last-minute activity in the kitchen. So this chapter has been specially designed to meet that challenge. The preparation sequence in each of the seven menus allows you to do all of the cooking in the electric fry pan at a sensible and sociable party pace.

Not only are these party plans practical, but the food is simply sensational. For brunchtime entertaining, you can choose a New Orleans menu of Peaches in Champagne, Eggs Sardou, and hot-from-the-frypan Beignets, or an Italian feast of soufflélike Herbed Omelet

Parmesan, Hot Sausage Antipasto, and Rum Tortoni. You can celebrate the Chinese New Year with the tender fried dumplings called Pot Stickers, Chinese Chicken and Vegetable Stir Fry, and light Almond Custard, which signifies good luck. If you dream of a sunny holiday, you can regale guests with a Greek or Mexican dinner. If you're lured by the seashore, serve a New England-style Steamed Shore Dinner and Blueberry Cream Cake. But if the evening is ripe for romance, you'll want to indulge the mood with a dramatic dinner of Apricot-Honey Glazed Duckling and Cherries Jubilee.

Chinese Dinner

Egg Drop Soup
*Potstickers
*Chinese Chicken and Vegetable Stir Fry
Steamed Rice
*Almond Custard

*Recipes Included

Potstickers

6	ounces lean ground beef or pork	1/8	teaspoon salt
1	cup shredded Chinese or green cabbage	1/8	teaspoon pepper
1/4	cup finely chopped celery	24	won ton or 6 egg roll wrappers
1	tablespoon finely chopped green onion and top		Water
1	tablespoon soy sauce	2 to 4	tablespoons peanut or vegetable oil
1	tablespoon cornstarch	2	cups chicken broth
1/4	teaspoon ground ginger		Soy sauce

Combine ground beef, cabbage, celery, onion, 1 tablespoon soy sauce, cornstarch, ginger, salt and pepper. Cut won ton wrappers into 3-inch rounds with cutter. Spoon about 1 1/2 teaspoons beef mixture on each won ton wrapper; brush edges with water. Fold wrappers in half and seal edges with tines of fork to make potstickers.

Heat fry pan at 375°. Add 2 tablespoons oil and potstickers; cook until golden on bottoms, about 3 minutes. Turn potstickers. Add chicken broth; cook, covered, at simmer, between Warm and 200°, until potstickers are tender and broth has evaporated, about 10 minutes. Continue cooking, uncovered, until bottoms of potstickers are golden, adding more oil, if necessary. Serve hot with soy sauce.

2 dozen.

TIP: Chinese cabbage and won ton and egg roll wrappers can be purchased in specialty food stores or large supermarkets.

Chinese Chicken and Vegetable Stir Fry

6 Chinese dried mushrooms
1/2 cup hot water
3 tablespoons peanut or vegetable oil
1 teaspoon sesame oil
4 boned, skinned chicken breast halves (about 1 1/2 pounds), cut into 1-inch pieces
2 1/2 cups diagonally sliced broccoli
1 cup sliced red or green pepper
3/4 cup diagonally sliced carrots
4 ounces sliced fresh or canned mushrooms
1 8-ounce can sliced water chestnuts, drained

2 green onions and tops, thinly sliced
2 tablespoons soy sauce
1 teaspoon sugar
1/8 teaspoon Chinese 5-spice powder (optional)
1/4 teaspoon salt
1/4 teaspoon pepper
4 ounces pea pods
1/2 cup cashews or peanuts, toasted
1 tablespoon sesame seed, toasted
Hot cooked rice

Combine dried mushrooms and hot water in small bowl; let stand until softened, about 15 minutes. Drain mushrooms, reserving liquid. Chop mushrooms coarsely, discarding tough centers.

Heat fry pan at 400°. Add oils and chicken; cook until brown. Remove chicken with slotted spoon; reserve. Add broccoli, red pepper, and carrots to fry pan; cook 2 minutes, stirring constantly. Add fresh mushrooms, water chestnuts, and onions; cook 2 minutes, stirring constantly. Mix soy sauce, sugar, 5-spice powder, salt and pepper; stir into fry pan. Add pea pods, reserved mushrooms with liquid and reserved chicken to fry pan; cook, covered, until vegetables are crisp-tender, 3 to 5 minutes. Sprinkle with cashews and sesame seed. Serve with hot cooked rice.

6 servings.

TIP: Chinese 5-spice powder can be purchased in specialty food stores or larger supermarkets. There is no substitute.

Almond Custard

3 cups milk
3 cups half-and-half
1 cup sugar
3 tablespoons all-purpose flour

3 tablespoons cornstarch
3/4 teaspoon almond extract
1 11-ounce can mandarin orange segments, drained

Heat fry pan at 400°. Add 2 1/2 cups milk, half-and-half and sugar; cook until boiling, stirring constantly. Mix flour, cornstarch and remaining 1/2 cup milk; stir into milk mixture. Reduce heat to simmer, between Warm and 200°; cook until thickened, stirring constantly. Stir in almond extract. Pour custard into serving bowl; cool to room temperature. Refrigerate, covered, until chilled, about 3 hours. Spoon custard into serving dishes; garnish with oranges.

6 servings.

Italian Brunch

Herbed Omelet Parmesan
Hot Italian Sausage Antipasto
Spinach, Sliced Pear and Pine nut Salad
Lemon Vinaigrette Dressing
Italian Bread
Rum Tortoni

*Recipes Included

Herbed Omelet Parmesan

Hot Italian Sausage Antipasto
Butter or margarine, softened
6 egg whites
1/8 teaspoon cream of tartar
6 egg yolks
1/2 teaspoon dried basil leaves

1/8 teaspoon dried tarragon leaves
1/4 teaspoon salt
1/8 teaspoon white pepper
2 tablespoons grated Parmesan cheese
Minced parsley

Make Hot Italian Sausage Antipasto; remove from fry pan and reserve. Clean fry pan.

Cut double thickness of aluminum foil 20 inches long; place in fry pan, allowing edges of foil to extend up sides of fry pan. Butter foil generously.

Beat egg whites and cream of tartar in large bowl until stiff, but not dry, peaks form. Beat egg yolks, basil, tarragon, salt and pepper in large bowl until thick and lemon colored, about 5 minutes. Stir about a fourth of the egg whites into yolk mixture; fold yolk mixture into remaining whites. Fold in 1 1/2 tablespoons cheese.

Heat fry pan at 250°. Pour egg mixture into fry pan; cook, covered, 30 minutes, or until omelet appears dry on top and springs back when lightly touched. Loosen edges of omelet with plastic or wooden spatula; lift from fry pan, using foil, and invert on serving platter. Sprinkle with remaining 1/2 tablespoon cheese and parsley; keep warm.

Return reserved antipasto mixture to fry pan; cook, covered, at 300° until heated, 3 to 4 minutes. Spoon over omelet or serve alongside.

4 servings.

Hot Italian Sausage Antipasto

1 pound mild or hot Italian sausage, cut into 2-inch pieces
2 cups coarsely chopped tomatoes
1 1/2 cups sliced mushrooms
1 medium zucchini, cut into 1/2-inch pieces
1 9-ounce package frozen artichoke hearts
1/2 cup sliced pitted black olives

1 clove garlic, minced
2 tablespoons lemon juice
1 teaspoon dried basil leaves
1 teaspoon minced parsley
1/4 teaspoon dried oregano leaves
Salt
Pepper

Cook sausage in fry pan at 300° until browned and no longer pink in the center, 8 to 10 minutes. Drain excess fat from fry pan. Stir in remaining ingredients, except salt and pepper; cook, covered, until vegetables are tender, 8 to 10 minutes, stirring occasionally. Season to taste with salt and pepper.

4 servings.

Rum Tortoni

1/2 cup angel food cake crumbs
1 cup whipping cream or half-and-half
1 egg, beaten
2 tablespoons sugar
Dash of salt
2 teaspoons cornstarch

2 tablespoons light rum
1 teaspoon vanilla
1/4 cup whipping cream, whipped
Slivered almonds, toasted
Red or green maraschino cherries

Cook angel food cake crumbs in fry pan at 225° until light brown, about 8 minutes, stirring frequently. Remove from fry pan and reserve. Mix 1 cup whipping cream, egg, sugar and salt until smooth; pour into fry pan; cook at 200° until slightly thickened, stirring constantly. Mix cornstarch and rum; stir into cream mixture until thickened, about 2 minutes, stirring constantly. Spoon mixture into bowl; cool to room temperature. Stir in vanilla; refrigerate until chilled, about 1 hour.

Fold whipped cream and reserved cake crumbs into cream mixture. Spoon into 4 paper-lined muffin cups; garnish with almonds and cherries. Freeze until hard, about 4 hours.

4 servings.

TIP: To make angel food cake crumbs, process 1-inch pieces of angel food cake in food processor or blender.

Mexican Dinner

Guacamole Dip with Tortilla Chips
*Mexican Flank Steak with Salsa
*Rice and Corn Casserole
Shredded Lettuce and Tomato Salad
*Sugared Cookies

*Recipes Included

Mexican Flank Steak with Salsa

1 1/2 pounds beef flank steak, excess fat trimmed	1/4 teaspoon dried marjoram leaves
1 cup tomato juice	1/8 teaspoon ground cumin
2 tablespoons distilled white vinegar	1/8 teaspoon pepper
1 tablespoon sugar	Mexican Salsa (see recipe, page 74)
1 teaspoon Worcestershire sauce	2 tablespoons vegetable oil

Pound flank steak with mallet until even in thickness (scant 3/4-inch thick). Score steak diagonally in diamond pattern on both sides, using sharp knife. Place steak in shallow glass baking dish. Mix tomato juice, vinegar, sugar, Worcestershire sauce, marjoram, cumin and pepper; pour over steak. Refrigerate 4 to 6 hours, turning steak occasionally.

Make Mexican Salsa; refrigerate until ready to use. Remove steak from marinade; reserve marinade. Heat fry pan at 300°. Add oil and steak; cook until browned on both sides. Add reserved marinade; heat at 400° until boiling. Reduce heat to simmer, between Warm and 200°; cook, covered, 30 minutes. Stir in Mexican Salsa; cook, covered, 30 minutes, or until steak is tender.

6 servings.

Mexican Rice and Corn Casserole

4 cups cooked rice	1/8 teaspoon ground cumin
1 10-ounce package frozen whole kernel corn, thawed	1/2 cup Monterey Jack cheese
1/2 cup sour cream or sour half-and-half	1/2 cup cheddar cheese

Combine rice and corn in fry pan; cook, covered at 350° until heated, about 5 minutes. Reduce heat to Warm. Stir in sour cream, cumin and sprinkle with cheeses; cook, covered, until cheese is melted, about 3 minutes.

6 servings.

Sugared Cookies

1/2 cup butter or margarine, softened	1/8 teaspoon salt
1/4 cup powdered sugar	1/3 cup finely chopped pecans
1/2 teaspoon vanilla	Powdered sugar
1 cup plus 2 tablespoons all-purpose flour	

Beat butter in small bowl until fluffy; beat in 1/4 cup sugar and vanilla. Mix in flour, salt and nuts. Shape dough into 3/4-inch balls; flatten with bottom of glass to 1/4-inch thickness.

Heat fry pan at 225°. Place half the cookies in bottom of fry pan; cook, with cover 1/2 inch ajar, until golden, about 15 minutes on each side. Remove cookies to wire rack. Repeat with remaining dough. Coat warm cookies generously with powdered sugar; cool and store in airtight container.

About 3 dozen.

137

Mexican Flank Steak With Salsa, Mexican
Rice and Corn Casserole, Sugared Cookies.

Greek Dinner

*Saganaki
*Greek Shish Kabobs
Rosemary Rice Pilaf
Tomato Wedges with Black Olives and Feta Cheese
Oregano Vinaigrette Dressing
Hard Rolls
*Honey-soaked Pastries
*Recipes Included

Saganaki

(Flaming Cheese)

1 pound Kasseri or Kefalotiri cheese, cut into 6 pieces, 1/2-inch thick
 Flour
2 eggs, beaten

2 tablespoons butter or margarine
2 tablespoon brandy
3 tablespoons lemon juice

Coat cheese lightly on all sides with flour; dip into eggs and coat again with flour. Heat butter in fry pan at Warm until melted. Add cheese; cook, covered, at 225° for 2 minutes on each side (cheese will become very soft, but should not be cooked long enough to melt). Add brandy; turn heat to Off and unplug cord from wall outlet. Flame cheese. Sprinkle lemon juice over cheese. Serve immediately.

6 servings.

TIP: Kasseri or Kefalotiri cheese can be purchased in specialty food stores or large supermarkets. If not available, mozzarella cheese can be substituted.

Greek Shish Kabobs

1 1/2 pounds boneless lean lamb or beef, cut into scant 1-inch cubes
24 mushrooms
2 medium zucchini, cut into 1/2-inch pieces
2 medium onions, cut into wedges
1/4 cup white wine vinegar
2 tablespoons olive or vegetable oil
1/2 teaspoon sugar

1 clove garlic, minced
1/2 teaspoon dried oregano leaves
1/2 teaspoon dried mint leaves
1/2 teaspoon salt
1/4 teaspoon pepper
 Hot cooked rice

Combine lamb, mushrooms, zucchini and onions in shallow glass baking dish. Mix remaining ingredients, except rice; pour over meat and vegetables. Refrigerate, covered, 4 to 6 hours, stirring occasionally. Drain.

Arrange meat and vegetables alternately on 12 metal skewers. Heat fry pan at 300°. Arrange skewers in fry pan; cook until meat is browned and cooked to desired degree of doneness, 2 to 3 minutes on each side for medium. Turn skewers halfway through cooking time. Serve with hot cooked rice.

6 servings.

Honey-Soaked Pastries

1   1/4-ounce package active dry yeast
3/4   cup warm water (110°)
2   tablespoons butter or margarine,
    melted
1 1/2   cups all-purpose flour

1/2   cup finely chopped pecans
1   teaspoon salt
    Honey Syrup
    Vegetable oil

Mix yeast and warm water; let stand 5 minutes. Stir in butter, flour, pecans and salt to make smooth dough; let stand, covered, 35 to 40 minutes.

Make Honey Syrup; pour into shallow baking dish. Clean fry pan.

Heat 1 inch oil in fry pan at 375°. Drop dough by teaspoons into oil; cook until golden, 2 to 3 minutes. Remove from oil with slotted spoon; drain on paper toweling. Place pastries in syrup in baking dish; let stand until soaked with syrup. Spoon pastries onto serving plates, spooning small amount of syrup over.

3 dozen.

Honey Syrup

1   cup water
1   cup sugar
1/4   cup honey

2   tablespoons lemon juice
1   tablespoon grated lemon rind

Mix all ingredients in fry pan; cook at 400° until boiling, stirring constantly until sugar is dissolved. Reduce heat to simmer, between Warm and 200°; cook until slightly thickened, 3 to 5 minutes.

About 1 1/2 cups.

Shore Dinner

Deep-fried Mushrooms with Tartar Sauce
*Steamed Shore Dinner
*Cream-Dill Sauce
Marinated Red and Green Pepper Rings
Crusty French Bread
*Blueberry Cream Cake

*Recipes Included

Steamed Shore Dinner

2 cups water	12 cherrystone clams
1 large onion, cut into wedges	6 fresh or thawed frozen halibut, haddock or cod fillets (about 4 ounces each)
1 bay leaf	
4 black peppers	18 medium shrimp in shells, uncooked
6 small unpeeled red potatoes, cut lengthwise into halves	12 mussels
	Cream-Dill Sauce
6 ears corn	Melted butter

Heat water, onion, bay leaf and whole peppers in fry pan at 400° until boiling. Add potatoes; reduce heat to simmer, between Warm and 200°; cook, covered, 8 minutes. Add corn and clams; cook, covered, 3 minutes. Add fish fillets, shrimp and mussels; cook, covered, until fish and vegetables are tender and cooked, about 5 minutes. Remove seafood and vegetables to serving platter; keep warm while making Cream-Dill Sauce. Strain cooking liquid and reserve for Cream-Dill Sauce. Serve Creamed Dill Sauce and melted butter for dipping.

6 servings.

Cream-Dill Sauce

Reserved cooking liquid from Steamed Shore Dinner	1/2 teaspoon dried dillweed
	Dash cayenne pepper
1/2 cup whipping cream or half-and-half	

Heat reserved cooking liquid in fry pan at 400° until boiling. Stir in cream, dillweed and cayenne pepper; cook until slightly thickened, about 2 minutes, stirring frequently. Serve hot.

About 1 cup.

Blueberry Cream Cake

1 9-ounce package yellow cake mix	1 1/2 cups milk
1 egg	1 teaspoon orange flavor liqueur or 1/4 teaspoon orange extract
1/4 cup water	
1/4 cup sour cream or sour half-and-half	1 21-ounce can blueberry pie filling
1 teaspoon grated lemon rind	1 teaspoon sugar
1 3 1/8 ounce package vanilla pudding mix	1/8 teaspoon ground cinnamon

Make cake mix according to package directions, using egg and water; mix in sour cream and lemon rind. Heat fry pan at 350°. Pour batter into greased and floured 8-inch square baking pan. Place pan on rack in fry pan; cook, covered, until toothpick inserted near center of cake comes out clean, about 1 1/4 hours. Cool cake on wire rack 5 minutes; invert onto serving plate.

Make pudding mix in fry pan according to package directions, using milk; stir in liqueur. Pour into small bowl; cool to room temperature. Refrigerate, covered, until chilled, about 30 minutes. Spread pudding over top of cake. Mix pie filling, sugar and cinnamon; spoon over pudding. Cut cake into wedges to serve.

1 cake

New Orleans Brunch

Peaches in Champagne
Eggs Sardou
Smoked Oyster Stuffed Cherry Tomatoes
Rémoulade Sauce
Beignets
*Recipes Included

Peaches in Champagne

1 cup water
1/2 cup sugar
1 cinnamon stick
6 whole cloves

2 whole allspice
1 8-ounce can peach slices, drained
1 25-ounce bottle champagne, chilled

Heat water, sugar, cinnamon stick, cloves and allspice in fry pan at 400° until boiling. Reduce heat to simmer, between Warm and 200°; cook 5 minutes. Add peach slices; cook 5 minutes. Spoon mixture into small bowl; cool to room temperature. Refrigerate several hours for flavors to blend.

Drain peach slices; divide peach slices into champagne glasses and pour champagne over.

6 servings.

Eggs Sardou

Creamy Hollandaise Sauce (see recipe, page 71)
Water
12 Eggs
Warm water

Creamed Spinach with Nutmeg (see recipe, page 28)
2 14-ounce cans artichoke bottoms, drained
Paprika

Make Creamy Hollandaise Sauce in fry pan; spoon sauce into small bowl and reserve. Clean fry pan.

Heat 2 inches water in fry pan at 400° until boiling; reduce heat to simmer, between Warm and 200°. Break 6 eggs, 1 at a time, into cup and gently pour into fry pan; cook until eggs are set, but still soft, about 2 minutes. Remove eggs from fry pan with slotted spoon; place in baking dish filled with warm water. Repeat with remaining eggs. Clean fry pan.

Make Creamed Spinach with Nutmeg in fry pan. Spread spinach mixture evenly in bottom of fry pan. Arrange 12 artichoke bottoms on spinach. Top artichoke bottoms with eggs. Spoon reserved Creamy Hollandaise Sauce over eggs and sprinkle with paprika; cook, covered, at Warm until heated through, 5 to 8 minutes. Serve immediately.

6 servings.

Beignets

1 16-ounce loaf frozen sweet bread dough, thawed
Vegetable oil

Powdered sugar

Roll dough on lightly floured surface into rectangle 1/2-inch thick. Cut into twelve 2-inch squares; cover lightly with towel and let stand until dough has doubled in size, about 45 minutes.

Heat 1 1/2 inches oil in fry pan at 375°. Add dough squares, several at a time; cook until golden, about 2 minutes on each side. Drain on paper toweling. Sprinkle with powdered sugar; serve warm.

1 dozen.

French Dinner

*Apricot-Honey Glazed Duckling
*Pecan Rice
Buttered Steamed Turnips
Curly Endive Salad with Hot Bacon Dressing
French Bread
*Cherries Jubilee

*Recipes Included
†Recipe on page 80

Apricot-Honey Glazed Duckling

4 pound frozen duckling, thawed,
   cut into fourths
Salt
Pepper
1 cup water
1/2 teaspoon chicken flavor instant bouillon

1/2 cup apricot preserves
2 tablespoons honey
2 tablespoons lemon juice
1/2 teaspoon grated lemon rind

Generously pierce skin of duckling pieces with fork. Heat fry pan at 300°. Add duckling; cook, covered, at 300° until well browned, about 8 minutes on each side. Remove duckling from fry pan; sprinkle lightly with salt and pepper. Drain fat from fry pan; discard.

Place duckling pieces, skin sides up, on rack in fry pan. Add water and bouillon; heat at 400° until water is boiling. Reduce heat to simmer, between Warm and 200°; cook, covered, until duckling is tender and juices are clear when thickest parts are pierced with a fork, about 1 1/4 hours. Remove duckling from fry pan. Clean fry pan.

Mix remaining ingredients in fry pan; cook at 200° until bubbly. Add duckling with skin-side down, coating pieces evenly with glaze; cook, covered, until glaze has thickened and duckling is golden, about 5 minutes. Arrange duckling on serving platter.

4 servings.

Pecan Rice

1/4 cup butter or margarine
1 cup thinly sliced celery
1/4 cup finely chopped onion
2 cups water
2 teaspoons chicken flavor instant
   bouillon
1/2 teaspoon dried thyme leaves

1/8 teaspoon ground mace
1 6 1/4-ounce package fast-cooking
   long grain and wild rice
1/2 cup pecan halves, toasted
Salt
White pepper

Heat butter in fry pan at Warm until melted. Add celery and onion; cook 2 minutes. Stir in water, bouillon, thyme and mace; heat at 400° until boiling. Stir in rice. Reduce heat to simmer, between Warm and 200°; cook, covered, until rice is tender and all liquid is absorbed, about 5 minutes. Stir in pecans; season to taste with salt and pepper.

4 servings.

TIP: If package of rice contains a seasoning packet, reserve packet for other use.

Special Techniques

This chapter highlights the heating efficiency, the generous contours, and the nonstick surface of the electric fry pan with three special techniques: stir-frying, steaming, and fat-free cooking. The results are very special, too—food with an unusual twist and a remarkable flair for all kinds of meals and occasions.

Stir-frying is fast cooking in a small amount of oil at high heat. Foods are cut into small pieces and stirred continuously; so they cook thoroughly in the shortest amount of time. The method is popular in China and other Far Eastern countries where fuel supplies are limited, but it can be applied to European-style dishes too. Meats and poultry are often marinated prior to stir-frying to ensure tenderness and uniform seasoning within the short cooking time. Vegetables are almost always added to the pan sequentially, starting with the firmest and leaving the most delicate for last, so that all are cooked just to crisp-tenderness. Once the primary ingredients have been stir-fried, they are usually combined and briefly heated in a sauce. One convenience of stir-fry recipes is that all preparations, including cutting up the food and mixing the sauce, can be done in advance, leaving only a few minutes of cooking to be done just before serving. For best results, be sure that the cooking oil is hot before you add the food and be careful not to overcook. The method is perfect not only for such Oriental favorites as Sweet-Sour Shrimp or Szechuan Beef and Peanuts, but also for freshest-tasting vegetable combinations, including Mixed Vegetable Curry and Mediterranean Peppers and Squash.

Steaming is most often associated with rich holiday puddings and New England-style brown bread. So the concept of steaming fish, poultry, and even stuffed cabbage may be new to you, and you may be surprised by the elegance of these foods. They cook quickly, retain delicate flavors, and remain perfectly moist. Placed directly on a rack and cooked over well-seasoned broth, wine, or a sauce, they become suffused with the fragrance of the liquid. Steamed puddings, cakes, and breads, by contrast, are steamed in covered containers placed on a rack over plain water. For either type of steaming, the rack can be almost anything that will support the food above the water—a cake cooling rack, wok steaming rack, or pressure cooker rack will work well, but other arrangements can be improvised from flat cans with the ends removed or canning jar lid rings or a disposable pie pan with holes punched in it. The technique's versatility is showcased in recipes as diverse as Wine-Steamed Cornish Hens with Tarragon, Beer-Steamed Bratwurst, and Apple-Steamed Pudding.

You don't have to be on a fat-free diet to appreciate the lighter appeal of foods pan-fried or sautéed without cooking oil. The technique is easy, thanks to the even heat and nonstick surface of the electric fry pan. And the fare is as tempting as Marinated Salmon Steaks with sweet-sour seasonings, Ham-Stuffed Chicken Breasts glazed with white wine, and Scallops St. Jacques scented with herbs and served in a bouquet of fresh vegetables.

Beer-Steamed Brats

1 **12-ounce can beer**
1 **teaspoon beef flavor instant bouillon**
1 **teaspoon dried rosemary leaves**
8 **fully cooked bratwursts
   or other sausages**
8 **hot dog buns**

3 **tablespoons mayonnaise or
   salad dressing**
3 **tablespoons Bavarian-style mustard**
3 **tablespoons finely chopped dill pickle**
3/4 **teaspoon prepared horseradish**

Heat beer, bouillon, and rosemary in fry pan at 400° until boiling. Reduce heat to simmer, between Warm and 200°. Arrange bratwursts on rack in fry pan; cook, covered, until hot through, 10 to 15 minutes. Wrap buns loosely in aluminum foil; place on rack in fry pan during last 5 minutes of cooking time.

Mix mayonnaise, mustard, pickle and horseradish. Arrange bratwursts in buns; spoon mayonnaise mixture over.

8 servings.

Hungarian Stuffed Cabbage

3/4	pound lean ground pork		1	teaspoon salt
1	cup cooked rice		1	16-ounce can tomatoes, undrained, coarsely chopped
1	egg, beaten			
1 1/2	tablespoons tomato paste		1	15-ounce can tomato sauce
1	clove garlic, minced		1	tablespoon tomato paste
3/4	teaspoon grated lemon rind		1	cup water
1/2	teaspoon caraway seed, crushed		2	teaspoons sugar
3/4	teaspoon salt		1	bay leaf
1/4	teaspoon pepper		1/8	teaspoon ground cinnamon
1	large head cabbage		1/4	teaspoon pepper
	Water			Chive Dumpling

Combine ground pork, rice, egg, 1 1/2 tablespoons tomato paste, garlic, lemon rind, caraway seed, 3/4 teaspoon salt and 1/4 teaspoon pepper until blended. Refrigerate.

Remove and discard tough outer leaves of cabbage. Carefully detach 16 large leaves and trim thick center spine from each. Combine 2 inches water and 1 teaspoon salt in fry pan; heat at 400° until boiling. Reduce heat to simmer, between Warm and 200°. Place half the cabbage leaves on rack in fry pan; cook, covered, until cabbage is beginning to soften, about 5 minutes. Rinse leaves under cold water and drain. Repeat with remaining cabbage leaves. Discard water. Clean fry pan.

Place 2 cabbage leaves, overlapping, on flat surface; spoon 3 tablespoons pork mixture on bottom half of leaves. Fold lower end of leaves over filling; fold sides in and roll up. Repeat with remaining cabbage leaves and pork mixture.

Combine remaining ingredients, except Chive Dumpling, in fry pan; heat at 400° until boiling. Reduce heat to simmer, between Warm and 200°; cook, covered, 5 minutes. Place rack in fry pan. Place cabbage rolls, seam sides down on rack; cook, covered, until cabbage is tender and pork mixture is no longer pink in the center, about 1 1/2 hours.

Make Chive Dumpling; form mixture into log about 8 inches long and 1 1/2 inches in diameter. Place log on piece of greased aluminum foil; place on top of cabbage rolls in fry pan during last 15 minutes of cooking time.

Arrange cabbage rolls on serving platter; slice dumpling and arrange next to cabbage rolls. Pass sauce to spoon over cabbage rolls and dumpling.

4 servings.

Chive Dumpling

1	cup plus 2 tablespoons buttermilk baking mix	1/3	cup cold milk
1	teaspoon dried chives		

Mix 1 cup of the buttermilk baking mix and chives in small bowl; stir in milk to moisten. Beat mixture vigorously 30 seconds. Coat dough with remaining 2 tablespoons baking mix and knead 10 times.

1 large dumpling

Steamed Vegetable Platter

2	cups chicken broth	1	medium sweet potato, cut into 3/4-inch slices
1	bay leaf	2	celery hearts, trimmed
1/2	teaspoon dried thyme leaves	1	10-ounce package frozen artichoke hearts, thawed
1/2	teaspoon dried marjoram leaves	8	ounces green beans
1/2	teaspoon dried rosemary leaves		Salt
4	medium carrots, cut diagonally into 2-inch pieces		Pepper
2	medium potatoes, peeled, cut into halves		Drawn Butter Sauce (see recipe, page 72)

Heat chicken broth, bay leaf, thyme, marjoram and rosemary in fry pan at 400° until boiling. Reduce heat to simmer, between Warm and 200°. Place all vegetables, except artichoke hearts and green beans on rack in fry pan; cook, covered, until vegetables are crisp-tender, about 25 minutes. Add artichoke hearts and green beans during last 10 minutes of cooking time. Sprinkle vegetables lightly with salt and pepper. Arrange vegetables on serving platter; keep warm. Discard broth mixture. Clean fry pan. Make Drawn Butter Sauce; pass to serve over vegetables.

8 servings.

Oriental Steamed Fish

1	dressed whole whitefish or other freshwater fish (about 2 pounds)	1	clove garlic, thinly sliced
1	teaspoon salt	3	tablespoons teriyaki sauce
2	slices fresh or canned ginger root (about size of dime)	3	tablespoons sake or dry white wine
	Water	1	teaspoon light brown sugar
3	tablespoons peanut or vegetable oil	1	teaspoon sesame or vegetable oil
1	teaspoon slivered fresh or canned ginger root	2	green onions and tops, sliced

Rub fish, inside and out, with salt and 2 slices ginger root; discard ginger root. Place fish on rack in fry pan. Add 1 1/2 inches water to fry pan; heat at 400° until boiling. Reduce heat to simmer, between Warm and 200°; cook, covered until fish is tender and flakes with a fork, about 12 minutes. Arrange fish on serving platter; keep warm. Discard water; clean fry pan.

Heat fry pan at 225°. Add oil, slivered ginger root and garlic; cook 2 minutes, stirring constantly. Spoon mixture over fish. Stir in teriyaki sauce, sake, sugar and sesame oil; cook 1 minute. Pour over fish; sprinkle with green onions.

4 servings.

Steamed Brown Bread

1	cup gingersnap crumbs	1	cup buttermilk
2/3	cup unbleached flour	1/3	cup dark molasses
2/3	cup whole wheat flour	3/4	cup raisins
1	teaspoon baking powder	1	tablespoon grated orange rind
1	teaspoon baking soda		Water
1/2	teaspoon salt		

Mix gingersnap crumbs, flours, baking powder, baking soda and salt in bowl; mix in remaining ingredients, except water, until blended. Spoon batter into 2 greased 16-ounce cans. Cover cans firmly with double-thickness aluminum foil.

Place rack in fry pan; place cans on rack. Add 1 1/2 inches water; heat at 400° until boiling. Reduce heat to simmer, between Warm and 200°; cook, covered, until toothpicks inserted in centers of breads come out clean, 45 to 60 minutes. Cool on wire rack 5 minutes; remove from cans and cool completely.

2 breads

146   **Wine-Steamed Fish with Red Pepper Sauce, Mushroom Salisbury Steaks, Lemon Chicken**

Steamed Fish with Red Pepper Sauce

1/2	cup cold butter, cut into pieces	2	dressed whole rainbow trout or other freshwater trout (about 12 ounces each)
1/2	cup finely chopped red pepper		Salt
1/4	cup thinly sliced green onions and tops		White pepper
1/4	teaspoon anise seed, crushed	1	tablespoon sour cream or sour half-and-half
1 1/2	cups dry white wine		
1	teaspoon lemon juice		

Heat 1 tablespoon of the butter in fry pan at Warm until melted. Add red pepper and onions; cook at 225°, 2 minutes. Stir in anise seed, wine and lemon juice; heat at 400° until boiling. Reduce heat to simmer, between Warm and 200°. Sprinkle cavities of fish lightly with salt and pepper. Place on rack in fry pan; cook, covered, until fish is tender and flakes with a fork, about 10 minutes. Remove fish to serving platter; keep warm.

Whisk remaining butter vigorously into cooking liquid, whisking in 2 small pieces at a time. Turn heat to Off; whisk in sour cream. Spoon sauce over fish.

4 servings.

Wine-Steamed Cornish Hens with Tarragon

	Tarragon Butter	1/4	cup finely chopped mushrooms
2	Cornish hens (1 to 1 1/4 pounds each)	1	green onion and top
	Salt	1 1/2	tablespoons cornstarch
2	cups water	3	tablespoons cold water
1	cup dry white wine	2	teaspoons brandy (optional)
1	teaspoon chicken flavor instant bouillon		White pepper

Make Tarragon Butter. Loosen skin over breasts of hens; spoon Tarragon Butter under skin, spreading evenly over breasts. Sprinkle cavities and outsides of hens lightly with salt.

Combine 2 cups water, wine, bouillon, mushrooms and green onion in fry pan; heat at 400° until boiling. Reduce heat to simmer, between Warm and 200°. Place hens on rack in fry pan; cook, covered, until hens are tender and juices are clear when thickest parts are pierced with a fork, about 45 minutes. Remove hens to serving platter; keep warm. Remove rack from fry pan. Cook liquid at 400°, 5 minutes. Remove green onion. Mix cornstarch with cold water and whisk into liquid in fry pan; cook at 200° until thickened, about 2 minutes, whisking constantly. Stir in brandy; season to taste with pepper. Pass sauce to spoon over hens.

2 servings.

Tarragon Butter

6	tablespoons butter or margarine-butter blend, softened	1	small clove garlic, minced
1/2	cup finely chopped mushrooms	2	teaspoons dried tarragon leaves
2	tablespoons finely chopped green onion and top	1/8	teaspoon pepper

Beat butter until fluffy; mix in remaining ingredients.

Makes about 2/3 cup.

TIP: Tarragon Butter is excellent spread on grilled meats, or melted and served over vegetables.

Teriyaki Chicken

1/3 cup teriyaki sauce

1/3 cup sake or dry sherry

1 tablespoon cornstarch

2 teaspoons grated grapefruit rind

1 clove garlic, minced

1 pound boned, skinned chicken breast, cut into 1/2-inch pieces

2 tablespoons peanut or vegetable oil

1 green onion and top, sliced diagonally into 1/4-inch slices

Hot cooked rice

Mix teriyaki sauce, sake, cornstarch, grapefruit rind and garlic; pour over chicken in shallow glass baking dish. Let stand 30 minutes. Drain chicken, reserving marinade.

Heat oil at 325°. Add chicken; cook until chicken is no longer pink in the center, about 4 minutes. Stir in reserved marinade; cook until thickened, stirring constantly. Sprinkle with onion. Serve with hot cooked rice.

4 servings.

Italian Beef on Noodles

3/4 cup beef broth

4 tablespoons olive or vegetable oil

3 tablespoons red wine vinegar

1 tablespoon Worcestershire sauce

1 tablespoon cornstarch

2 teaspoons sugar

1 teaspoon dried red pepper

1/4 teaspoon dried basil leaves

1/4 teaspoon dried marjoram leaves

1 clove garlic, minced

3/4 pound beef flank or round steak, thinly sliced

1 medium onion, sliced

1 large green pepper, sliced

Hot buttered egg noodles

Mix beef broth, 1 tablespoon oil, vinegar, Worcestershire sauce, cornstarch, sugar, red pepper, basil, marjoram and garlic in shallow glass baking dish; add beef, stirring to coat pieces evenly. Refrigerate, covered, 2 to 3 hours, stirring occasionally. Drain beef, reserving marinade.

Heat fry pan at 225°. Add remaining 3 tablespoons oil, onion and green pepper; cook until tender, 3 to 4 minutes, stirring constantly. Stir in beef; cook at 350° until beef is brown, about 3 minutes, stirring constantly. Stir in reserved marinade; cook until thickened, 1 to 2 minutes, stirring frequently. Serve beef mixture over hot buttered noodles.

4 servings.

Mixed Vegetable Curry

3 tablespoons olive or vegetable oil

1/2 cup chopped onion

1 clove garlic, minced

1 tablespoon curry powder

1/2 teaspoon ground cumin

1/2 teaspoon coriander seed or 1/4 teaspoon ground coriander

1/4 teaspoon ground cinnamon

1/4 teaspoon ground ginger

1/16 teaspoon cayenne pepper

1 small head cauliflower (about 12 ounces) cut into flowerettes

1 large potato, peeled, cut into 1/2-inch cubes

4 ounces green beans, cut into 1 1/2-inch lengths

2 large carrots, cut diagonally into 1/4-inch slices

1/3 to 1/2 cup water

1/4 cup raisins

1/4 cup frozen peas, thawed

Salt

Heat fry pan at 225°. Add oil, onion, garlic, curry, cumin, coriander, cinnamon, ginger and cayenne pepper; cook 2 minutes, stirring constantly. Stir in cauliflower, potato, beans and carrots; cook 4 minutes, stirring constantly. Add 1/3-cup water; cook, covered, until vegetables are crisp-tender, about 4 minutes, adding more water, if necessary. Stir in raisins and peas; cook until heated, about 2 minutes, stirring constantly. Season to taste with salt.

6 servings.

Szechwan Beef and Peanuts

1 egg white, beaten
1 tablespoon dry sherry
1 tablespoon soy sauce
1 tablespoon cornstarch
1/2 teaspoon sesame oil (optional)
1 pound beef flank steak, cut across the grain into 1/8-inch slices
2 tablespoons peanut or vegetable oil
1 to 1 1/2 teaspoons minced fresh or canned ginger root

1 clove garlic, minced
1/4 to 1/2 teaspoon dried red pepper
1/2 cup water
1/4 teaspoon beef flavor instant bouillon
3 green onions and tops, cut into 2-inch pieces
1/3 cup unsalted cocktail peanuts
Hot cooked rice

Mix egg white, sherry, soy sauce, cornstarch and sesame oil; pour over flank steak in shallow glass baking dish, stirring to coat pieces evenly. Let stand 30 minutes. Drain beef, reserving marinade.

Heat fry pan at 225°. Add oil, ginger root, garlic and red pepper; cook 1 minute. Add beef; cook at 325° until beef is brown, about 2 minutes, stirring constantly. Stir in water, bouillon and reserved marinade; cook until sauce has thickened, about 1 minute. Cut onion pieces lengthwise into fourths. Stir onions and peanuts into beef mixture; cook 1 minute. Serve over hot cooked rice.

4 servings.

Sweet and Sour Shrimp

Vegetable oil
1 pound peeled, deveined, uncooked shrimp
Cornstarch
2 tablespoons peanut or vegetable oil
1 large green pepper, cut into 1-inch pieces
1/4 cup finely chopped onion
1/4 cup drained canned bamboo shoots
1 clove garlic, minced
1 teaspoon minced fresh or canned ginger root
1 15 1/4-ounce can pineapple tidbits, undrained

1/4 cup rice wine vinegar or distilled white vinegar
2 teaspoons soy sauce
3 tablespoons sugar
1/2 teaspoon sesame oil (optional)
1 tablespoon cornstarch
2 tablespoons cold water
1 large tomato, cut into wedges
Salt
Hot cooked rice

Heat 1/4 inch vegetable oil in fry pan at 350°. Coat shrimp lightly with cornstarch; cook in fry pan until browned, about 2 minutes on each side. Drain shrimp on paper toweling; discard oil. Clean fry pan.

Heat fry pan at 225°. Add oil, green pepper, onion, bamboo shoots, garlic and ginger root; cook 2 minutes, stirring constantly. Drain pineapple tidbits, reserving juice. Stir in reserved juice, vinegar, soy sauce, sugar and sesame oil; heat at 400° until boiling. Reduce heat to simmer, between Warm and 200°. Mix 1 tablespoon cornstarch and cold water; stir into fry pan. Cook until thickened, stirring constantly. Stir in shrimp, pinneapple tidbits and tomato; cook until heated, about 2 minutes. Season to taste with salt. Serve with hot cooked rice.

4 to 6 servings.

TIP: 1 pound thawed frozen cod fillets can be substituted for the shrimp. Cut cod into 1-inch pieces; press lightly with paper toweling to remove excess moisture. Coat lightly with cornstarch; cook as above.

Pork Sate

1/4 cup soy sauce

2 tablespoons dry sherry

2 tablespoons sugar

2 cloves garlic, minced

1/2 teaspoon ground ginger

1 pound boneless lean pork, cut into pieces 1 × 1 × 1/4 inch

1 cup flaked coconut

1 1/4 cups very warm water (120°)

1/3 cup chopped onion

1 clove garlic

1/2 teaspoon dried coriander leaves

1/4 teaspoon dried red pepper

1/4 cup water

1/3 cup creamy peanut butter

2 tablespoons vegetable oil

1 small cucumber, thinly sliced

1 small onion, thinly sliced

Rice wine vinegar or distllied white vinegar

Mix soy sauce, sherry, sugar, 2 cloves garlic and ginger; pour over pork pieces in shallow glass baking dish, stirring to coat pieces evenly. Let stand 30 minutes. Drain pork; discard marinade.

Process coconut and 1 1/4 cups very warm water in food processor or blender until smooth, 1 to 2 minutes; strain mixture into fry pan, discarding coconut. Process onion, 1 clove garlic, the coriander, red pepper and 1/4 cup water in food processor or blender until smooth, about 1 minute; stir into mixture in fry pan. Heat at 400° until mixture is boiling. Reduce heat to simmer, between Warm and 200°; cook 4 minutes, stirring frequently. Stir in peanut butter; cook until mixture thickens, 1 to 2 minutes, stirring constantly. Pour into serving bowl; keep warm. Clean fry pan.

Heat fry pan at 325°. Add oil and pork; cook until meat is brown and no longer pink in the center, 2 to 3 minutes, stirring constantly. Transfer meat to serving bowl.

Place cucumber and onion in small bowl; sprinkle with vinegar and toss to coat lightly. Serve meat with peanut butter sauce for dipping. Garnish with cucumber mixture.

4 servings.

Lemon Chicken

1/3 cup sugar

1 tablespoon cornstarch

1/4 cup lemon juice

1/4 cup rice wine vinegar or distilled white vinegar

1 teaspoon soy sauce

1 teaspoon grated lemon rind

1 pound boned, skinned chicken breast, cut into 1-inch pieces

2 tablespoons peanut or vegetable oil

2 cups snow peas

1 cup thinly sliced carrots

1/2 cup water

1/4 teaspoon chicken flavor instant bouillon

1/2 cup blanced whole almonds

1/4 cup thinly sliced green onions and tops

Salt

White pepper

Hot cooked rice

Mix sugar, cornstarch, lemon juice, vinegar, soy sauce and lemon rind; pour over chicken in shallow glass baking dish. Let stand 15 minutes. Drain chicken, reserving marinade.

Heat fry pan at 325°. Add oil and chicken; cook until brown, about 4 minutes, stirring constantly. Remove chicken from fry pan and reserve. Add snow peas and carrots; cook 2 minutes, stirring constantly. Stir in reserved marinade, water and bouillon; heat at 400° until boiling. Reduce heat to simmer, between Warm and 200°; cook until sauce is thickened, about 2 minutes, stirring constantly.

Stir in reserved chicken, almonds and onions; cook until heated, about 2 minutes. Season to taste with salt and pepper. Serve with hot cook rice.

4 servings.

Greek-Style Spinach and Rice

3 tablespoons olive or vegetable oil
1/3 cup pine nuts or slivered almonds
1 10-ounce package frozen spinach, thawed
1 medium cucumber, peeled, cut lengthwise into halves, seeded
1 clove garlic, minced

1/2 teaspoon dried oregano leaves
1/4 teaspoon dried mint leaves
1/4 teaspoon pepper
2 cups cooked rice
Salt

Heat fry pan at 250°. Add oil and nuts; cook until golden, 1 to 2 minutes, stirring constantly. Drain spinach well between paper toweling. Slice cucumber halves into arcs. Add spinach, cucumber, garlic, oregano, mint and pepper; cook 2 to 3 minutes, stirring constantly. Stir in rice; cook until heated, about 2 minutes. Season to taste with salt.

4 servings.

Artichoke Hearts Provencale

2 tablespoons olive or vegetable oil
1/2 cup chopped mushrooms
1/4 cup chopped onion
1 9-ounce package frozen artichoke hearts, thawed

1/4 teaspoon dried tarragon leaves
1/8 teaspoon pepper
1/2 cup cherry tomatoes, cut into halves
2 tablespoons grated Parmesan cheese

Heat fry pan at 225°. Add oil, mushrooms and onion; cook until onion is tender, about 3 minutes, stirring constantly. Stir in artichoke hearts, tarragon and pepper; cook until artichoke hearts are tender, 3 to 4 minutes, stirring frequently. Stir in tomatoes and cheese; cook 1 minute.

4 servings.

Mediterranean-Style Peppers and Squash

2 tablespoons vegetable oil
1/2 cup chopped onions
1 clove garlic, minced
1 cup sliced mushrooms
1 medium green pepper, cut into 1/4-inch strips
1 medium red pepper, cut into 1/4-inch strips
1 large yellow squash, cut into pieces, 1 1/2 × 1/4 × 1/4 inch

1/2 teaspoon dried basil leaves
1/2 teaspoon dried rosemary leaves
1/2 teaspoon dried marjoram leaves
1/4 teaspoon dried thyme leaves
1 large tomato, chopped
Salt
Pepper

Heat fry pan at 225°. Add oil, onion and garlic; cook 1 minute. Stir in mushrooms; cook 1 minute, stirring constantly. Add peppers; cook 2 minutes, stirring constantly. Stir in squash, basil, rosemary, marjoram and thyme; cook until vegetables are crisp-tender, 2 to 3 minutes, stirring constantly. Stir in tomato; cook 1 minute. Season to taste with salt and pepper.

4 servings.

Marinated Salmon Steaks

1/2 cup orange juice
1/4 cup sake or dry white wine
1/4 cup soy sauce
  2 teaspoons packed light brown sugar
  1 clove garlic, minced

3 star anise
1/8 teaspoon pepper
4 salmon steaks or other fish steaks, 3/4 inches thick

Mix orange juice, sake, soy sauce, sugar, garlic, anise and pepper; pour over salmon steaks in shallow glass baking dish. Refrigerate, covered, up to 1 hour, turning fish 2 or 3 times. Drain fish, reserving marinade.

Heat reserved marinade in fry pan at 400° until boiling. Reduce heat to simmer, between Warm and 200°. Add fish; cook until fish is tender and flakes with a fork, about 4 minutes on each side. Transfer fish to serving platter; spoon remaining marinade over.

4 servings.

Eggs Foo Yong

4 eggs, beaten
1 teaspoon soy sauce
1/8 teaspoon anise seed, crushed
1/8 teaspoon white pepper
1 cup fresh or drained canned bean sprouts

1/2 cup chopped mushrooms
2 tablespoons finely chopped green onion and top
Soy sauce

Mix eggs, 1 teaspoon soy sauce, anise seed and pepper in bowl until blended; mix in bean sprouts, mushrooms and onion. Heat fry pan at 225°. Spoon egg mixture into fry pan, using 1/4 cup egg mixture for each patty; cook, with cover 1/2 inch ajar, until egg mixture is set, 2 to 3 minutes. Turn; cook about 1 minute. Remove cooked patties from fry pan; repeat with remaining egg mixture. Serve with soy sauce.

4 servings.

Scallops St. Jacques

1 pound sea or bay scallops
1 tablespoon lime juice
1/8 teaspoon pepper
1/2 cup dry white wine
1 cup chopped seeded tomato
1/2 cup sliced mushrooms
1 clove garlic, minced

1 cup sliced cucumber
1/2 cup chopped green pepper
1 teaspoon dried chives
1/2 teaspoon dried chervil leaves
Salt
Hot cooked rice

Sprinkle scallops with lime juice and pepper; reserve. Heat wine, tomato, mushrooms and garlic in fry pan at 400° until boiling. Reduce heat to 350°. Stir in reserved scallops, cucumber and green pepper; cook, covered, until scallops are tender, 2 to 4 minutes. Stir in chives and chervil; season to taste with salt. Serve with hot cooked rice.

4 servings.

Mushroom Salisbury Steaks

1	pound lean ground beef	1 1/2	cups beef broth
1	tablespoon tomato paste	2	cups sliced mushrooms
1	tablespoon dried chives	1 1/2	tablespoons cornstarch
1/8	teaspoon ground nutmeg	1/3	cup dry white wine or water
1/2	teaspoon salt	1/16	teaspoon ground nutmeg
1/16	teaspoon pepper		

Mix ground beef, tomato paste, chives, 1/8 teaspoon nutmeg, salt and pepper; form mixture into 4 oval patties. Heat fry pan at 225°. Add beef patties; cook to desired degree of doneness, 5 to 7 minutes for medium, turning patties occasionally. Remove patties from fry pan. Drain fry pan.

Add beef broth to fry pan and heat at 400° until boiling. Reduce heat to simmer, between Warm and 200°. Add mushrooms; cook, 3 minutes, stirring occasionally. Mix cornstarch and wine; stir into broth mixture until thickened. Stir in 1/16 teaspoon nutmeg. Add beef patties; cook, covered, until heated through, about 2 minutes.

4 servings.

Ham-Stuffed Chicken Breasts

4	boned, skinned chicken breast halves, (about 1 1/2 pounds)	3/4	teaspoon Dijon-style mustard
1	cup dry white wine		Salt
1/2	cup shredded Swiss cheese		Pepper
1	egg white	2	ounces thinly sliced baked ham

Pound chicken breasts with flat side of mallet until even in thickness; place in shallow glass baking dish and pour wine over. Let stand 30 minutes, turning chicken occasionally. Drain chicken, reserving wine.

Mix cheese, egg white, and mustard. Sprinkle chicken breasts lightly with salt and pepper. Arrange ham on chicken breasts; divide cheese mixture on ham. Roll up chicken breasts, jelly-roll style; secure with wooden picks.

Heat fry pan at 250°. Place chicken breasts in fry pan; cook with cover ajar 1 inch, until chicken is browned and juices are clear when thickest parts are pierced with fork, about 8 to 10 minutes. Add reserved wine; cook until wine is nearly evaporated, 4 to 5 minutes, turning chicken to glaze.

4 servings.

Conversion to Metric Measure

WHEN YOU KNOW	SYMBOL	MULTIPLY BY	TO FIND	SYMBOL
teaspoons	tsp	5	milliliters	ml
tablespoons	tbsp	15	milliliters	ml
fluid ounces	fl oz	30	milliliters	ml
cups	c	0.24	liters	l
pints	pt	0.47	liters	l
quarts	qt	0.95	liters	l
ounces	oz	28	grams	g
pounds	lb	0.45	kilograms	kg
Fahrenheit	°F	5/9 (after subtracting 32)	Celsius	C
inches	in	2.54	centimeters	cm
feet	ft	30.5	centimeters	cm

Liquid Measure to Milliliters

1/4 teaspoon	=	1.25 milliliters
1/2 teaspoon	=	2.5 milliliters
3/4 teaspoon	=	3.75 milliliters
1 teaspoon	=	5 milliliters
1-1/4 teaspoons	=	6.25 milliliters
1-1/2 teaspoons	=	7.5 milliliters
1-3/4 teaspoons	=	8.75 milliliters
2 teaspoons	=	10 milliliters
1 tablespoon	=	15 milliliters
2 tablespoons	=	30 milliliters

Fahrenheit to Celsius

F	C
200°	93°
225°	107°
250°	121°
275°	135°
300°	149°
325°	163°
350°	177°
375°	191°
400°	205°
425°	218°
450°	232°
475°	246°
500°	260°

Liquid Measure to Liters

1/4 cup	=	0.06 liters
1/2 cup	=	0.12 liters
3/4 cup	=	0.18 liters
1 cup	=	0.24 liters
1-1/4 cups	=	0.3 liters
1-1/2 cups	=	0.36 liters
2 cups	=	0.48 liters
2-1/2 cups	=	0.6 liters
3 cups	=	0.72 liters
3-1/2 cups	=	0.84 liters
4 cups	=	0.96 liters
4-1/2	=	1.08 liters
5 cups	=	1.2 liters
5-1/2 cups	=	1.32 liters

Index

Index

Index

Index

Index

Index